# THE HAWAIIDIET™

# *The* HAWAIIDIET™

TERRY SHINTANI, M.D., J.D., M.P.H.

WITH A FOREWORD BY DR. BOB ARNOT,
CHIEF MEDICAL CORRESPONDENT FOR NBC

POCKET BOOKS
New York   London   Toronto   Sydney   Tokyo   Singapore

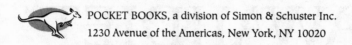 POCKET BOOKS, a division of Simon & Schuster Inc.
1230 Avenue of the Americas, New York, NY 10020

Library of Congress Cataloging-in-Publication Data

Shintani, Terry T., 1951–
    The Hawaiidiet / Terry Shintani ; with a foreword by Bob Arnot.
      p.    cm.
    Includes bibliographical references.
    ISBN 0-671-02666-6
    1. Reducing diets.   2. Cookery, Hawaiian.   3. Vegetarianism.
  I. Title.   II. Title: Hawaii diet.
  RM222.2.S5273   1999
  613.2—dc21                             99-26473
                                               CIP

First Pocket Books hardcover printing June 1999

10 9 8 7 6 5 4 3 2 1

POCKET and colophon are registered trademarks of
Simon & Schuster Inc.

*Designed by Laura Lindgren*

Printed in the U.S.A.

This book is dedicated to our Almighty Father,
the Great Physician who is the source of all healing.

# Contents

# Foreword

$\mathcal{I}$ first met Dr. Shintani early in 1991, when I interviewed him for a national TV show about his work with the Native Hawaiian people. I was most impressed with the health and diet program originated by him, which forms the basis of this book.

The most memorable part of my interview was a conversation with one of Dr. Shintani's patients. Big Eddie, a man of Native Hawaiian ancestry, stood six-feet-five and at one time weighed 425 pounds. At the time of the interview, he had trimmed down to 274 pounds. He was delighted with the difference in his life and health. We stood on a bluff overlooking the beautiful blue Pacific Ocean, and talked about the devastating problems the Native Hawaiian people face with regard to health and obesity. Big Eddie was diabetic, like so many other Native Hawaiians. The incidence of diabetes and other chronic health problems among Native Hawaiians is one of the highest in the world.

Because I had been a diabetes researcher at one time, I was especially interested in the fact that Big Eddie had once required regular shots of insulin but was by then no longer on medication. As a result of his tremendous weight loss, he had all but conquered his life-threatening illness—and he had done it through diet alone. This was impressive indeed.

Dr. Shintani has had similar results with many of his other patients, and also with other types of chronic illnesses. In many cases, this program is so effective that it can actually eliminate the need to take medication for problems such as heart disease, high cholesterol, hypertension, and other chronic illnesses.

Dr. Shintani is definitely on to something. Anyone trying to conquer bad health and obesity needs to look seriously at his work. His message of restoring health and achieving an ideal weight is based on his belief that we all need to return to the whole, unrefined diets of our ancestors: fresh fruits, fresh vegetables, and whole, unprocessed grains.

And there's more. The ancient Hawaiians believed that all health is forged from the principles that harmonize spiritual, mental, emotional, and physical well-being. You'll find this message incorporated throughout the pages of this book, as it relates not only to Hawaii but to all of us. With this book, the spirit of Hawaii and the principles of the HawaiiDiet™ are made available to us all. These principles may change your life.

Dr. Bob Arnot
Chief Medical Correspondent, NBC News
Author of *Dr. Bob Arnot's Revolutionary Weight Control Program*

# Introduction

"In the beginning, God created the heavens and the earth."

In the Hawaiian chant of creation, the *Kumulipo*, Sky Father (*Wakea*) and Earth Mother (*Papa*) mate and, through this mating, create all things.

Similar creation beliefs are found in many cultures throughout the world, from the Asians to the Native Americans, from prehistory through the present day. The understanding that everything is born of a common source—and is therefore connected to everything else—is fundamental to most of the great religions, philosophies, and cultures of the world.

Modern-day science is beginning to agree. When it comes to issues of diet, lifestyle, and spiritual faith, our ancestors were correct after all. The HawaiiDiet™ is a measured attempt to show us that we can achieve good health by integrating spiritual values, diet, and lifestyle in a way that allows us to make the most of the cutting-edge principles of modern science.

The HawaiiDiet™ was conceived in part as a response to the high rates of death from chronic diet-and-lifestyle-related diseases among the Native Hawaiians. These diseases include heart disease, hypertension, arthritis, asthma, allergies, cancer, diabetes, stroke, gastritis, and many other chronic conditions that are reaching epidemic proportions in our society.

Part of the research began with my initial interest in traditional diet and with my private practice. Another major part of it began as the

Waianae Diet Program in Waianae, Hawaii, a region that contains the largest Native Hawaiian population in the world.

In the Waianae coastal community, there is great poverty—at least from a material perspective. This sets the stage for poor health. But the people there are also blessed with great wealth from a spiritual perspective. If nurtured properly, spiritual strength may set the stage for the recovery of good health. The success of the Waianae Diet Program is a realization of some of this potential. Because of the dramatic improvement of the participants' health, and because of the ease with which most of them achieved weight loss, I constantly receive requests for the diet program from all over the world.

This program is called The HawaiiDiet™ in honor of the land where it was born, and also because of the spirit of the Hawaiian people. Their ancient wisdom embraces universal concepts common to traditional cultures from all over the world and can therefore provide a road map to world health.

The Hawaiian spirit of *aloha,* or universal love, embraces people from a variety of cultural backgrounds and enjoys ethnic cuisines from all over the world. In keeping with this spirit, I utilize foods from many cultures. In my private medical practice, I use the same principles when dealing with people from outside Hawaii as I do when dealing with Native Hawaiians. We achieve the same excellent results. In other words, this is a program that can be used and enjoyed by anybody, anywhere in the world, even though it was founded in Hawaii.

## SELF-TRANSFORMATION AND TRADITIONAL DIET

My first encounter with what I call traditional diet was in the mid-1970s. At that time, I changed my diet in an attempt to improve my energy level. The results astounded me. My energy level increased dramatically and in a matter of days I went from sleeping nine hours per day to five hours per day. I lost thirty-five pounds effortlessly. I felt better than I had felt for years. I was following a strict vegetarian diet based on whole foods from traditional cultures around the world.

Although my personal preference is still for a fully vegan diet, which is a diet that contains no animal products whatsoever, the HawaiiDiet™ is not strictly vegetarian, reflecting the traditional practices of the majority of people around the world.

I was so surprised by what was happening to me that I began to seriously wonder: Why weren't the physicians and health care professionals at the university and in my community talking about the importance of diet in one's health and overall lifestyle? Was there any hard scientific data that backed up what I sensed was happening to me?

These questions intrigued me so much that I finally changed careers. I left the field of law and went to medical school. But medical school didn't offer much information with regard to nutrition or the *prevention* of disease. After finishing medical school, I earned a master's degree in nutrition and, shortly thereafter, became board certified in preventive medicine.

A major interest of mine had always been the effect of traditional diet upon health around the world.

In this book, I define "traditional diets" as those diets that cultures have followed for centuries prior to the industrial revolution. This includes those cultures that mingled with others but that still follow the diets of their ancestors.

The diets from both these indigenous and mingled cultures have been studied and documented by a number of researchers. Most of the information on traditional diets comes from studies done in places where there has been little modernization and where the current diet reflects the dietary pattern from centuries ago in that same area. Other information comes from data gathered in countries where dietary records of some kind were kept prior to the changes in diet that occurred with modernization.

I learned almost everywhere I looked that those cultures that were moving away from traditional diets were the same cultures that were rapidly developing epidemics of diet-related disease. Fortunately, studies began to emerge that indicated that many of these diet-related diseases could be reversed by returning people to their traditional, culture-based diets. In America, too, there was mounting evidence in the nutritional and preventive-medicine communities that most of our common diseases could be both prevented and reversed through a return to the traditional diet of our own ancestors.

## PUTTING THEORY INTO PRACTICE

When I returned to Hawaii in 1987, I immediately began to apply this theory in my private practice. My approach was to use diets that had no cholesterol and were about ten percent fat, in keeping with my over-all approach of modeling the program after typical traditional diets. My goal was to prescribe a good diet and a healthy lifestyle as a means to weaning people off their medications. I also wanted to help them avoid unnecessary surgeries. In general, I wanted to maximize the health and well-being of my patients, even those who did not show symptoms of an already established disease.

Shortly after I began working with this program in private practice, I also took a position at the Waianae Coast Comprehensive Health Center (WCCHC). I felt that there was a great need for my services in that community and that my background in nutrition would be useful in a population suffering from high rates of nutrition-related disease.

Since this center is located in the community with the largest Native Hawaiian population in the world, it is therefore the largest provider of primary health care to Native Hawaiians in the world—caring for some ten thousand Native Hawaiian people. This population has many serious health problems, most of which are related to the modern American diet and lifestyle.

Obesity—that is, the condition of being significantly overweight (usually defined as being more than twenty percent over one's ideal body weight)—is a serious health problem in the United States. It is even worse in certain subpopulations. For example, in the Native Hawaiian population, the prevalence of obesity is a staggering sixty-four percent. This is one factor that contributes to Native Hawaiians' rates of death from heart disease, cancer, stroke, and diabetes, which are among the highest in the nation.

At WCCHC, I was able to use the same approach toward solving these problems that I also used in private practice. The Native Hawaiian people had long since abandoned their traditional diet, for a variety of reasons, but it was still possible to reconstruct that diet. I was given an opportunity to work with the Native Hawaiian people and others to help them return to their traditional diet, which was infinitely more healthy than the high-fat, low-fiber Westernized diet that had taken its place.

I was convinced that ancient Hawaiian cultural principles, representing universal truths such as *lokahi*, or wholeness, were a key to getting people to maintain the diet and to truly adopt a healthy lifestyle. I was blessed to be working for a community-owned health center that shared my conviction. The WCCHC board voted to allow me to spend time developing this project, the Waianae Diet Program, despite the fact that we had no funds to support it. Fortunately, the Waianae Coast community joined in the support of the program and the project began with sheer *aloha* from the community. In addition, a catalyst appeared. I became aware of a research project that held views similar to mine. This other project was known as the Molokai Diet Study. It was the first research project to measure the effect of the traditional Hawaiian diet on blood cholesterol levels. Although the results were unpublished at that time, the project provided credibility for my concept and encouraged me to continue my work.

## THE HAWAIIAN PARADOX

When we finally implemented the Waianae Diet Program, it was a strict three-week, holistic program that used traditional Hawaiian foods and was based upon universal concepts of health as embodied in Hawaiian cultural healing principles. The results were startling. The average weight loss was seventeen pounds in three weeks, while people ate as much as they wanted; cholesterol levels fell 14.1 percent. (See Appendix 3I). Some individuals' diabetes came under control so quickly that they had to be carefully monitored in the beginning while they were completely weaned off their insulin and other medication. The most startling outcome was that the participants wound up losing weight while eating more food, and controlling blood sugar while eating more carbohydrates. This is what I call the Hawaiian paradox. The results were published in the *American Journal of Clinical Nutrition*, and the program won the highest national award for health promotion in a community, awarded by the Secretary of Health and Human Services. We have been fortunate enough to have the program featured in *Newsweek,* on CNN, on CBS, NBC, and in the *Encyclopedia Britannica 1995 Medical and Health Annual,* among numerous other publications.

## WHY THE HAWAIIDIET™?

In 1997, I and others initiated a similar program, known as the Hawaii-Diet™ program, which provided additional impetus for this book. The participants in the program included Hawaii's governor, the Honorable Benjamin J. Cayetano, and other community leaders, including residents of the Hawaiian Homestead—known as Papakolea. (Hawaiian Homesteads are plots of land that once belonged to the Hawaiian monarchy but that have now been set aside by the state to provide housing for the Native Hawaiian people. One must have fifty percent or more of Hawaiian blood to qualify for Homestead land.) The results of this program were even more remarkable, with cholesterol levels falling by a dramatic average of twenty-four percent in just a matter of three weeks. Blood sugar levels were so well controlled that one person with diabetes no longer needed the ninety units of daily injected insulin that she had previously required.

Many of my readers know that I am a vegetarian, despite the fact that some of the diets I prescribe are not vegetarian. The HawaiiDiet™ is in part based on traditional cultural eating patterns from around the world, and most of these diets included animal products, albeit in very small amounts (an average of seven ounces per week). In fact, this low-level consumption of animal products suggests that the vast majority of our ancestors were primarily vegetarian. The HawaiiDiet™ follows this eating pattern for the first two weeks, and in the last week is strictly vegetarian. This provides a convenient transition to a long-term plant-based diet if the dieter wishes to continue this way.

As for other nonessential food items, such as oil and sweeteners, the HawaiiDiet™ does allow them on occasion, in keeping with traditional dietary patterns. However, there should be no mistake: The HawaiiDiet™ does not consider these foods to be ideal and recommends minimal use of them. I feel that the focus on traditional diets as a model for this book may reduce the consumption of animal products to a greater extent than if I were to advocate a strict vegan program. Preliminary results, including the fact that Governor Cayetano's son adopted a vegetarian lifestyle as a result of this diet, indicate that our general strategy for promoting a plant-based diet is effective.

I invite you to try the HawaiiDiet™ and see if you might improve your own health and lose some excess pounds. Perhaps you might become part of a movement to restore not only your own health, but also the health of the community and ultimately the health of the whole world.

# PART ONE

# Getting to Know the HawaiiDiet™

# ONE

# Taking the First Step Toward Changing Your Life

*C*ongratulations. By picking up this book, you have taken the first step toward changing your life. The purpose of this book is to help you maximize your health and, in the process, minimize your weight. It will give you a new perspective on health by letting you look through the lens of some universal principles embodied in six basic Hawaiian healing concepts. It will describe the science behind the health effects of the HawaiiDiet™ and will show you how to make the revolutionary concept I call the Hawaiian paradox work for you. It will also provide you with a step-by-step nutrition plan, complete with more than one hundred fifty delicious recipes, as well as useful tools to help you stay with the diet for years to come.

## WHAT'S IN THIS DIET FOR YOU?

What, exactly, can you expect from this health program? This simple step-by-step plan will help you:

- Control weight while eating more food
- Control blood sugar while eating more carbohydrates
- Control blood cholesterol while eating more fats

- Live healthier and longer
- Minimize, with the help of your doctor, your need for medications
- Adjust your diet to suit your genetic type

If you are like most people, you've probably already tried dieting, only to find that it doesn't work in the long run. For most people, even if they do lose weight it returns as soon as they step away from the iron-clad discipline that most diet regimens require.

This program is not a diet in the conventional sense of the word. It is, rather, a program that shows you how to lose weight by maximizing your health. Whereas most weight-loss diets rely upon deprivation and rigorous willpower, the HawaiiDiet™ utilizes your natural enjoyment of eating. It shows you how to replace unhealthy, fat-promoting foods with healthy, delicious foods that satisfy in every way.

You may be confused by the nutrition information that is going around these days. First people say carbohydrates are bad, then they say they are good. They say that fat is bad for you, but then they're not so sure—maybe it's the sugar. Some "experts" say that protein is good for you, but then a book comes out that says that animal protein promotes heart disease. The HawaiiDiet™ helps to clear up this confusion through an integration of ancient wisdom and modern science.

On the other hand, perhaps you are more concerned about your health than about your weight. Maybe you are battling a health problem, such as high blood pressure, high cholesterol, or diabetes. Or you may just not feel up to par and want your energy back. Whatever your reasons for wanting to embark upon this program, you'll learn some fascinating lessons about health and weight control. You'll learn:

- Why our health care system is failing
- Why the original Native Hawaiians and other premodern populations were trim and healthy
- What it was about Hawaiian food that helped people control their weight, blood sugar, and cholesterol
- How to find foods that help you lose weight with Dr. Shintani's Mass Index of food (SMI)
- How the HawaiiDiet™ can be helpful to people of any ethnic group

- Six traditional Hawaiian principles of health
- How to use the HawaiiDiet™ pyramid to balance your diet
- How the application of these principles can help you achieve optimal health

Add all these together, and you can see that the HawaiiDiet™ makes it possible for you to eat all the delicious food you want, from any ethnic cuisine, while still losing weight and restoring your health.

## MANY OTHERS HAVE SUCCEEDED: SO CAN YOU!

In these pages, you'll see that others are succeeding at this program, or have already succeeded—people such as Mary T., whose heartwarming story is representative of what this diet can do for you. At age forty, Mary was already taking eighty units of insulin and she was at high risk for serious complications from diabetes. She went on the Hawaii-Diet™ and lost fifty-six pounds. Seven years later, she maintains that same weight, although she "eats everything in sight."

Ten days after Mary started our program, she stopped her twice-a-day insulin injections (under very close physician's supervision) and hasn't needed a single injection since. She says, "I have more energy, I sleep less. This diet has literally changed my life."

On the HawaiiDiet™, Hawaii's governor, Benjamin Cayetano, reduced his cholesterol from 234 milligrams per deciliter (mg/dl) down to 162 mg/dl. His "good cholesterol," or high density lipoprotein (HDL), increased from 26 to 32. His triglycerides (blood fats) fell 534 points, from a very high 617 mg/dl to a normal level of 83 mg/dl (the optimal range is 50 to 150 mg/dl).

Cholesterol levels are indicators of risk of heart disease, as are levels of triclycerides. "Good cholesterol," or HDL (high density lipoprotein), is distinguished from "bad cholesterol," or LDL (low density lipoprotein). HDL helps your body transport cholesterol out of the arteries, whereas LDL facilitates the transformation of cholesterol into plaque in the artery walls. Thus, the goal is to have a high HDL and low LDL, and also low triglycerides.

"I lost thirty pounds in just twenty-one days," said Albert M., a participant in one of my early programs several years ago. "I couldn't believe it. I was eating all this food and the weight still came off."

Ellen K. told me, "This is the greatest diet in the world," as she stepped on my office scale. She had lost sixty pounds after years of failing on every other diet. She looked better than she had in years, her skin was glowing, and she had new vitality and a renewed zest for life.

## WHAT IS THE HAWAIIDIET™?

### 1. The HawaiiDiet™ Is a Whole-Person Program
The HawaiiDiet™ emphasizes the health of the whole person, including spiritual, mental, emotional, and physical aspects, through a focus on food and diet. It includes exercise, stress reduction, and an understanding of universal principles embodied in traditional Hawaiian beliefs and a faith in God. When all of these aspects of life are in harmony, your health is maximized. When your health is maximized, your excess weight disappears automatically. Energy levels increase and you become more effective in every way.

### 2. The HawaiiDiet™ Is a No-Deprivation Eating Program
There is no calorie-counting or portion-size restriction on the Hawaii-Diet™. It is an "all you can eat" health program that emphasizes the type of food eaten rather than the quantity. When we fed participants traditional Hawaiian food, they kept losing their excess weight. The HawaiiDiet™ simply shows you how to lose weight and eat until you're satisfied. In fact, in our studies people wind up eating more food than ever and still losing weight.

### 3. The HawaiiDiet™ Integrates Modern Science with Ancient Wisdom
The HawaiiDiet™ employs the best of both worlds: It seeks to integrate ancient wisdom with modern science. Leading-edge research from nutritionists and physicians is beginning to support the value of the HawaiiDiet's™ approach. New information on the benefits of eating whole grains, vegetables, and fruit shows us why our ancestors rarely

suffered from chronic diet-related diseases that plague us today, and why they rarely had problems with obesity. They knew something that we are only beginning to learn.

### 4. The HawaiiDiet™ Is Based upon Traditional Eating Patterns

In my research into traditional diets, I began to see that, with few exceptions, the healthiest cultures ate a diet similar in macronutrient content to that of the ancient Hawaiians, and also practiced lifestyle principles similar to those of ancient Hawaii.

(Macronutrients are calorie-containing nutrients, including carbohydrates, protein, fats, and alcohol; micronutrients are mostly vitamins and minerals.) The macronutrients in the diets of the healthiest cultures consisted of large volumes of unrefined carbohydrates, moderate amounts of protein (mostly from vegetable sources), and few fats. To simplify the application of these examples, a diagram known as the HawaiiDiet™ pyramid is used to assist in the selection of types and combinations of foods. The pyramid shows that the majority of foods you select should be plant-based foods high in whole complex carbohydrates and very low in fat and cholesterol.

For example, in the first two weeks of a recent program I conducted, participants were allowed to eat an average of seven ounces of protein per week, in the form of fish or poultry. This reflects the fact that traditional diets, such as those of ancient Asia, included roughly this amount of animal products. In the third week, the diet is strictly vegetarian. This reflects the fact that most premodern humans ate no flesh on most days.

### 5. The HawaiiDiet™ Is Not a One-Diet-Fits-All Program

Because the HawaiiDiet™ is based on traditional diets from many cultures, it recognizes that individuals may be genetically adapted to various dietary patterns. For example, a higher-fat Mediterranean-style diet may be acceptable for individuals who are adapted to such a diet. Using tools such as the Spectrum of Diets diagram, the HawaiiDiet™ allows for the tailoring of the diet to fit individual needs and genetic makeup. (See Appendix 3F.)

### 6. The HawaiiDiet™ Uses a Wide Variety of Foods

Because the HawaiiDiet™ embraces traditional eating patterns from cultures around the world, the choices of foods are virtually endless. The diet can be made up of foods that are available in your local supermarket and are simple to prepare, or it can be made up of foods that are exotic and prepared by a gourmet chef. Thus, the Hawaii-Diet™ can be used by anyone and incorporated into one's daily routine for the rest of one's life.

### 7. The HawaiiDiet™ Uses Foods That Are Filling

The SMI, or Shintani Mass Index, helps you select common everyday foods that have the characteristics of the traditional Hawaiian foods that helped keep people slim for generations. The index number of any given food represents roughly the number of pounds it takes of that food to provide one day's worth of calories, or the number of calories required to maintain weight. This is a way of describing how much of the food will fill your stomach and make you feel satisfied in relation to the number of calories it provides. For example, corn has an SMI value of 6.5. In other words, it takes 6.5 pounds of corn to provide one day's worth of calories. By contrast, a cheeseburger has an SMI value of 2.1 (which means it takes 2.1 pounds of cheeseburger to provide one day's worth of calories). By comparing these numbers, we can deduce that corn is more filling and satisfying than cheeseburger, because for the same number of calories, your stomach will be much fuller from the calories in corn.

To simply this concept, let's look at it another way. If you eat 677 calories of cheeseburger, how full is your stomach? This much cheeseburger probably weighs about one-half pound. Therefore, the average stomach will still have plenty of room for more food. Now, if you eat 677 calories of corn, how full is your stomach? You've eaten about 1.5 pounds of corn, so your stomach is much fuller. If you go to a really high SMI food, such as grapefruit, and eat 677 calories, you've eaten about five pounds—if you can eat that much. Your stomach will be ten times as full as it would have been with that much cheeseburger. Satisfaction of hunger occurs when your stomach is full enough to signal the brain to stop eating. Thus, the higher the index number, the more likely the food is to help you *lose* weight. The lower the number, the more likely the food is to help you *gain* weight.

## NO MORE DEPRIVATION, NO MORE COUNTING CALORIES

During the course of this program, you will focus upon the positive aspects of health and weight control. You will not be worried about deprivation. You won't be focusing upon all the things you should not do. Instead, you will be focused upon all the delicious meals and recipes that have been carefully selected for you. You will be focused on foods that satisfy your hunger. The HawaiiDiet™ will help you to discover how to optimize your health no matter what your age, sex, ethnic makeup, or regional background. Even though the Hawaii-Diet™ was conceived partially in response to the high rates of death from chronic diet-and-lifestyle-related diseases among Native Hawaiians, the same health crisis is occurring right now in all of America. Nearly seventy percent of deaths in this country are from diet-and-lifestyle-related diseases.

This figure comes from the mortality statistics issued by the office of the Surgeon General. The figures break down this way: The number one cause of death is heart disease (about thirty-three percent of all deaths every year); the number two cause is cancer (twenty-five percent); the number three cause is stroke (seven percent). Seventh in line is diabetes (2.4 percent); and the tenth leading cause of death is atherosclerotic disease other than heart disease or stroke (1.2 percent). These are all nutrition-related diseases. If you add all these percentages together, they equal 68.6 percent.

## HOW EASY IS THE HAWAIIDIET™?

How easy is it to make a quick meal at home? Or to dine on the creations of some of the best chefs in Paradise? In other words, the HawaiiDiet™ is both easy and tasty. In the recipe section, you'll find a whole range of dishes, from simple to gourmet. In addition to recipes devised by some of Hawaii's award-winning consumer science teachers (home economists), you'll also find dishes from world-class chefs such as Roy Yamaguchi, Peter Merriman, and Mark Ellman.

You can make your recipe choices based on the HawaiiDiet™ pyramid and the SMI. With the range of recipes provided and with these two handy program aids, you'll soon find yourself eating delicious, traditional meals based on cuisines from Pacific to European to Asian—a wonderful reflection of the diversity of Hawaii's multicultural society. Whether you're a seasoned cook or just a beginner, you'll find recipes here that work for you.

# TWO

# *Why the HawaiiDiet*™?

*W*hy should you or anyone else interested in health and weight control be interested in Hawaii? Because the Hawaiian paradox carries important insights about how food can help promote health and induce weight loss, and because the healing tradition and principles of Hawaii show us how we can regain optimal health.

## HAWAI'I: THE ALCHEMY OF LIFE

Hawaii has a powerful healing tradition inherent in its location and culture. Much of this tradition is preserved in the carefully guarded knowledge of the ancient *kahuna* (which means the keeper of the secret), who could perform legendary feats of healing with herbs, chants, and other methods. There are strong similarities between ancient Hawaiian healers and the anointed healers found in the Bible. "In the beginning was the Word," according to John 1:1. In fact, the Bible tells us that God literally spoke creation into existence with the words "Let there be light" (Genesis 1:3). Ancient Hawaiian tradition also held that words carried great power. In fact, one of the methods of healing used by the *kahuna* was the call, or *kahea*.

The word *Hawai'i* is an example of a word that has great power. Translated into English, it means "the breath (*ha*) and water (*wai*) of life from God (*i*)." It is a life-giving word, a virtual formula for the alchemy of life itself. The name, in a way, speaks of the global role Hawaii—this paradise on earth—plays as a place of healing.

## HAWAII: A PLACE TO INTEGRATE ANCIENT PRINCIPLES WITH MODERN SCIENCE

People are now recognizing the healing power in Hawaii and the climate that surrounds it. It is the perfect mix of East and West, a blend of ancient and modern, a merging of the physical and spiritual. It has the purest air and water of any industrialized state. It has the best weather, and many experts believe it is also a strong source of healing energy.

Hawaii is also in the unique position of being a part of the United States, the most technically advanced nation in the world, and also of having a rich tradition of ancient healing arts that still survives today. It is a crossroads where the healing arts of Asia and other nations have flourished. At a time when we are searching the world for answers to the ultimate question of how best to heal this nation and our people, we need not look beyond our borders to find a rich tradition of spiritual healing and ancient wisdom.

## THE FAILURE OF OUR HEALTH CARE SYSTEM

The new approach to health and weight control offered by the Hawaii-Diet™ is timely because our health care system is failing us. Today we are faced with a continued crisis in health care. Costs continue to spiral out of control, and health care is moving beyond the financial reach of the average person. We now spend an annual $1.2 trillion to support our health care system and this staggering amount rises each year, faster than the inflation rate. The irony is that, in truth, our so-called health care system is really not a health care system at all. It is a *dis-ease*-care system. In other words, our system does virtually nothing to prevent disease and responds only when someone becomes sick.

This flaw is indicative of a more profound deficiency in our whole shortsighted mindset toward health care. We focus primarily on symptoms rather than causes, on palliation rather than cures.

# MOST MODERN MEDICATIONS CURE NOTHING

America's shortsightedness in dealing with health problems leads to another serious flaw in our health care system—our choice of treatment methods. We choose medicines and surgery—in other words, artificial chemicals or the practice of removing body parts and diseased tissue—as the chief methods of treatment. The problem with surgery is that the underlying problems are seldom fixed, since they are usually systemic in origin. As far as medications are concerned, with the exception of antibiologic agents, practically all of our medications cure nothing. Does diabetes medication cure diabetes? Does high blood pressure medication cure high blood pressure? Does asthma medication cure asthma, or does arthritis medication cure arthritis? The answer to all these questions is no. These and practically all other medications for chronic conditions merely deal with symptoms or aftereffects of diseases.

This symptomatic approach means that patients require more and more medication to achieve results. To be sure, the medications do some good and are necessary to mitigate the discomfort and the damage caused by these diseases. But the simple fact that patients need to take diabetes medication or high blood pressure medication or other medications for the rest of their lives should clearly tell us that they are not getting any healthier. They have their symptoms palliated and the damage from the disease lessened to some extent but they remain ill for the rest of their lives. There is something very wrong with a health care approach that accepts such a low standard of health as "good medicine." Certainly the healing *kahuna* of ancient Hawaii would not have accepted it.

# THE AMERICAN DIET DISASTER

Fortunately, many people do see the underlying cause of the health care crisis. They realize that the main causes of disease in this country are diet and lifestyle. In fact, nearly seventy percent of us die from of diet-and-lifestyle-related diseases. (See Appendix 3A.)

The top three causes of death—heart disease, cancer, and stroke (as well as diabetes, the sixth leading cause of death)—are largely diet-related. A review of the dietary factors that contribute to the risk of contracting these diseases reveals that some of the nutritional and preventive recommendations we have been given over the past fifty years have been disastrous to our health. For years, we have been told to eat lots of meat because protein is healthy for us. Then we find that meat is high in cholesterol and saturated fat and increases the risk of heart disease. Next, we are told to eat more chicken, only to find that there is as much cholesterol in chicken as there is in beef. We are told to eat more cheese as a way of avoiding other animal products, only to find that cheese has similarly high levels of cholesterol and fat. We are told to eat margarine made from corn oil instead of butter, only to find that the trans-fatty acids in margarine (abnormal fats created in the process of hydrogenating oil to produce margarine) are probably as detrimental as butter. Recently, several new diets have claimed that carbohydrates are more of a problem than fat because of their effect on blood sugar and insulin. Yet our studies show good control of blood sugar and insulin with a high-carbohydrate diet. Nutrition and diet information is still conflicting and confusing. It is fraught with misleading conclusions drawn both by professionals and by the press.

To some extent, the nutrition-related diseases mentioned above are also related to obesity. There is some debate as to how directly related obesity is, but no one disputes that obesity is a risk factor for a number of chronic health conditions. Obesity is an obsession with the American people. Weight loss is one of the largest industries in this country. Unfortunately, modern approaches to treating obesity have been generally unsuccessful, if not disastrous. The fen-phen fiasco, in which heart valve problems developed among people taking a combination of weight-loss drugs, is a good example.

In this instance, two drugs, Fenfluramine (fen) and Phentermine (phen), were used in combination for weight control. Soon, certain conscientious physicians began to notice heart valve problems—some fatal—in people taking this combination of drugs. Though the association was not proof of causation, there was enough evidence to warrant caution, and this resulted in the discontinuation of this combination of medications. This is only one example among many of failed attempts to produce long-term weight loss by discovering a "magic bullet."

## A TRAGIC IRONY

In ancient times, the image of the Native Hawaiians as paragons of natural health was accurate. The chronic diseases that plague today's world were rare in the ancient Hawaiian people, as was obesity. They were naturally trim and athletic. Before they were subject to Western influences, the Hawaiian population flourished, nurtured to health in an environment of pure water, a warm climate, and lush vegetation.

Even today, the inherent healthiness of the land remains. Hawaii is even known as the Health State. Hawaii is in fact the healthiest state in the U.S., from the standpoint of longevity. Careful analysis, however, indicates that those people who are most long-lived are not Native Hawaiians but more recent immigrants—Asians and Caucasians—who seem to have lower rates of many chronic diseases. The various reasons for this include diet and lifestyle habits, genetic resistance to certain diseases, and socioeconomic status.

As for the people native to this beautiful land, we must tell a different, sadder story. The tragic irony is: While Hawaii is statistically the healthiest state in the U.S., the Native Hawaiian people have the worst health in the nation. (See Appendix 3B.)

## HAWAII AS A METAPHOR

The Hawaiian experience provides a powerful metaphor that helps to explain the global epidemic of chronic disease. Fortunately, this metaphor includes both the problem and the solution. Let's look first at what we can learn from this situation about the cause of chronic disease. Then we'll explore how the misfortunes of the Native Hawaiian people can also happen—in fact *are* happening—to the rest of us.

The key difference is one of magnitude. It is as if the health problems of the Native Hawaiians are reflective of what happens to all people when they abandon their own culture and way of life—the ways of their ancestors. Over time this has resulted in a staggering death rate from chronic disease for Native Hawaiians—as it has and will for most of the modernized world.

However, by examining what happened to the Native Hawaiian people, we see a striking contrast between ancient Hawaiian people and modern Native Hawaiians. To arrive at a full and functional solution, we need to know what, exactly, kept the Native Hawaiian people healthy in the past. Would a return to those ways tend to reverse chronic diseases in the rest of us, even as it has done for the Native Hawaiians who have returned to traditional ways?

Perhaps the most evident change from ancient times to modern times is the astonishing increase in obesity among the Native Hawaiian people. In preindustrial times, Native Hawaiians were described as "thin," "graceful," and "nimble." One eighteenth-century writer described the Native Hawaiian people in this way: "The common people are of a thin rather than full habit." Today, the Native Hawaiian people have the highest prevalence of obesity in the nation, estimated at sixty-four percent. (See Appendix 3C.)

Because of the sharp contrast between ancient Hawaiians and modern Native Hawaiians, we wanted to find out what they were eating in previous centuries that kept them both slim and healthy. Some of us went into the initial phases of our research expecting to find that modern Native Hawaiians were grossly overeating. Or perhaps Hawaiians of the past were somehow able to curb their appetites as a result of some quality found in their food, or perhaps as a result of exercise.

## THE HAWAIIAN PARADOX

I had hypothesized that Native Hawaiians would actually have eaten more food in ancient times than they do now. I believed this for two reasons. First was the very nature of the food itself during ancient times. I believed there was some inherent quality in the food that made it nutritionally superior to what the Native Hawaiian people are eating today. I felt that there must be something about the wholeness of the food during ancient times—the fact that it was unprocessed, not ground up into flour, or altered significantly by taking away parts of the food or adding artificial ingredients—that gave the foods a health-inducing quality. This, I believed, allowed Native Hawaiians to eat more food without suffering obesity or the ill effects of excessive caloric intake. I also believed this was a key difference between ancient and modern diets.

Second, I thought that because these foods were unprocessed, the actual bulk, or mass, of the food was greater than the mass of the foods you might find in our typical modern American diet. In other words, I believed that the mass-to-energy ratio—that is, how much weight and volume a food has in relation to the number of calories contained in that food—was an important factor in both ancient and modern diets.

When we analyzed the premodern diet carefully, we indeed found that ancient Hawaiians ate *more* food in terms of weight than what we eat today. In other words, we learned from historical and anthropological accounts what foods were eaten by ancient Hawaiians and estimated how much (in grams) of these foods was eaten in order to provide an adequate amount of calories per day. We then compared this amount to how much food (in grams) we typically eat today. The surprising result was that the Native Hawaiians—who have the world's highest levels of obesity in modern times—ate much more food in ancient times, but, incredibly, weighed much less. This phenomenon is what I call the Hawaiian paradox, which can be summed up as follows: Native Hawaiians have among the highest rates of obesity in the world in modern times. However, in ancient times, the Hawaiians ate much more food but they weighed much less.

We then took this Hawaiian paradox principle and applied it in our modern-day HawaiiDiet™ program. The question was: If we fed modern Native Hawaiians who were overweight traditional Hawaiian foods, could we allow them to eat more food but still lose weight? This was very important to us because of our concern about the high rates of chronic disease associated with obesity among Native Hawaiians. We wanted to see if traditional Hawaiian foods could help Native Hawaiians who are afflicted with modern illnesses to regain their health, while at the same time controlling yet another major factor in optimizing health, which was their weight.

We also wanted to explain why Native Hawaiians were slim in ancient times and so very obese today, and we wanted to discern whether there was something about traditional Hawaiian food that had some health-inducing weight-controlling properties. In order to do this, we tested the effect of these foods on a group of modern-day Native Hawaiians. Twenty participants agreed to stay on a strictly traditional Hawaiian diet for a period of twenty-one days. There was no calorie restriction on this diet and they were allowed to eat until satisfied.

The results were startling. While we fed the participants a large amount of traditional Hawaiian food, they lost weight—an average of seventeen pounds in three weeks. When we measured the amount of food they were eating on the program, we found that it was an average of 4.1 pounds of food per day compared to an average of 3.6 pounds per day while not on the program. Yet every participant lost weight on the program. (See Appendix 3D.)

The confirmation of the fact that a traditional Hawaiian diet could induce weight loss even while participants ate as much of it as they wanted provided a fundamental validation of a key principle behind the Hawaiian paradox. We also needed to understand what it was about the traditional foods themselves that induced weight loss. Once we knew this, it would be possible to show people of every ethnic background how they could lose weight while eating more food. We could, in fact, provide a simple compass to point people in the direction of good health and weight loss.

The "compass" that I used was the SMI index. By using this index, we could select foods from any culture or locality that would help induce weight loss and translate this weight-controlling ability to any cuisine, from American to Italian, Chinese, and everything in between.

The effect of applying this Hawaiian paradox to health and weight control was particularly remarkable because of the people who demonstrated these results. We came to understand that if this methodology is demonstrably effective with the Native Hawaiian population—a group that has the highest obesity rates in the nation—then it should work equally well or even better for people of other ethnic backgrounds who do not have such a propensity to gain weight.

## ANOTHER HEALTH BENEFIT
## OF THE HAWAIIAN PARADOX

A second element of the Hawaiian paradox is related to blood sugar and insulin levels, an emerging field in the study of health and obesity. Some experts now believe that at least part of the obesity problem in America is due to excessive carbohydrate consumption, which leads to chronically high blood sugar levels. This, in turn, leads to both diabetes and weight gain.

But, paradoxically, the HawaiiDiet™ controls blood sugar while the dieter is consuming a high carbohydrate diet (up to seventy-eight percent of total caloric intake). In some cases, this control is so effective that people with adult-onset diabetes can reduce or eliminate their need for insulin (with the help of their physician). Studies indicate that the blood sugar response in humans to carbohydrates depends not only upon the quantity of carbohydrates but also on how intact or how finely ground the carbohydrates are. For example, potatoes ground into flour cause a greater rise in blood sugar and insulin than do whole potatoes. (See Appendix 3H.) The HawaiiDiet™ features mostly unprocessed, whole foods that have not been ground up, refined, or otherwise tampered with. This is why, with the HawaiiDiet™, you can eat a lot of carbohydrates yet still control blood sugar, insulin, and weight.

By offering hands-on, practical solutions to the problems of weight loss and the reversal of disease, we have helped many Native Hawaiians successfully return to the diet and lifestyle they abandoned as they adapted to Western influences. We have also shown that the Hawaiian experience has broader applications. By using ancient ways to cure modern diseases, we see how low-tech, inexpensive approaches are more effective than high-tech, high-cost solutions when it comes to preventing and even reversing the major killer diseases of Western society.

# THREE

# Ancient Ways for Modern Health

## (With Kahu—Traditional Practitioner—Kamaki Kanahele)

*I*n my work with the Native Hawaiian community, I have had the privilege of being in close contact with Native Hawaiian healers. I have some training in Oriental medicine and, to my great delight, I found that the fundamental principles I had learned in my training were very similar to those of the native healers of ancient Hawaii. This was further evidence to me that the truths found in these ancient principles were universal and that they applied to all peoples.

Through the Hawaiian community, I began to learn a revealing and fundamental truth. We must regain a basic understanding of nature, of life in all its aspects, and of the fundamental, underlying causes of the diseases that threaten and disturb this life. This healing must begin with individuals, then broaden to include our communities. In this way, we can come to address the problems of our nation and the earth itself. Health and healing can become an abiding principle.

But how do we start such a quest? We can start by understanding some of the fundamental principles followed by the healers of ancient Hawaii.

# RETURNING TO THE SOURCE OF HEALTH

Whether our ancestors originated in Hawaii, Europe, Asia, Africa, the Americas, one of the myriad islands all over the world, or some other place, certain universal principles link us all to tradition. These general principles are embodied in the Hawaiian culture, and so we have used this culture as a model. But remember that these principles are not exclusive to Hawaii. If you search hard enough in your own culture, you will probably find the same fundamental principles. In these pages, you will learn the Hawaiian version of what are often universal, ancient, traditional belief systems. You will recognize the underlying humanity and value in the ancient wisdom. If you want to return to your own cultural traditions, you can simply find your own cultural equivalent. Or you can easily adapt the traditions of ancient Hawaii to the practical aspects of your own modern lifestyle.

My descriptions of these concepts are necessarily offered from the perspective of a health care professional whose understanding of the Hawaiian culture comes from my work in the community and with my adopted Native Hawaiian family. The true Hawaiian healers have a deeper understanding of these concepts and may explain them better than I can. Therefore, I encourage any serious student of the medical arts to seek such an expert. Return to the source, in nature and in natural wisdom, so you may gain as much understanding of these concepts as possible. Take them into your heart, just as our ancestors did.

## THE POWER IN THE WORD

In ancient Hawaii, there was no written language. All of their history was oral, passed down from generation to generation and largely kept in the form of chants. The ancient chants can still be heard, in certain places and contexts. They are both eerie and strangely beautiful. They evoke a feeling of unity with a spiritual world that is beyond what we know with the senses. Words, whether chanted or spoken, were considered to be of great importance, and words were considered to have great power. In an earlier section of this book, I pointed out that one of the healing arts is the art of *kahea,* or the call—in other words, healing by words. This is an important principle to understand.

Another important aspect of the Hawaiian language is that in the healing and spiritual arts, words have double meanings; that is, they contain underlying messages. In traditional Hawaiian culture, it is said that words have a *kaona,* which is a "hidden meaning" or the "underlying meaning of a word or phrase." In Hawaiian healing, it is often the hidden meaning that is most important. The meanings of words can be seen as a metaphor for the spiritual (hidden) and physical (overt) aspects of healing. Much ancient Hawaiian wisdom finds a parallel in current concepts of medicine, wherein the mind and the body join together to determine both physical and spiritual health.

Let me describe some of these ancient principles in terms of certain words that have power in their hidden meanings. If you integrate this wisdom with the practical and scientific information in this book, you will greatly enhance your HawaiiDiet™ experience, and you will find yourself making certain lifestyle changes (in addition to dietary changes) that will lead you to long life and good health. In fact, many who follow this diet undergo a change in spirituality. In other words, this diet program may help you in many ways. You'll never know how it can benefit you until you try.

## ANCIENT PRINCIPLES OF THE HAWAIIDIET™

*1. Kumu:* The Source

When it comes time to solve difficult problems, an ancient saying in Hawaii is used by lay persons and traditional healers alike. The saying *Nana i ke kumu* means "Look to the source" (Look [*nana*] to [*i*] the [*ke*] source [*kumu*]).

This saying has roots that go as far back as the ancient creation chant of early Hawaii, the *Kumulipo* ("the dark source," which is similar to the darkness in the book of Genesis in the Bible). In times of difficulties, wise elders would advise people to "look to the source." The literal meaning is obvious. It means that in order to solve a problem, you should first seek the root cause or the source of the problem and then deal with that. *Kumu* also means teacher. Thus, the phrase also means to go to the master teachers if you need assistance in finding the answer to a problem. This phrase can also mean looking to a place where there is a certain spirit, or *mana,* so you can have the opportunity to absorb this energy as a source of inspiration or healing. For example, Hawaii has become a place where people come for healing partly because of the spiritual energy that many feel here.

The phrase *Nana i ke kumu* contains another, deeper meaning, or *kaona.* Since ancient Hawaiians believed that there is one almighty God and that God (*io* or *i*) is the source of all healing, the phrase carried a spiritual meaning as well and suggested that one seek the Lord, or the source, in one's search for healing. As described above, the word *Hawai'i,* translated into English, means "the breath (*ha*) and water (*wai*) of life from God (*i*)"—the formula for life itself and a perfect formula for health. If we understand this concept of looking to the source, and if we understand that God is ultimately the source of everything, we will see that everything is connected, or bound by a common ancestry—the Lord himself. Once we see this, then we will begin to understand what is meant by the principle of *lokahi*—the principle that everything is connected.

## 2. *Lokahi:* Oneness, Wholeness, Unity

*Lokahi* literally means "consensus." From a health perspective, it means "harmony," "oneness," "wholeness," and that "all things are connected." In the deepest sense, *lokahi* means that we are connected to everyone and everything—whether person, land, the larger universe, or God.

If we understand this principle, we begin to unlock the wisdom of the ages. This principle is a fundamental piece of the fabric of all the great cultures of the world and is the foundation of Hawaiian healing. In modern times, we have forgotten this principle. If we internalize this principle and begin to incorporate it into our daily thoughts, actions, and prayers, we will come to some startling and revealing conclusions about health and how we may initiate self-healing.

For example, if we understand *lokahi,* we will realize that because of this interconnectedness, our total health ultimately depends upon the health of our spiritual, mental, emotional, and physical beings. It is also dependent on the health of our relationship to the environment and to everyone around us. And, with regard to diet, health is intimately related to what we eat. Through the principle of *lokahi*, we are connected to that food. In the most literal, physical sense, we become what we eat.

If we understand *lokahi*, we will also realize that the optimal solution to health involves healing the whole person and not just prescribing a certain pill or cutting out a part of the body. We must first seek the reason for the illness. In fact, we must know the meaning of early symptoms. Simply taking pills to mask the symptoms and forgetting about the underlying disease is not the answer. Such a simplistic response neglects the whole-person aspects of health. The result is that the solution remains incomplete, and the underlying disease lingers, albeit with its symptoms covered up. If we were to simply apply the concept of *lokahi*, or wholeness, we would quickly see that most of today's modern illnesses are caused by our own actions, not only as individuals but also as a society. Knowing this, we could then begin to shape our attitudes and to make plans toward changing the ways in which we maintain health and how we deliver health care.

The concept of *lokahi* gives us one of the most fundamental principles of the HawaiiDiet™. It points out that if we are to be as healthy, or as whole, as possible, then the food we eat should also be as whole as possible. In other words, whole grains are preferred over whole-grain flour, and whole-grain flour is preferred over white refined flour or sugar. In the HawaiiDiet™, the SMI is a good representation of this principle because it encourages us to eat whole, unrefined foods. By using this table, people find that their weight comes off naturally.

Remember that whole foods are those that are as close to their original state as possible. For example, whole corn is preferable to cornbread, and cornbread is preferable to corn oil or corn syrup, which are examples of the most highly refined forms of corn products.

Once we know the relationship between the concept of *lokahi* and diet, we are on our way to health. The next step is to know how to apply this underlying principle.

3. *Pono:* Justice, Righteousness

From the perspective of health, *pono* means a "proper balance of all aspects in nature." If we establish *pono,* or righteousness, in relation to the laws of the universe that govern our health, disease will disappear and health will be restored. This includes eating the right foods, thinking the right thoughts, and doing the right things, always with *aloha* in our hearts and always mindful of the gifts of life and health that God has given us. When we are not righteous in our ways, consequences result due to the forces of nature, and continue to occur until justice is restored.

Traditional ways of eating were almost always centered on starchy staples, such as wheat, rye, barley, corn, rice, potatoes, and, in Hawaii, taro. These served as the central foods and were then supplemented with an abundance of vegetables.

Today, in America, we center our diet on animal products. What is considered a main dish is beef, pork, chicken, or fish. Thus, our current way of eating is not *pono,* because it involves excessive killing of animals, which puts us in great disharmony with nature. The result is our own premature death. Put more simply, humans are the leading cause of death in animals because we unnecessarily slaughter them for food. At the same time, animals are the leading cause of death among humans, because we eat them in great excess and we pay a massive price in heart attacks, strokes, cancers, and other health problems. This is one example of the concept of *pono,* or supreme justice.

In addition to our unhealthy reliance upon animal products, the animals themselves are taken out of balance with nature by the ways in which they are raised and slaughtered. Artificial growth hormones are added in some instances in order to enhance the size, weight, and maturing time of the animals. Floods of antibiotics are pumped into them in order to counter the unhealthy conditions in which they are reared and killed. Other unnatural practices often confuse the natural biochemical structure of the animals, and in turn this influences our own bodies when we eat them.

We can see that, by the principle of *pono,* what we do to harm the world in turn harms us. But what we do positively comes back to us in a positive way. Once we apply this principle of *pono* and reestablish wholeness in ourselves—including spiritual, mental, emotional, and physical aspects—we improve our health. If we do this properly, ailments naturally disappear and we begin to feel much better than before. If we eat and live in harmony with our environment according to the traditional cultural ways of our ancestors, health returns.

Our research demonstrates a dramatic improvement of health in those who follow the *pono,* or properly balanced, way of eating. In keeping with the principle of *pono,* we come to know and practice the balance among all aspects of diet and lifestyle.

### 4. *Aloha:* Universal Love

The common meaning of *aloha* is the well-known salutation of "hello," "good-bye," or "love." In a deeper sense, it means the love for everyone and the embracing of all people, creatures, and things. It is the spirit of loving unconditionally and giving unconditionally that characterizes the Hawaiian spirit. The deeper spiritual translation of *aloha* is "the joining of heaven and earth"; *alo,* "face to face," and *ha,* "breath of life." Together it is a powerful statement of wishing that the forces of nature and the spirit of God be with someone.

Although *aloha* has many usages, all usages stem from the concept of universal love. Universal love permeates the fundamental spirit of Hawaiian culture. It is an inherently nonjudgmental culture, and therefore the ways of all cultures are embraced, respected, and accepted. What is therefore known as the *aloha* spirit is in fact largely responsible for the multicultural harmony now found in Hawaii. Many cultures have migrated to Hawaii from all over the world. Though most outsiders see Hawaii as a tropical paradise, Hawaii is among the most cosmopolitan of all places in the world, with a preponderance of well-educated, well-traveled people. Hawaii is often described as a cultural melting pot. I prefer to call it a cultural tossed salad, where the blend works well and creates a delightful mix of flavors, yet each element retains its original character and each individual cultural flavor remains unique. You will see this principle reflected in the multicultural nature of the recipes in this book, and in the HawaiiDiet™ program in general.

The Spirit of *Aloha* is to give and to give endlessly. In Western culture we have the concept of "give and take." In Hawaiian culture, the concept is to give and keep giving. While this may not make sense in the Western mind, from a Hawaiian perspective the concept of "oneness" is understood. It is believed that everything and everyone is connected and so whatever you give eventually comes back to you. Furthermore, if the concept of *mana* is understood, we see that even if the return does not come back in the physical realm, it does so in the spiritual realm.

One traditional Hawaiian health practitioner described a life-changing incident that captures the essence of *aloha*. He had a good relationship with his parents, and when his mother passed on and then his father died a year later, he grieved as any son would. Then his mother, whom he loved very much, came to him in a dream. She gently told him: If you want to send us your love, then love everyone—for we are now in God, and God is in everyone. Thus, the spirit of *aloha* means to love everyone, for in truth what you are loving is the spirit of God in everyone. This is the Hawaiian way.

If we make these principles a part of our lives and take care of our health based on the application of these principles, we may undergo an inner transformation. We may begin to intuitively understand nature and the universe as our ancestors did. As a result, we may gain some insight into the true nature of things. Our bodies, minds, and spirits will begin to resonate with nature. We will then realize that there is a "spirit" or a "life force" in every thing and in every living creature. In other words, there is *mana* in everything.

## 5. *Mana:* Life Force, Spirit

*Mana* is a universal concept found in the great civilizations of the world. In China, it is called *chi*. In Japan, it is called *ki*. In India, it is called *prana,* and in the Christian religion it is simply the spirit of God in all people and things.

This life force is recognized in all things, whether animate or inanimate. It is a force akin to the Westernized belief that there is a spiritual world that lies beyond all things physical that plays itself out on the physical stage. The spiritual, unseen aspects of everyone and everything are respected. For example, in Hawaiian tradition, if you offer food to a passing stranger, you are in fact offering food to the spirit of God within that person. This is a beautiful concept, comparable to the biblical passage: "Let brotherly love continue. Do not neglect to show hospitality to strangers, for thereby some have entertained angels unawares" (Hebrews 13:1–2).

If we regain the understanding that the ancient Hawaiians possessed of the nature of the universe, we will see the answer to many difficult problems that afflict our society today. In ancient Hawaii, the idea of a life force in all beings and things was second nature. If we also come to this realization, then many of the principles of the Hawaii-Diet™ will become intuitive and an integral part of our being.

Once we fully understand these five concepts—*kumu*, the source; *lokahi*, oneness; *pono*, righteousness; *aloha*, universal love; *mana*, life force—we can begin to learn what to do with them. For example, the realization of the existence of *mana* in food can help keep us motivated to stay on the HawaiiDiet™ because knowing that the life force in food adds to our own life force gives us another reason to eat whole natural foods. We learn the ancient Hawaiian arts of manifesting reality so that we can enhance our contribution to all of life within God's plan.

### 6. 'Ano 'Ano: The Seed of All Things

'Ano 'ano literally means "seed." In the HawaiiDiet™, there are several underlying meanings to this word.

For example, the seed concept is also biblical. Exhortations to plant seeds of faith and love are found throughout the Holy Book. In what is known as the parable of the seed in Luke 8, we are told that the Word of God is like a seed. And the human body is also described as a seed that will ultimately become pure spirit, in 1 Corinthians 15.

In most Hawaiian teaching, *'ano 'ano* describes a method used by some *kahunas*, or priests, to help create a reality by planting a seed of thought in one's mind and nurturing it into physical reality. It is similar to what we could now call visualization. Hawaiian masters teach us that there are seven steps necessary to translate a thought into reality:

1. Sit quietly and search your soul, see truly what it is you desire, then make sure it is in harmony with God's plan. Pray, and if it is in God's plan, He will give you what you ask.

2. Ask for guidance to ensure that what you want is good for all involved.

3. State clearly, in detail, the condition that you want with words, numbers, data. Be specific about what you want. Remember that words have power.

4. See this end result in full detail with color, sound, and action. Remember, "Faith is the assurance of things hoped for, the conviction of things not seen" (Hebrews 11:1).

5. Feel what it will be like to have this desired result come to fruition.

6. Do not tell others except those who are absolutely committed to your success about the seed you have planted.

7. Pray for the results each day with the words you have chosen and give gratitude as you see and feel this result being accomplished.

These seven steps have great power. They are a recipe for the manifestation of reality on this earth. Knowing how to make them work is a great responsibility. Most of all, we must exercise these seven steps in order to further worthy objectives that fall within God's plan, for in the end all else is meaningless.

If we faithfully do these things every day, and adopt these principles into our lives with faith, then all things are possible. And then, coming full circle, we become the seed—the 'ano 'ano for the future of health and peace in our communities and the world.

## THE ANSWER IS SIMPLE

From a Hawaiian perspective, the answer to the Hawaiian paradox is obvious. The reason why popular diets fail is that they neglect the concept of wholeness by focusing on one nutrient or concept at a time. For example, diets focusing on calorie restriction fail because they ignore the hunger drive; diets focusing on fats allow too much white flour and sugar; diets focusing on sugar allow too much animal protein; diets focusing on protein allow too much fat, and diets claiming to create a balance focus only on calorie restriction. The HawaiiDiet™ avoids these problems by enabling the dieter, with the help of the SMI index and the HawaiiDiet™ pyramid, to choose whole foods that are filling and nutritious.

With an understanding of Hawaiian healing principles, the answer to the health problems of America is obvious. Clearly, our health care system is failing because we fail to follow the wisdom in the phrase *Nana i ke kumu* (look to the source). Our health care system doesn't get at the *causes* of disease, which, in America, are in most cases related to bad diet and unhealthy lifestyle. The explanation of what is wrong is also simple from a Hawaiian perspective. The problem with our diet and lifestyle is that they are not *pono,* or "righteous," with nature—too much fat, too much meat, too much refined and chemicalized food. Finally, the answer to what we must do to fix this problem is clear. We must achieve *lokahi* (oneness) with nature. We must eat foods that are as close to nature and to the land as possible.

From a Hawaiian perspective, these conclusions are obvious. But for the modern Western mind, the "science" behind weight loss and the diet plan must be explained. The next chapter will explain some of the scientific research and principles behind my conclusions.

# FOUR

# *Integrating Modern Science with Ancient Ways*

*O*besity is a key health problem that afflicts America in general and the Native Hawaiian people in particular. Since the 1950s, obesity has been defined as the condition of being twenty percent (or more than 20 percent) heavier than one's ideal body weight. One's ideal body weight could be found in charts published by the Metropolitan Life Insurance company, which became the gold standard for defining obesity. Another standard for the definition of obesity is Body Mass Index. This is a standard that has been accepted by the National Heart Lung and Blood Institute and other organizations. BMI is calculated by taking weight in kilograms divided by height in meters squared. BMI numbers are preferred by many researchers because it is a better way to assess health risk than is body weight alone. A BMI number greater than or equal to twenty-five is considered "overweight." A BMI number greater than or equal to thirty is considered "obese." (See Appendix 4.)

According to this new measure, more people than ever are obese, and not only in the Native Hawaiian community. Some studies indicate that three-fourths of American adults are too heavy, even though they may not meet the criteria for being obese. The obesity epidemic is also spreading among America's children. The problem is so severe that former surgeon general C. Everet Koop recently stated that if he had remained in office, he would now launch the same attack on obesity that he once did on smoking. From a Hawaiian healer's perspective, obesity is an early sign of being unhealthy. Indeed, modern statistics show that obesity is a condition that is associated with a number of diseases.

# THE TRADITIONAL
# HAWAIIAN DIET AS A MODEL

The main staple foods of preindustrialized Hawaii were taro (a starchy root much like a potato), and poi, which is a mashed form of taro made into a smooth pudding by mixing it with water. Native Hawaiians also ate sweet potatoes, breadfruit, and yams as staple foods. They also consumed the greens that went along with these staples, such as taro tops and sweet potato greens. The traditional Hawaiian diet also included large amounts of other vegetables and some fruit. There was some fish and other seafood in the diet, depending on how close an individual lived to the ocean or to an ancient aquaculture site. There was also a limited amount of chicken and even some wild pig on special occasions. Those who lived inland were largely vegetarian, and there were no flour products, like bread, or sugar products, like candy. All food was eaten in its whole, natural state, with no processing, refining, or other substantial alteration of its original form. Foods were cooked by broiling, steaming, boiling, baking, or roasting. Food was never fried. In fact, there was no concept of cooking oil or frying pans prior to contact with Westerners. An analysis of the nutrient mix reveals that the traditional Hawaiian diet was approximately ten percent fat, seventy-eight percent carbohydrate, and twelve percent protein.

This is in sharp contrast to a typical American diet, which is between thirty-six and forty-two percent fat, forty-three to forty-nine percent carbohydrate, and approximately fifteen percent protein. This is a drastic change from ancient times. It is no wonder that obesity and health problems result from such a diet.

The difference in nutrient intake is significant, but what is even more radically different is the actual bulk amount, or mass, of food that we consume today as compared to ancient times. Today, though we are generally more overweight, we in fact eat less food than in the old days. As we have seen throughout, this is one of the startling conclusions of the HawaiiDiet™. When we compare the total weight of the foods that were eaten in the traditional Hawaiian diet to a typical American diet, we find that the modern American diet weighs much less.

What special quality in the ancient foods kept Hawaiians slim in ancient times even though they ate more food? Analyzing the nutritional content of poi gives us an excellent clue. A quarter pound of poi provides a little less than sixty-nine calories. Yet it is full of complex carbohydrates and fiber, and derives only one percent of its calories from fat. Because, on the average, a sedentary man or active woman requires about 2,500 calories per day, by this standard he or she would require 9.1 pounds of poi to get one day's worth of calories. Thus, it is virtually impossible to become fat by eating this food. In looking at other traditional foods of Hawaii, we found a similar pattern. A quarter pound of sweet potato provides about ninety-six calories. In order to obtain one day's calories from this food, you would have to eat about 6.5 pounds of it. Taro leaves would provide a day's worth of calories only if you ate twenty-one pounds of them. Hawaiian mountain apples would do the same with about 9.5 pounds.

## TRADITIONAL HAWAIIAN FOODS INDUCE WEIGHT LOSS

The average person will not eat six or nine or twenty pounds of any food. Research indicates that people eat about 2.6 to 4.1 pounds of food before they feel satisfied. Native Hawaiian people remained slim because their foods provided enough bulk to fill them and satisfy their hunger before they could ingest too many calories. Of course, we have to consider that Native Hawaiians' ancestors were much more active than are most Native Hawaiians today. But clinical testing even without added exercise demonstrates that these foods by themselves can induce weight loss.

Here's a typical traditional Hawaiian meal:

|       | *Weight* | *Calories* | *Fat*    |
|-------|----------|-----------|----------|
| Taro  | 4 oz.    | 161       | 0.12 gm. |
| Poi   | 8 oz.    | 151       | 0.3 gm.  |

|  | Weight | Calories | Fat |
|---|---|---|---|
| Sweet potato | 8 oz. | 314 | 1.2 gm. |
| Taro greens (cooked) | 7 oz. | 42 | 0.5 gm. |
| Mountain apple | 5 oz. | 81 | 0.5 gm. |
| Fish | 2 oz. | 75 | 0.7 gm. |
| Seaweed | 1 oz. | 13 | 0.2 gm. |
| Total | 35 oz. | 837 | 3.5 gm. |

Here's a typical modern American meal:

|  | Weight | Calories | Fat |
|---|---|---|---|
| Cheeseburger | 8.5 oz. | 677 | 40 gm. |
| French fries | 4.3 oz. | 400 | 22 gm. |
| Total | 12.8 oz. | 1077 | 62 gm. |

Most researchers are concerned only with the individual nutrients—that is, the calories, fat, protein, etc.—in a particular food. But from the perspective of "wholeness," we look at the whole diet and at nonnutritive aspects of the food as well. One of the most neglected aspects of food is its weight or mass. When you look at the comparison tables above, it is quite obvious that the difference between the weight of the foods in the traditional diet and the weight in the modern diet is enormous. In this example, a traditional Hawaiian meal weighs nearly three times as much as an American meal, yet has fewer calories and less than one-tenth the fat.

How does this affect us? When we eat a typical modern American diet, it turns out to be such a small amount of food in terms of weight or mass that our stomachs remain empty and hunger is not completely satisfied. At the same time, most of these low-weight foods also contain high amounts of energy potential, or calories. Because we have not eaten enough actual bulk, or mass, we begin to crave more food and wind up ordering a dessert of some kind. By contrast, the traditional Hawaiian meal is so bulky and weighs so much (while at the same time generally containing far fewer calories) that when we eat such a meal we are so full that we either can not finish the whole meal or it is a long time before we want to eat another meal. Because we are full and stay full longer, the total amount of calories we ingest decreases, even though we have eaten more food. This, to some extent, explains the Hawaiian paradox. If we eat truly authentic Hawaiian food, it is likely that we will eat more food but take in fewer calories. As a result, we experience an unexpected (and paradoxical) weight loss. Thus, the characteristic that makes traditional Hawaiian food induce weight loss is a high mass-to-energy ratio.

## THE MASS-TO-ENERGY RATIO

As we have seen throughout, the mass-to-energy ratio is a key to the SMI, and therefore to the HawaiiDiet™. Foods have volume, or mass, or bulk: that is, an apple is larger and weighs more than a doughnut. Therefore, it has more mass.

At the same time, foods also have units of energy that we call calories. These two quantities are not proportional. In other words, just because a food is large does not necessarily mean that it has a lot of calories—though it does have more mass. The mass-to-energy ratio, then, is merely the ratio, or relationship, between a food's mass and its energy potential, or calories. The apple's mass-to-energy ratio will be larger than that of a doughnut because the apple is larger in mass, or bulk, though lower in calories. The higher the mass-to-energy ratio of a food, the fuller you become, because the bulk fills your stomach and signals your brain that your hunger is satisfied. At the same time, by relying on high-mass-to-energy foods, you are ingesting fewer calories and usually fewer fats and refined carbohydrates. In addition, foods that have a high mass-to-energy ratio are higher in fiber and much more rich in vitamins and other health-supporting antioxidants and phytochemicals, or plant products.

## IS THIS CONCEPT APPLICABLE
## TO EVERYDAY FOODS?

Is there something special about Hawaiian foods that makes this phenomenon unique? I almost wish this were true because then Hawaii could corner the market on weight-loss foods. But in reality, this is only partially true. Traditional Hawaiian foods are excellent for weight control because they are unusually high in bulk (that is, in actual mass) compared to the number of calories they contain. In general, traditional Hawaiian foods tend to have a higher mass-to-energy ratio than most other traditional foods.

But what if you don't eat poi, sweet potatoes, or other traditional Hawaiian favorites? There are countless other foods that are more commonly available and that serve us just as well.

If we look at how people have been eating around the world over the years, we can learn something about obesity in general. With the Hawaiian paradox in mind, and considering the mass-to-energy ratio of foods, it becomes apparent that as nations become modernized, their populations have actually been eating more foods that are low in mass-to-energy ratio, such as fats, sugars, and refined flour products.

These foods are little more than calories with the rest of the food stripped away. This provides very little bulk and does not fill up the stomach and cause the stomach walls to stretch. The result is that when foods of this kind are consumed, the stomach remains partially empty and you remain hungry. In order to satisfy hunger, you eat more food, usually foods that are similarly low in mass-to-energy ratio. By the time hunger is satisfied, you have eaten an excessive amount of calories. This continued cycle results in obesity.

# DR. SHINTANI'S
# MASS INDEX OF FOOD (SMI)

Most people are interested in calories per serving or calories per ounce of food. I'm more interested in the amount of weight there is in the food *per calorie*. I have calculated the mass-to-energy ratio of a variety of common foods and expressed the number in a simplified manner. The resulting table is, as previously mentioned, Dr. Shintani's Mass Index of Food, or the SMI. You'll find this on page 271. This table helps you find foods that will help you lose weight and satisfy your hunger.

The SMI applies this concept of high mass-to-energy ratio to all foods in a way that is simple to understand. The SMI assigns a number to each food. The higher the number, the more helpful the food is. As previously stated, the U.S. government estimates that the average adult male or active adult female needs about 2,500 calories per day in order to maintain her or his body weight. This will vary from person to person, depending on height, level of activity, special needs, and so on. But how many pounds of food equals 2,500 calories? This is the question that the SMI answers for you at a glance.

Let's look at a couple of weight-loss foods to start with. Broccoli, for instance, is one of the best. This is a high-bulk, low-calorie food that is chock-full of nutrients. Its SMI value is 17. What does this mean? It means that you'd have to eat seventeen pounds of broccoli (about one hundred cups) in order to get your 2,500 calories for the day.

But maybe you don't like broccoli (and you certainly don't like that much of it). Don't worry. There are many weight-loss foods that you'll learn to rely upon. For example, even though you'd have to eat thirty-one apples or thirty ears of corn or twenty-four potatoes in one day in order to get your 2,500 calories, you can mix and match among them. In fact, there is a whole cornucopia of delicious and varied foods just waiting to help you shed those pounds. You can eat all you want of such foods as fresh corn on the cob, certain whole-grain dishes, some delicious soups and casseroles, and a number of pilafs and stir-fried dishes.

No one would expect you to eat seventeen pounds of food in a day, whether it's broccoli or strawberry shortcake. But can you eat five pounds of food in a day? Six? Ten? How much food do you need to eat to be properly nourished and healthy? How much do you dare to eat, if you're trying to watch your weight?

In my own research into weight loss, I've found that the average person eats between three and 4.1 pounds of solid food per day. Other research supports our conclusions. For example, another research project, conducted at the University of Alabama, found that people are satisfied when they eat somewhere between 2.6 and 4.1 pounds of food per day. Keep the number 4.1 in mind as we proceed. It's going to be important, because foods that rank at or above this number on the SMI are foods that will help you lose weight. Furthermore, they tend to be healthy foods because they are generally high in fiber and high in key nutrients.

In my seminars, I like to talk about broccoli versus cheeseburgers when I'm explaining the SMI. I realize that broccoli may not be one of your favorite foods, and I'm not suggesting that you grab a stalk of broccoli every time you get hungry for a cheeseburger. I know that wouldn't work. But broccoli is such a simple and elegant food to work with, and the comparison with cheeseburgers really makes the point.

For example, two cheeseburger meals (with fries and a milk shake) equal 2500 calories. Seventeen pounds, or one hundred cups, of broccoli also equal 2500 calories. But the bulk of the broccoli is much greater than that of the burgers and fries. In other words, you can eat two cheeseburgers with fries in a day—easily—and still be ready for a steak and potatoes at day's end. But after you finish the seventeen pounds of broccoli? You won't have room for another bite for the rest of the day.

Hundreds of other foods also make perfect replacements for the high-fat, high-calorie, low-bulk foods that are getting us all into trouble. All of these foods—and dozens of others—can take the place of those two cheeseburger meals. Soon you'll be combining all these foods into tasty, satisfying weight-loss meals.

| Food | SMI Value |
| --- | --- |
| Potatoes | 9.6 |
| Corn | 6.5 |
| Cabbages | 22.76 |
| Cucumbers | 32.79 |
| Peaches | 16.50 |
| Radishes | 32.14 |
| Oranges | 15.61 |
| Tomatoes | 27.32 |
| Lettuce | 39.02 |
| Green beans | 21.85 |

Another example is corn. It takes 6.5 pounds of corn to provide one day's worth of calories for an average man or average active woman. Other common examples are oatmeal (9.9 pounds), potatoes (9.6 pounds), and apples (9.4 pounds).

The fact that it's almost physically impossible to eat that amount of high-bulk food in a day means that no matter how hard you try, you *won't* eat 2,500 calories worth, even in combination. You can eat all you want and you're still bound to lose weight. Furthermore, none of these foods have the saturated fat or other unhealthy ingredients that you'd find in that cheeseburger meal, or in most of the other foods we eat. In fact, they all contain wonderful, and wonderfully varied, nutrients that will help you on the road to good health.

The HawaiiDiet™ concept of filling the stomach to produce weight loss finds scientific support in an unexpected field—the surgical intervention of obesity. The problem of morbid obesity in America has been so perplexing that in severe cases, stomach surgery is used in order to help induce weight loss. The concept is very simple but drastic. In order to reduce the caloric intake of a morbidly obese person, a portion of the stomach is either cut away or stapled off with surgical staples. This reduces the volume of the stomach so that the stomach stretches more quickly with less food than it would ordinarily require. The stretching of the stomach induces a feeling of fullness through receptors in the stomach wall that send signals to the brain through the vagus nerve. A sensation of satiety is also induced because stretching the stomach causes a release of gastrointestinal hormones such as cholecystokinin, which is known to cause a feeling of satisfaction.

Of course I'm not recommending the surgical method. All I'm saying is that this intervention demonstrates that the concept of filling the stomach to induce weight loss works. So if it works, why not make use of this mechanism by using the natural stomach-stretching qualities of real food? Wouldn't this be a much simpler method?

## DOES THE HAWAIIDIET™ WORK FOR ALL ETHNIC GROUPS?

If this program and these principles work with Native Hawaiians, who have among the most difficult problems with obesity in the world, they should work with anyone. But just why do Native Hawaiians have such a propensity to gain weight during modern times? There are several theories. Perhaps Native Hawaiians adapted over the years to a diet that was unusually high in bulk and low in calories. Perhaps they adapted in this way because at one time they were forced to live on foods from which it was difficult to obtain calories, so that they had to learn to use calories more effectively. This may explain why today's Native Hawaiian people tend to gain weight so readily with modern American foods that are very low in mass-to-energy ratio. If it is true that Native Hawaiians gain weight more readily on modern foods than do people of most other ethnic backgrounds, perhaps is also true that those of other backgrounds should lose weight more quickly by using traditional Native Hawaiian or similar foods. This concept should work as well or even better on those who are not Native Hawaiian.

## IS THE HAWAIIDIET™ HEALTHY?

Losing weight can be accomplished in a healthy way or an unhealthy way. Weight control means nothing if the foods recommended increase your risks of chronic disease. With the HawaiiDiet™, there is no guessing whether it is healthy or not because it was designed primarily to improve health. The proof is in our results. A diet that helps improve health does so by lowering risk factors. Measuring lipids and blood sugar are good ways to evaluate the healthfulness of a diet. The results in the 1997 HawaiiDiet™ test group were as follows.

During a three-week time period, average cholesterol in the participants' blood decreased 23.6 percent, from an average of 205 milligrams per deciliter (mg/dl) to 157 mg/dl. At the beginning of the program, there were eleven people with cholesterol counts higher than 200. At the end of the program, there was only one person whose cholesterol count was higher than 200.

Average triglycerides (blood fats) decreased 36.3 percent, from an average of 238 mg/dl to 152 mg/dl. One person's triglycerides decreased 863 mg/dl, from 988 mg/dl to 125 mg/dl. Another person's triglycerides decreased from 617 mg/dl to 83 mg/dl.

Blood sugar in those with diabetes or borderline diabetes fell an average of thirty-one percent, from an average of 177 mg/dl to 122 mg/dl. This drop resulted even though the four participants on medication for diabetes were able to reduce their medications, including one who got off ninety units of insulin.

Average blood pressure fell from 130/79 to 120/75. This resulted even after eliminating one person's blood pressure medication as soon as his blood pressure dropped to normal levels, and also after reducing the blood pressure medications of two other people.

## HOW DOES THIS DIET COMPARE TO OTHER TRADITIONAL DIETS?

When we compare the HawaiiDiet™ to other traditional diets, we can see that the very low fat content of the HawaiiDiet™ matches the diets of countries where heart disease rates are low. In fact, when we compare dietary fat intake of different countries, the lower the fat intake, the lower the heart disease rate.

The HawaiiDiet™ is similar in a number of ways to some of the healthiest diets in the world—the diets of Asia. These diets, which include Japanese, Chinese, traditional Southeast Asian, and so on, are similarly low in fat, high in complex carbohydrates, and moderate in protein. International studies have demonstrated that the nations that have the lowest rates of chronic diseases, such as heart disease and diabetes, are nations that have dietary profiles similar to traditional Asian and Pacific models.

### Traditional Japanese Diet

One excellent example of a healthy diet similar to that of ancient Hawaii is the Japanese diet. We took great interest in the Japanese diet because as a nation, Japan has the population with the longest life span in the world and the largest well-documented segment of people surviving to be more than one hundred years of age. Japan has also had consistently low rates of heart disease. They also have low rates of diabetes and low rates of the cancers that are common in the U.S., such as lung cancer, prostate cancer, breast cancer, and colon cancer.

The typical traditional Japanese diet consists of rice as its main staple and makes use of large amounts of vegetables, fruit, seaweed, and small amounts of seafood and an occasional piece of chicken or pork. From a macronutrient perspective, the traditional Japanese diet was also high in carbohydrate (seventy-eight percent), very low in fat (nine percent), and moderate in protein (thirteen percent). The foods are high in fiber, low in cholesterol, and low in saturated fats.

*Traditional Chinese Diet*

In the 1980s, a massive research project studying the relationship between diet and disease known as the Chinese diet study was conducted by a multinational team from Cornell University, Oxford University, and the University of Beijing headed by Dr. T. Colin Campbell. This study, involving more than one hundred villages, revealed that the Chinese diet was also associated with low rates of chronic diseases, as was the Japanese diet. In some areas in China, heart disease was virtually nonexistent. While many of the foods were quite different from the Japanese diet, the center of the diet was the same—rice—and an overall similar dietary pattern emerged in terms of the macronutrient content. The Chinese diet averaged 14.5 percent fat and about 10.5 percent protein, with the remaining seventy-five percent of calories coming from carbohydrates. Meat, poultry, or fish sources averaged less than one ounce per day.

Typically, in epidemiological studies, the countries that had the lowest rates of heart disease were the Asian countries whose diets are based largely on rice and whole foods of plant origin with very little if any meat. Numerous studies have confirmed that a very low-fat diet can help to reduce cholesterol, triglycerides, and blood pressure. There are even studies that demonstrate that a low-fat diet can reverse existing atherosclerotic plaques, or hardening of the arteries, and eliminate the need for bypass surgery.

In these studies, the way cholesterol is typically controlled is by (1) reducing the intake of saturated fat, (2) reducing the intake of fats and oils of all types so that the total fat intake is low, (3) reducing the intake of cholesterol by eliminating or greatly reducing the intake of animal products, and (4) increasing the intake of foods containing soluble fiber, such as oatmeal, whole wheat, brown rice, and other whole grains. The HawaiiDiet™ does all these and more.

## Mediterranean Diets

The one exception to this rule of a high-fat diet being associated with high rates of heart disease is Greece, and in particular the island of Crete. There, the rate of heart disease was as low as the lowest rate of coronary disease in any of the countries studied. The Seven Countries Study, a monumental study on the relationship between nutrition and coronary disease in the United States, Yugoslavia, Finland, Italy, the Netherlands, Greece, and Japan, involved a total of 12,763 participants and was sponsored by the U.S. Public Health Service, the American Heart Association, and similar associations and organizations in the participating nations. The study began in 1958 and continued through the 1960s and early 1970s. (See Appendix 3F.) The anomaly of the Greek population stimulated interest in traditional Mediterranean diets and the use of olive oil. Careful analysis reveals that a country's level of modernization or industrialization provides a better explanation for disease rates than does the level of dietary fat. Subsequent studies indicate that as Crete modernizes, coronary disease also rises, despite little change in total fat intake. The reasons for this are as yet unknown, but many speculate that the high whole-vegetable and fruit content of traditional diets—i.e., foods high in mass-to-energy ratio—provided certain nutrients such as vitamins and phytochemicals that protected people prior to modernization. The more industrialized a nation, the more likely it is that their population will suffer from a high rate of heart disease. In other words, the farther populations stray from the ways and the diets of their ancestors (their "source"), the worse their health becomes.

In Crete, despite having a high-fat diet, the population, which is still largely nonindustrialized, follows the diet of their ancestors. Even though this diet was relatively high in fat, due to the use of olives and olive oil, the vegetable and fruit content was high, and thus the people ate foods that were high in mass-to-energy ratio. The carbohydrates in their diet were also different in that they were largely unrefined. They were made up of whole grains, such as wheat, rye, barley, buckwheat, or rice, or coarsely ground grains, such as very coarse whole-wheat bread. Adaptation of the Cretan population over many years to this type of diet, combined with other aspects of their lifestyle, may be just as important as the food itself in determining their low rate of heart disease. However, the anomaly of the Cretan diet bears further research, and is in fact receiving a great deal of attention in the nutrition community and has made Mediterranean-style diets popular in some circles.

There is an additional concern with regard to very low-fat diets. There are some reports now that link unusually low levels of cholesterol with hemorrhagic stroke. Hemmorhagic stroke is a result of bleeding in the brain, in contrast to the strokes caused by blocked arteries in the brain. In this regard, a higher-fat diet may have an advantage over a very low-fat diet. However, this is a concern only for some individuals. Do not use this as an excuse to continue eating excessive dietary fat, for the number of studies that show that fat can be harmful to your health far exceed the number of studies that indicate otherwise.

## DIET AND CANCER

In addition to being helpful in weight loss and the control of cholesterol and triglycerides, low-fat diets appear to be important in the prevention of cancer. Cancer is the number two killer in America. It currently kills one in four Americans, despite our best efforts with early diagnosis, technology, surgery, and chemotherapy. Internationally, there is a strong correlation between the modernization of diet and mortality from those cancers that are most common in the U.S. In the early 1980s, the National Cancer Institute finally acknowledged that poor diet was the leading cause of cancer. It makes sense, then, that eating a good diet would be the number one way to prevent cancer. In studies comparing cancer rates around the world, it appears that incidences of some of the most common cancers in America, such as breast cancer, prostate cancer, and colon cancer, are much lower in places that are less industrialized and, judging by the low fat content, presumably still following their ancient traditional diets.

While the direct association between dietary fat and breast cancer is disputed, and certain studies indicate no relationship between dietary fat and breast cancer, other studies tend to confirm a relationship between both saturated and unsaturated fats and breast cancer. However, there is some question as to whether or not monounsaturated fats will contribute to cancer as do saturated fats and polyunsaturated fats.

Monounsaturated fats are those types of fats that are found in olive oil, macadamia nut oil, and canola oil. Polyunsaturated fats are found in vegetables oils such as corn oil and safflower oil.

Whether this relationship holds up or not, what is not disputed is that the further away from its traditional diet a population goes, the higher its rate of breast cancer and some other forms of cancer that are common in America today.

## DIET AND DIABETES

Diabetes is another disease that is more common in modernized nations than in nations that are still following their traditional dietary patterns. While Japan, for example, has become as industrialized as the U.S., the nation has been slow to change its diet away from its usual rice-centered fare. Meanwhile, prior to industrialization, many of the people of Japan migrated to the U.S. Their descendants have become part of the mainstream culture here and have to a large extent adopted the American diet and lifestyle. The difference in the rate of diabetes is striking. In Hawaii, where the diet is mostly modernized but still has some of the aspects of the traditional Japanese diet, the diabetes rate among immigrant Japanese is two hundred percent higher than the rate in Japan. In Washington, D.C., where the diet is essentially the same as the modern American diet, the diabetes rate among immigrant Japanese population is three hundred percent higher than the rate in Japan. Thus, these studies show that Americans of Japanese ancestry are not protected by their ethnic makeup and they are affected by their diet in a manner similar to the way Americans of European ancestry or of African ancestry are affected.

Another consideration is blood sugar. If you have diabetes, the management of blood sugar is of great importance. A number of researchers have suggested that people with diabetes have great difficulty handling carbohydrates. In our research, we have found just the opposite. Roughly one third of the people on our program do extremely well and I am able to get them off insulin very quickly with our high-carbohydrate diet, some of them within a matter of days. Another forty percent of our participants respond gradually. And the rest, with a few exceptions, respond very slowly. There are a few rare patients who don't seem to be able to improve their blood sugar with our low-fat version of the HawaiiDiet™. For those who have tried the Pacific-style HawaiiDiet™ and who do not see a good response, I advise them to try the Mediterranean-style HawaiiDiet™ and gradually increase their intake of monounsaturated fats, such as extra-virgin olive oil, macadamia nut oil, or good-quality canola oil.

## THE HAWAIIDIET™ PYRAMID

In order to develop guidelines for the HawaiiDiet™, we compared our research with information on diets around the world. From looking at the relationship between diet and disease, we concluded that the common characteristics of a healthy diet are as follows:

- The diet is centered on whole, unrefined complex carbohydrates
- The foods are moderate to high on the SMI index
- Most or all calories come from vegetable sources
- Most or all protein comes from vegetable sources
- No more than one ounce of animal flesh is eaten per day
- The diet has little or no added fat
- The diet has very little saturated fat
- The diet contains some monounsaturated fat in as whole a form as possible for those adapted to higher-fat diets
- Dairy products, refined fats, oils, sugars, and alcohol are optional but only in small amounts

In order to express these concepts as simply as possible, I designed the HawaiiDiet™ pyramid. As I said, it is modeled after the USDA Food Guide Pyramid so that health professionals who are accustomed to the pyramid format can use it effectively. However, there are a number of differences between the HawaiiDiet™ pyramid and the USDA pyramid.

The USDA Food Guide Pyramid is an improvement over the old four basic food groups dietary model. But in my opinion and that of many other scientists, it is not good enough. Here is what it looks like:

**The USDA Food Guide Pyramid**
A Guide to Daily Food Choices

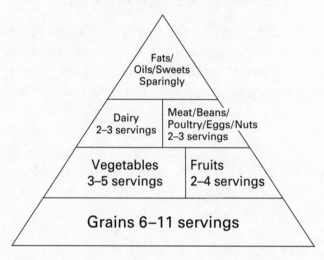

The USDA's pyramid provides for the daily use of dairy and meat, as you can see. In my opinion, and in the opinion of many other scientists, the USDA is much too liberal with dairy and meat groups. Less would be better for the purpose of preventing heart disease, certain cancers, and other chronic diseases. Compare it to:

**The HawaiiDiet™ Pyramid**
A Guide to Daily Food Choices

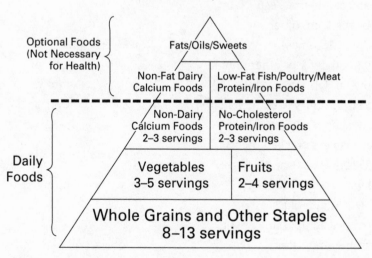

## UNDERSTANDING
## THE HAWAIIDIET™ PYRAMID

The HawaiiDiet™ pyramid helps to ensure that the nutrients you obtain from food are adequate. The following table shows, in another form, how the HawaiiDiet™ pyramid differs from the USDA pyramid. I recommend the HawaiiDiet™ pyramid as your guide for daily use.

| Food Groups | Servings in USDA Food Guide Pyramid | Servings in HawaiiDiet™ Pyramid |
| --- | --- | --- |
| Grains and other main staples (Potatoes, corn, taro, oats, millet, buckwheat, brown rice) | 6–11 | 8–13 |
| Vegetables (Squash, tomatoes, onions, broccoli, mushrooms) | 3–5 | 3–5 |
| Fruit (Apples, oranges, bananas, papaya) | 2–4 | 2–4 |
| Non-dairy calcium foods (Watercress, mustard greens, seaweed, cabbage, broccoli, turnip tops, kale) | | 2–3 |
| No-cholesterol protein/iron foods (Beans of all kinds, especially soybeans, tofu, other soy products, legumes) | | 2–3 |
| Dairy (Skim milk or other nonfat or low-fat dairy products) | 2–3 | never or rarely |
| Meat/Fish/Poultry (Cod, perch, scrod, snapper, halibut, fresh tuna, skinless chicken breasts) | 2–3 | never or rarely |
| Fats/Oils/Sweets (Canola, olive, and macadamia nut oils; maple syrup, molasses, brown rice syrup, barley malt, blackstrap molasses) | sparingly | never or rarely |

# DO OUR GENES DETERMINE
# WHAT FOODS WE SHOULD EAT?

The question "Do our genes determine what foods we should eat?" was the title of a *Newsweek* article (August 9, 1993) that featured our program. It is a good question. There are genetic differences among people and the way their bodies respond to food, in terms of cholesterol levels, blood sugar levels, allergies, and other responses. Probably the most obvious difference lies in how much fat people retain as a result of what they are eating. We all know of families in which one sibling is slim and another sibling is overweight, even while growing up on the same food and eating at the same table.

In my practice, I often see examples of how some individuals can become very large on ordinary food and how other individuals have difficulty gaining weight even while eating large quantities of food. I routinely have patients who weigh more than three hundred pounds and some who weigh more than six hundred pounds. I once had a patient walk into my office at 677 pounds. The largest patient I ever had the privilege of treating weighed more than 890 pounds. Many people see these individuals as having a deep-seated behavioral problem of overeating or sheer gluttony. Yet if a lottery company were to offer a million dollars plus an unlimited amount of food to anyone who could reach four hundred pounds, it would be impossible for ninety-nine percent of the population. This is because of their lack of genetic ability to gain that much weight. I know this not only because of my experience, but also because in the 1950s, research was done that demonstrated that people could not gain weight beyond a genetically set limit. It cited one case in which a subject was given an incentive to try to gain as much weight as he could. He gained twenty-eight pounds only to find that he could not gain the twenty-ninth pound, despite eating more than seven thousand calories per day. In other words, this study indicates that people are genetically limited in terms of how large they can become. We are all affected by our genes and diet.

Faced with examples such as these, there is a great temptation to just throw our hands up and say, "Why bother to try? It's all in the genes anyway." Let me dispel this myth immediately. What you need to know is that everyone is affected by genes and everyone is affected by diet. This principle is well illustrated by what happens in genetically similar mice when they are fed diets with different quantities of fat. In one study, the mice were broken up into different groups and allowed to eat as much as they wanted of a feed with a set amount of fat, carbohydrate, and protein. The amount of protein remained the same in each feed, but each feed had a different amount of fat, offset by increasing or decreasing the amount of carbohydrate. The results showed that the higher the fat in the diet, the higher the fat in the mice. It clearly showed that diet makes a difference in quantity of body fat.

However, the research also clearly showed that genes do make a difference. Many of the mice in this experiment became very obese when eating a high-fat diet, but some of them remained slim. Genes protected some of the mice from becoming obese, but in others, genes for extreme obesity were expressed as a result of the high-fat diet.

This study illustrates two important points. First, it shows that a change in diet, such as a change to a low-fat diet, will affect even those with genes that program them to be very obese. In other words, diet can override the effect of genes, or, put in still another way, diet can prevent the expression of the genes for obesity. Second, the study shows that within this genetically similar group of individuals, a wide variation in the response to high-fat diets occurred. Most individuals responded in an average way, gaining some weight when there was an increase in dietary fat. Yet some of them remained slim and others became very obese.

This variation is found in many other aspects of nature. Variation within a species is one of nature's ways of ensuring the adaptation and survival of a species through changing times and conditions. In animals and humans, one of the most obvious expressions of variation is size, i.e., weight and height. This variation generally applies to most other measurable biological characteristics, including the many that relate to human health.

## ETHNICITY IS NOT
## THE BEST INDICATOR OF IDEAL DIET

Back to the question: Do our genes determine what we should eat? The answer is to some extent, yes. But ethnicity is not the only element determined by genes. While it is tempting to say that people whose ancestors are from the Mediterranean should eat a Mediterranean-style diet and people from the Pacific should eat a Pacific-style diet, this is not very useful because of the wide variation within ethnic groups. The truth is that people are more similar *between* cultures than they are *within* cultures. We must recognize that within each group there will be individuals who respond well to a low-fat diet and those who will respond well to a higher-fat diet. In addition, people with genes that make them prone to obesity are more similar to people in other cultures who also have those genes than they are to others in their own culture or ethnicity who tend to be slender.

Still, we know that ethnicities have certain general tendencies with regard to weight. For example, Polynesians and certain Native Americans tend to become more obese than other ethnic groups on the modern American diet. But, within these and other ethnic groups, we find a subpopulation that tends to be vastly overweight, another that tends to be slender, and the majority who fall somewhere in the middle of the other two groups. Thus, ethnicity or race is only a rough prediction of how an individual will respond to a diet. It is an even poorer prediction of other seemingly related characteristics, such as the level of cholesterol or triglycerides.

## BLOOD TYPE IS NOT
## A GOOD INDICATOR OF IDEAL DIET

Recently, there has been popular interest in the use of blood type as a predictor of what diet one should eat. However, using blood type as a predictor doesn't work very well. The genes for blood type and the genes that determine obesity, cholesterol levels, and propensity for diabetes do not necessarily travel with each other; therefore, they cannot be measured as effects of one another. In reality, the literature cited by proponents of the "blood-type diets" is very old (from the 1950s and 1960s) and shows only a weak correlation between blood type and coronary disease. More modern studies indicate that the relationship between blood type and risk of heart disease barely reaches the level of statistical significance. In addition, one of the best heart disease research projects in the world, the Framingham Heart Study, shows no correlation between blood type and risk of heart disease. In other words, at best, blood type is a poor predictor of how a group will respond to a certain diet. If it is a poor predictor of how groups of people will respond, it is certainly an even worse predictor of what an optimal diet should be for an individual.

## SOME INDICATORS OF THE IDEAL DIET

There are better ways to determine the best diet for an individual. In general, the best way to see how one responds to a diet is based on objective measures. One of them is body weight. If you have a problem with obesity (and presuming you don't have an underlying condition that causes your obesity) a low-fat, high-SMI diet is optimal. If you don't have a weight problem, a higher-fat diet may be okay from the perspective of weight control. Whether this is a good idea in general is another question altogether. Low body weight does not necessarily mean that you have low cholesterol or a low risk of heart disease or other diseases. But at least it is a foundation for good health. However, you should pursue good health at the same time that you pursue sensible weight control. Remember: Thinness does not inherently equal good health.

Cholesterol levels are another good indicator of what type of diet suits you best. At the same time, they are another widely varying factor in individuals. Slimmer people tend to have lower cholesterol, but not necessarily. Cholesterol levels are often independent of weight. I have had patients with high cholesterol levels who are very trim (think of Jim Fixx, the marathoner who appeared to be slim and fit but who died of a heart attack); and I have had four-hundred-pound patients with cholesterol levels in the 160s. On the other hand, if your cholesterol is too low, say, in the 140s or lower, there is some concern that you might be at an increased risk of hemorrhagic stroke. While this is not a frequently occurring disease in America, those who have very low cholesterol, especially if they have a family history of hemorrhagic stroke, should consider keeping their cholesterol levels higher than 150 by adopting a higher-fat diet. They can do this by using the Mediterranean-style HawaiiDiet™.

Another indicator of what type of diet might suit you best is your blood sugar response. In most people, this is not commonly tested. Blood sugar is usually tested only if there is a reason to suspect glucose intolerance or diabetes. For those who are also overweight, I always try the low-fat Pacific-style HawaiiDiet™. If there is an indication that these individuals' blood sugars don't respond well to their diets, I first try to be sure that they are following the diet as diligently as possible and try to move their food selections up the SMI scale. If that doesn't seem to work, then I move toward the Mediterranean-style Hawaii-Diet™.

## MATCH THE HAWAIIDIET™ TO YOUR GENETIC TYPE

We return to the question: What is the best diet for you? There's no pat answer. For most people a low-fat, whole plant–based diet represented by the Pacific Style HawaiiDiet™ (excluding optional foods) is ideal. The best way to determine what works best for you is to try it yourself and see. It is also helpful to have your physician record your weight, test your blood, and take your family history. Based on these factors, he or she can give you some recommendations. In general, the diet program outlined in this book works for everyone, because it has room for variation. In order to determine what style of the HawaiiDiet™ you should be on, consider the following criteria. Remember that these are general guidelines that I use based on my reading of the current scientific literature. Remember also that the diets have room for variation between the two styles of eating and can slide along the spectrum of these diets.

Consider the Pacific-style HawaiiDiet™ if any of the following apply:

- You want to lose weight
- You have high cholesterol or cardiovascular disease
- You have a family history of breast, prostate, or colon cancer
- You have high blood sugar

Move toward the Mediterranean-style HawaiiDiet™ if at least three of the following apply:

- You don't need to lose weight
- You have very low cholesterol (below 150)
- You have a family history of hemorrhagic stroke
- You have tried the Pacific-style diet and your blood sugars don't respond well

If you don't have access to information about your family history and blood test results, and your main concern is your weight, one simple way to decide what type of HawaiiDiet™ to follow and how much fat you can tolerate is to match your BMI (Body Mass Index) to the SMI of your foods. Body Mass Index is a modern way of measuring obesity by dividing your weight (in kilograms) by your height (in meters) squared.

In other words, the higher your weight in relation to your height, the higher the SMI values of your food choices should be. The Pacific-style HawaiiDiet™ features foods higher in SMI value than the Mediterranean style. Thus, if you are overweight, you should follow a low-fat Pacific-style HawaiiDiet™ and choose higher SMI foods. If you are slim, you can follow a Mediterranean-style HawaiiDiet™ and choose somewhat lower SMI foods. In this way, you can optimize the diet for your specific needs.

# FIVE

# The Scientific Basis of the HawaiiDiet™

This chapter concerns the food components that scientists call macronutrients: carbohydrates (including dietary fiber), fats, and protein. It also provides additional information about micronutrients, such as vitamins, minerals, and phytochemicals (including antioxidants).

## CARBOHYDRATES

Carbohydrates have been the principle source of calories for humans throughout history. Carbohydrates provide the fuel that in turn provides most of the energy that has allowed the human race to thrive over the millennia. The traditional Hawaiian diet was centered on whole starchy staples (starch is one form of complex carbohydrate), such as taro, poi, and sweet potato. The principal source of calories in most ancient cultures was similarly centered on whole complex carbohydrates, such as whole grains and potatoes. The HawaiiDiet™ includes all of these whole staple foods as the main source of energy.

*Types of Carbohydrate*
There are two types of dietary carbohydrates—starches and sugars. Starches are actually long chains of sugar molecules linked together into one big strand-like macromolecule. Starches are also known as

complex carbohydrates. Sugars are either single molecules (monosaccharides, such as glucose and fructose) or pairs of sugar molecules (disaccharides, such as sucrose and maltose). Sugars are also known as simple carbohydrates. They all provide about four calories per gram. When carbohydrates are in whole foods that are made up primarily of carbohydrates, and they are left intact, as they are in brown rice, they provide about one calorie per gram. In this book, the word "refined" refers to foods that have been milled, ground, processed, or divided with parts of them removed, like white flour, white rice, etc. There are refined complex carbohydrates (white flour, in contrast to whole potatoes) and there are refined sugars (white sugar, in contrast to fruit sugar). Please keep these distinctions in mind, as they are important in explaining the Hawaiian paradox.

*The Carbohydrate Controversy*
Recently, carbohydrates have been the source of some controversy. A few decades ago, carbohydrates were thought to be one of the causes of obesity. If weight loss was the goal, people were advised to avoid carbohydrates.

At that time, experts indicated that meats were the healthiest foods. In the 1950s and 1960s, as a result of advertising and the recommendations of "experts," America went on a binge of animal-product consumption. Sales of meats, eggs, and cheeses boomed as never before. Then came the gradual realization that cholesterol, which is only found in animal products, and saturated fats, which are found in abundance in animal products, may contribute to the development of heart disease.

As emerging research indicated that dietary fat was even more important than dietary cholesterol in increasing blood cholesterol levels and the risk of heart disease, the scientific community began recommending a low-fat diet. But the calories lost by avoiding fat had to be replaced with other calories. A number of health organizations, such as the American Heart Association, began to advise a higher level of consumption of carbohydrates in order to replace those lost calories. I agree with these recommendations. However, there is both a beneficial way and a detrimental way of consuming carbohydrates.

Some authors of low-fat diet plans essentially suggest that all you have to do is count fat grams and you will automatically lose weight and be healthier. In other words, they recommend that you can reduce dietary fats yet eat an unlimited amount of carbohydrates in any form, including white sugar and white flour, and still not gain weight. The low-fat craze has resulted in a whole mini-industry producing low-fat, high-carbohydrate foods, from low-fat packaged foods, such as low-fat cheeses, to a line of low-fat snacks and artificial fats. While some of these foods are definitely an improvement over what we have been eating, there is evidence that many of these foods have gone too far. For example, studies on artificial fats indicate that blood levels of retinoids, that is, a class of plant-based nutrients that may play a part in cancer prevention, decreased significantly in individuals consuming artificial fats.

Recently, we have come full circle and many experts are now concerned that carbohydrates are not as benign as once thought. It has been assumed for some time that carbohydrates have a negative effect on people who have diabetes or borderline diabetes because carbohydrates (some of them, at least) increase blood sugar. This has some logical basis, because carbohydrates are nothing but starches and sugars, and starches are nothing more than long chains of sugars that are broken down into individual sugar molecules before they are digested. Moreover, some studies comparing high carbohydrate diets and low carbohydrate dies indicate that diets high in carbohydrates tend to raise blood sugar more than diets with fewer carbohydrates. A number of researchers and authors have used such studies to say that all diets high in carbohydrates are bad.

This is unfortunate because such a conclusion is an overgeneralization of the results of the research. These scientists would have difficulty explaining why, in Asia and ancient Polynesia, people ate up to eighty percent carbohydrates and still remained slim and free of diabetes. Careful analysis indicates that the carbohydrates used in these studies were primarily simple or refined carbohydrates, such as bread, muffins, juice, or fruit. But because the HawaiiDiet™ emphasizes whole foods, the carbohydrates are taken in more slowly and are digested more slowly, thus reducing the glucose load on the body within a given amount of time. This difference in the type or form of the foods may explain why, in practice, other studies' results are contrary to the experience and the results of the HawaiiDiet™ program.

*Dietary Fiber*

While most people don't think of dietary fiber as a carbohydrate, structurally it is a carbohydrate. However, in the context of nutrition it is not referred to as a carbohydrate because it is not digestible and provides no nutritional value. But it merits inclusion here because most high-carbohydrate foods, such as whole grains and fruit, are also high in fiber.

One of the most important factors that makes the Hawaiian paradox work in your favor is dietary fiber, which has no calories, vitamins, or minerals and is not even absorbed. Despite fiber's nonnutritive nature, high-fiber diets are associated with lower risk of heart disease, colon cancer, diabetes, and a variety of gastrointestinal diseases. Fiber has also been shown to help in promoting a sense of fullness.

What is dietary fiber? Dietary fiber is the substance that makes up the structural part of plants, grains, fruit, seeds, and other plant-based foods. There are two main types of dietary fiber. Soluble fiber is the type that dissolves in water and becomes a gel-like substance. Pectins (the stuff that makes jelly gel) and gums are in this category. These substances are known to control cholesterol by binding it in the gut and carrying it out in bowel movements. Soluble fiber is found in whole grains, beans, fruit, and vegetables.

Insoluble fiber is the type that does not dissolve in water. This type of fiber, along with soluble fiber, expands in the stomach and creates a sensation of fullness that helps to reduce the intake of calories.

All whole plant-based foods contain some insoluble fiber. These include fruits and vegetables, but one of our richest sources is whole grains, including whole-grain breads and cereals. The outer coatings of grains are especially rich in insoluble fiber, which is one reason why many people take bran as a supplement. Insoluble fiber also increases stool bulk and lowers the transit time through the intestines. Both types of fiber seem to reduce the rate of absorption of sugar into the bloodstream by diluting the concentration of sugar in the gastrointestinal tract.

The HawaiiDiet™ encourages the consumption of foods that are high in fiber, because foods that are high on the SMI index have a high mass-to-energy ratio, and such foods typically have a lot of fiber. This is one of the reasons that people on the HawaiiDiet™ experience weight loss while feeling full and and experience blood sugar reduction while eating more carbohydrates.

### Carbohydrates and Blood Sugar

Control over blood sugar and insulin occurs as a result of a reduction in glucose load—that is, the amount of glucose being absorbed over a specific period of time. Nowhere is this more dramatically apparent than in some of our patients with diabetes who are taking insulin. All but a very few of them see a reduction in their blood sugar level. Why does this occur? Research on blood sugar response to food intake gives us some indication. One of the ways scientists assess the healthfulness of a food is to measure its glycemic index. The glycemic index is a measure of how much a person's blood sugar rises over a certain period of time (usually two to four hours) after the ingestion of one hundred calories of a food. The higher the glycemic index, the higher the blood sugar. In some studies, scientists have concluded that one of the most important factors in predicting how high the glycemic index will be is the surface area of the food. The more finely a food is ground, or the more highly refined a food is, the more likely it is to have a high glycemic index because grinding it increases its surface area. Those foods that have a high SMI value usually have a small surface area and thus a low glycemic index.

This indicates that it makes a big difference whether a food is whole, like baked potatoes, or refined, like bread. Research done on the difference between potatoes and potato flour illustrates this point. When people eat whole potatoes, their blood sugar rises. However, when they eat potato flour, their blood sugar rises much higher, as does their blood insulin level. The same holds true with rice and rice flour. (See Appendix 3G.) In other words, the more refined, the more finely ground a food is, the more likely it is to have a high glycemic index and raise insulin levels.

The reduction in insulin carries with it additional benefits. Insulin is a hormone that promotes obesity. The reduction in insulin levels appears to help people, at least in theory, in their efforts to lose weight. Weight loss on the HawaiiDiet™ is well documented. How much insulin control plays a part is uncertain. Whatever the mechanism, some combination of the multiple aspects of the HawaiiDiet™ seems to reduce blood sugar levels, reduce insulin requirements in those with blood sugar problems, and induce natural weight loss in those who are overweight.

### Carbohydrates and Cardiovascular Risk

Some experts have gone as far as to say that carbohydrates increase the risk of heart disease. Recent studies do indicate that an increase in carbohydrates results in a decrease in high-density lipoprotein (HDL), also known as good cholesterol. Some of these studies indicate that high-carbohydrate diets also result in high triglyceride, or blood fat, levels. As a result of these and other studies, some diabetes educators have been encouraging selected patients to reduce their carbohydrate intake.

However, the HawaiiDiet™ yields results that are contrary to the theory that a high-carbohydrate diet increases the risk of cardiovascular disease. Our research indicates that, with a high-carbohydrate diet, not only does a person's cholesterol level improve, but triglycerides are dramatically reduced. And while the "good cholesterol" levels are also reduced, this is in relation to a large overall decrease in total cholesterol, and an even greater reduction in the "bad cholesterol" levels. This translates to decreased coronary risk.

## FATS

In keeping with traditional dietary patterns from around the world in populations that have low rates of chronic diseases, the typical HawaiiDiet™ is, for most people, very low in fat—especially the Pacific-style HawaiiDiet™ because in Hawaii and the Pacific, including eastern Asia, traditional diets were uniformly low in fat.

### Do Fats Make You Fat?

Probably the best reason to avoid dietary fat is that substantial evidence indicates that dietary fat promotes obesity. The evidence is found in population studies, animal studies, research on nutrients and biochemical pathways, and in clinical trials.

Metabolic studies indicate that fats promote obesity in at least two different ways. First, fat, a substance used by plants and animals for storing energy, is the highest of all foods in calorie concentration. In other words, it is lighter in weight and occupies less space than other foods, yet contains more calories, so you get more storage potential with a smaller amount of weight and space. Second, because over millions of years of evolution the body has chosen fat as its best energy-storage option, it has devised a very efficient metabolic pathway for converting dietary fat to body fat. It requires a mere three calories to convert every one hundred calories of dietary fat into body fat, which means that ninety-seven calories of every one hundred fat calories we eat, if they are not used, will be stored as fat. Carbohydrates, on the other hand, are stored very inefficiently. In order to turn one hundred calories of carbohydrate into fat, or stored energy, it takes fully twenty-three calories, leaving sixty-seven calories to be burned or stored. This is still substantial, but nowhere near as dramatic as the dietary-fat-to-body-fat ratio.

Carbohydrate overfeeding studies indicate that dietary carbohydrate, even when taken in excess of necessary calories, results in very little fat production. This is the type of study that helped to create the notion that you could eat as much carbohydrate as you want and still lose weight, as long as fat grams were kept to a minimum. This is only partially true, however. Further studies indicate that if carbohydrates are taken in the wrong form, i.e., as refined (non-whole) foods like sugar and flour, they have an adverse effect on "good cholesterol" and may induce high levels of insulin, which promotes the production of fat.

*Do Fats Satisfy Hunger?*

Some experts argue that fats curb obesity by curbing hunger. They assert that the secretion of the gastrointestinal hormone cholecystokinin, which induces a feeling of satiety, is caused by fats when they reach the stomach. This may be true, but because of the high calorie concentration of fat, the actual satiety value, calorie for calorie, is not as good as it is with foods that are low in fat and high in bulk. Studies on the comparative satiety effect of foods indicate that satiety per calorie is inversely proportional to the amount of fat eaten. In other words, the higher the fat content of a food, the lower the per-calorie satisfaction you get from it. It is only a small logical step to the conclusion that eating fat causes people to become fat simply because, calorie for calorie, it isn't as satisfying as other foods.

### Why Low-Fat Diets Are Not Enough

At one time, some proponents of low-fat diets suggested that all you had to do to lose weight was count fat grams and limit your intake of them to a certain number per day. While there is some truth to the concept that limiting fat grams can induce weight loss, it is not the only criterion for optimal weight loss or optimal health.

If low fat is the sole criterion for a diet, there remains too much leeway in what the rest of the diet includes. We need to ensure that a diet is generally healthy and produces the desired weight while enhancing, rather than harming, health. For example, a meal made up of a cola and jelly beans has no fat in it. Some people who are attempting to follow a low-fat diet may mistake this for a healthy meal. In reality, it is not only devoid of nutritional value, it is also associated with higher risks of cardiovascular disease, because it lowers HDL cholesterol and raises triglycerides.

Foods that have a high SMI value are also generally low in fat, in addition to promoting a slower absorption rate of sugar and an overall decrease in glucose load. The result of selecting foods on this basis is that you will have a diet that is high in carbohydrates but that does not affect insulin levels in an adverse way. In this way you can reap the benefits of a low-fat diet and still avoid the problems posed by a refined-carbohydrate diet. (See Appendices 3I and 3J.)

### Essential Fatty Acids

Is there an adequate amount of essential fats (or essential fatty acids, as scientists call them) in the HawaiiDiet™? Fatty acid is simply a scientific term for individual fat molecules. There are two essential fatty acids that humans need in order to survive. One of them is linoleic acid and the other is linolenic acid. The requirement for these nutrients is very small, approximately a gram per day (about the weight of a raisin). The minimum amount of total fat required in our diet is about fourteen grams per day. Most sources of dietary fats include some essential fatty acids along with other types of fat. In other words, essential fatty acids are abundant in whole foods. Adding refined oils to your diet in order to make sure you are getting enough of them is not necessary.

*Polyunsaturated Fats*
As the scientific community began accumulating data indicating that saturated fats cause an increase in cholesterol and thus an increase in the risk of heart disease, it began to promote vegetable oils as a healthy alternative to animal fats. Once again, researchers discovered that in the countries where there was a high saturated fat intake, there was also a high blood cholesterol level and a high rate of coronary disease. In countries where polyunsaturated fat intake was high, there tended to be lower cholesterol levels and lower rates of coronary disease. Other researchers whose studies corroborated these findings concluded, among other things, that not only were saturated fats associated with a higher risk of cardiovascular disease but also that a proportionally higher intake of polyunsaturated fats was associated with lower risk of cardiovascular disease. Nutritionists began evaluating food and diets based on a polyunsaturated-to-saturated fat ratio. This is often described as the P:S ratio.

Experts began to recommend that we should not only reduce our consumption of meat products, which are high in saturated fat, but we should also use vegetable oils, which are naturally high in polyunsaturated fats, to replace animal fats and oils. As a result, the food industry began promoting vegetable oils as "healthy oils." Margarine, which is made from vegetable oil, is a good example of a product touted as healthy because of its polyunsaturated fat content.

One major problem was overlooked, however. Margarine manufacturers have to partially hydrogenate the vegetable oil so that it will remain solid at room temperature. This is the only way that margarine can hold its texture. Hydrogenate means saturate. In other words, manufacturers turn a portion of the polyunsaturated oil into saturated fat. Even worse, in the process, some of the polyunsaturated fats turn into abnormal fats not found in nature. These are known as trans fats. These trans fats actually raise cholesterol and increase the risk of heart disease nearly as much as regular saturated fats.

Another overlooked yet insidious problem is the risk of cancer associated with polyunsaturated fat. This is one of the pitfalls of the reductionistic form of modern medicine, which isolates one field of specialty from the others. Experts studying heart disease promoted the benefits of polyunsaturated fats. Experts studying cancer had some grave concerns about the possibility that polyunsaturated fats might raise the risk of breast cancer and other forms of cancer because studies on tumors in mice indicated that polyunsaturated fats promoted the growth of tumors as much as or more than saturated fats did, and epidemiological studies indicated that the higher the amount of saturated *or* polyunsaturated fat in the diet, the higher the breast cancer rates.

*Monounsaturated Fats*
The Mediterranean diet deserves special attention with regard to its fat content. In that region of the world, the fat is mostly monounsaturated—a type of fat found in olive oil and in good quality canola and macadamia nut oils. This fat is relatively healthy when compared to saturated, polyunsaturated, and trans fats. Comparative studies have indicated that cholesterol is reduced by monounsaturated fats when it replaces animal fat in the diet. Actually, polyunsaturated fats also lower cholesterol, but monounsaturated fats cause a relative rise in the "good" cholesterol, the HDL, and so their overall effect is considered to be the most favorable. However, this occurs only when monounsaturated fats *replace* animal fats in the diet but not when monounsaturated fats are *added* to a meat-centered diet. In our HawaiiDiet™ research, we have demonstrated that if monounsaturated fats are simply added, and no saturated fat is decreased, cholesterol levels actually increase.

There is some debate as to whether the heart-healthy effect of monounsaturated fats is a result of the oil in which they are contained or whether these fats are simply nontoxic. Some believe that what is healthy about monounsaturated fats is that extra-virgin oil still has many nutrients in it from the mother plant. While it is tempting to say that eating monounsaturated fats is healthy, we must be careful to note that it has only been shown to be healthy in the context of a diet that is already rich in other heart-healthy factors, such as antioxidants. You must also be aware that any time you eat fats, you are eating them instead of eating whole plant-based foods; i.e., you are consuming "empty calories" devoid of fiber and beneficial nutrients. The other caution I have in relation to olive oil is that it, like any fat, is highly concentrated in calories, at nine calories per gram, and therefore promotes weight gain in those who are susceptible.

### Omega-3 Fatty Acids

What we know about omega-3 fatty acids is due to the study of the traditional diet of the Greenland Eskimos. Researchers knew that the Eskimos of Greenland have relatively low rates of heart disease. This was surprising because this population eats large amounts of fish, seal, walrus, wild game, and the blubber and fat that is found on these animals of the Arctic. Apparently, there is something in their diet that protects them from heart disease, even though that diet should raise cholesterol, promote atherosclerosis, and increase the rate of heart disease.

Subsequent research indicates that all the fish and animal foods that the Eskimos eat have one very special ingredient that the flesh consumed by Europeans and Americans does not have. The Eskimo diet is rich in a type of oil known as omega-3 fatty acids. One of the reasons the fish and animals eaten by the Eskimos have omega-3 fatty acids is that these animals feed in the wild. Land animals such as caribou eat wild plants and leaves, and sea animals feed on seaweed and other animals that in turn feed on wild sea plants. The source of the omega-3 fatty acids seems to be the chloroplast membranes of green plants. Domesticated animals have almost no omega-3 fatty acids in them, because they are fed artificially rather than in the natural way they were intended to eat.

Researchers found that omega-3 fatty acids have three important effects on blood chemistry that help prevent heart disease. First, they thin the blood by inhibiting the first step in clotting, which is the aggregation of tiny blood particles known as platelets. This helps prevent the final precipitating event that triggers sudden heart attacks—a blood clot that forms on the rough edges of a cholesterol deposit and blocks the narrowed opening. This explains why Eskimos have such low rates of heart disease. (This also explains why they also have very high rates of hemorragic stroke. Thus, omega-3 fatty acids shouldn't be recommended without a warning.)

A second important effect of omega-3 fatty acids is that they somehow have a dramatic effect in reducing triglyceride levels, at least in some individuals. This means that one can actually reduce blood fats by replacing animal fat in the diet with an increase in omega-3 fatty acids. However, omega-3 fats have the same high calorie content as any fat and will contribute to obesity in most people. A better way to reduce triglycerides is to reduce total fat intake. A third effect that omega-3 fats have is that they reduce blood cholesterol slightly and thus reduce the risk of heart disease.

These findings caused researchers to conduct studies on the benefits of eating fish. Their results were reported in a 1985 issue of the *New England Journal of Medicine*. In this study, people who ate one to two fish meals per week had lower rates of coronary disease. This conclusion must be read in context, however, because this result only occurs when meat is replaced with fish. Other studies indicate that an even better way to avoid heart disease is to avoid all cholesterol and most fats, regardless of their source.

### What About Cholesterol?

Cardiovascular disease is by far the leading cause of death in this country. It is directly related to blood cholesterol levels, and in fact these levels are the most important risk factor for heart disease. Heart disease is so connected to cholesterol levels that experts can say with confidence that for every one percent increase in cholesterol in the blood there is a two percent increase in risk for heart disease. This is why it is so important for you to understand cholesterol in your diet and cholesterol in your blood.

The most important risk factor for heart disease is total cholesterol when levels are low enough. The importance of total cholesterol in determining risk of coronary heart disease is demonstrated by the fact that in the Framingham Heart Study, heart attacks virtually disappeared when cholesterol levels dropped below 150 mg/dl. At this low cholesterol level, heart disease risk disappeared, regardless of other risk factors, including obesity, diabetes, smoking and low HDL levels.

### The Hawaii/Pacific Diet Lowers Cholesterol More Than the Mediterranean Diet

There is some controversy over whether a very low fat diet, such as the Hawaii/Pacific style diet, or a diet with higher monounsaturated fat, such as the Mediterranean style diet, is best for coronary disease. The best data on the control and reversal of coronary disease indicate that very low fat diets are more effective in controlling cholesterol than higher fat diets. In order to demonstrate the comparative effect of traditional diets on cholesterol, we conducted a direct comparison between the very low fat "Hawaii/Pacific" style diet and the "Mediterranean" style diet in a research project called the "Hawaii Diet Study." We found that while both styles of diet lowered total cholesterol, the very low fat Hawaii/Pacific style diet controlled total cholesterol better than the Mediterranean style diet.

One surprising finding was that monounsaturated fats seemed to cause an increase in cholesterol when added to the diets of participants on a very low fat diet. This is contrary to the common notion that monounsaturated fats always cause a decrease in cholesterol. We found that when participants switched from a very low fat Hawaii/Pacific style diet to a higher fat Mediterranean style diet, their cholesterol levels increased. We attributed the rise in cholesterol to the added fats, mostly monounsaturated fats from olive oil in the Mediterranean style diet. The cholesterol levels still remained much lower than what they were on their usual standard American diet, and the good cholesterol (HDL) levels were better, so the Mediterranean style diet and its olive oil still provided an improvement against coronary risk. However, it apparently did not provide as much improvement as the Hawaii/ Pacific style diet.

I put the topic of cholesterol in the midst of our discussion about dietary fat because cholesterol falls into the same chemical category as fats. This category is known as lipids, or substances that are not soluble in water. Its inability to be dissolved in water is one of the reasons cholesterol can be a problem. Insolubility in water means that the body cannot dispose of it easily. The body cannot store cholesterol in fat cells or burn it for fuel. Thus, when cholesterol accumulates in the bloodstream, this waxy substance must be discarded in unusual ways. Unfortunately, one of the ways is that cholesterol gets transported into the blood vessel walls. It is this accumulation that can eventually lead to the blockage of arteries that nourish vital organs. Serious disease or death may result from this blockage.

### Good Cholesterol, Bad Cholesterol

Because cholesterol cannot be dissolved in water, it must be carried in the bloodstream in clusters of molecules known as lipoproteins. Cholesterol is identified by the type of these clusters in which it is transported. The ones you should know about are the high-density lipoproteins (HDL), also known as "good cholesterol," and low-density lipoproteins (LDL), also known as the "bad cholesterol." The important thing to know is that the good, or HDL, cholesterol is carrying cholesterol *out* of the arteries, and the LDL cholesterol is transporting cholesterol *into* the arteries. Thus, the higher the HDL the better and the lower the LDL the better.

National guidelines tell us that 200mg/dl is the highest healthy level of cholesterol in a person's blood. In my opinion, this is not good enough. A substantial number of heart attacks still occur when a person's cholesterol level is below 200mg/dl. Experts making this recommendation are using an American standard. If we take a broader world view, we see that in places where traditional diets are still followed, such as China, cholesterol levels are much lower. Heart disease is almost nonexistent in places where blood cholesterol is very low. If your cholesterol is around 160 mg/dl or less, your heart disease risk is extremely low. If it is 150 mg/dl or less, your risk of heart disease is virtually zero. This is the conclusion of both the Chinese diet study and the Framingham Heart Study (both landmark studies in the field). I believe that a cholesterol level of 150mg/dl is a better standard than the 200 mg/dl recommended by most American experts.

If your cholesterol level rises above these counts (as it does in most Americans), your level of HDL becomes a better predictor of heart disease than overall cholesterol. In general, it is best to have an HDL above 45 mg/dl. It is also best to have a low level of "bad cholesterol," or LDL. Ideally, your LDL should be less than 100 mg/dl. Some laboratories rate cardiovascular risk by dividing your overall cholesterol count by your level of HDL.

The average cholesterol-to-HDL ratio is about 4.4. If your ratio is higher than 4.4, your risk is higher than average. If your ratio is lower than 4.4, your risk is lower than average. In other words, the lower the number, the better. Ideally, this ratio should be less than 3.

*Triglycerides*

Triglycerides are fats in the form in which they are transported and stored (as opposed to the form in which they are eaten). Triglycerides are present in body fat and in the blood. They are made up of a backbone of a three-carbon sugar molecule to which is attached three fat molecules—each fat molecule attached to a carbon atom of the sugar molecule. This structure should help you remember how to reduce triglycerides—by reducing the fat and sugar you eat. Triglycerides are a risk factor (along with cholesterol) for heart disease. The higher your triglycerides, the higher your risk of heart disease. The lower you can keep your triglycerides, the better. Research indicates that the Hawaii-Diet™ lowers triglyceride levels and thus reduces another risk factor for heart disease.

# PROTEIN

Protein in the HawaiiDiet™ is moderate in quantity and less than the amount in a typical modern American diet, in keeping with traditional dietary patterns around the world. For example, you'll remember that in ancient Hawaii the principal foods were taro, poi, and sweet potato.

Most of the rest of the food in Hawaii came from other plant sources, such as assorted vegetables and greens, fruit, and sea vegetables. Fish and seafood were certainly a part of the diet, but most of the population lived too far from the ocean to obtain a regular supply. Other healthy populations had similar diets, albeit with regional variations.

In China, which is and has been throughout history the most populous country in the world, the animal protein intake was approximately seven ounces per week, based on the information collected in the Chinese diet study. In Japan, the amount of protein that came from animal products, including seafood and eggs, was similarly low. In the Mediterranean, including locations in Greece where the life span is way beyond the average and the heart disease rate is low, a similarly small amount of animal protein was found in the diet. In all of these cultures, most of the meals were without any animal protein at all.

There are certain populations that eat primarily animal proteins— for example, populations in the far north, such as the Greenland Eskimos, or hunter-gatherer populations in Africa and South America. We did not rely on these diets as models because these peoples did not thrive in large numbers and they are not known to have had very long life spans. While some experts recommend a Paleolithic, Stone-Age type of diet, which, presumably, was based on large amounts of low-fat animal products and a small amount of carbohydrates, we felt that this diet allowed people to survive in harsh conditions rather than flourish in large numbers over long periods of time. Moreover, we felt that if this type of diet was good for modern humans, there should be large numbers of people around the world who follow this dietary pattern and remain trim and free of the diseases that plague Americans today. This is not the case.

### The Protein Myths

Two protein myths endure in this country. The first is that we need a lot of protein to be healthy. The second is that animals are better sources of protein than plants because vegetable proteins are incomplete proteins.

We don't need a lot of protein to thrive. In fact, in this country we most likely consume a significant excess of protein. The U.S. government's Recommended Dietary Allowance indicates that an average woman between the ages of twenty-five and fifty needs about fifty grams of protein, or less than two ounces, per day (one gram is about the weight of a raisin and fifty grams is about 1.8 ounces). Americans actually consume much more. In 1980, the average amount of protein consumed by Americans was between seventy-five and one hundred grams per day.

Studies now indicate that depending on your size and level of activity, you may need as little as thirty grams of protein per day. The the minimum requirement may actually be lower, because the RDA allows for a wide margin of safety. (The requirement is higher for large people and for those engaged in strenuous exercise.)

In addition, for decades, people believed that vegetable proteins were "incomplete" proteins and had to be combined with one another to be sure that amino acids, the building blocks of protein, would be available in adequate quantities so that proteins could be properly formed. Today, we realize that such a perspective is simply wrong. Calculations of essential amino acids and total protein from vegetable sources indicate that whole plant-based proteins are adequate by themselves. Now, even the American Dietetic Association, in its consensus statement on vegetarian diets, indicates that vegetable-based protein is just as complete as animal protein.

### The Ketogenic Diet

Certain proponents of one type of popular high-protein and high-fat diet go as far as to say that carbohydrates should be almost eliminated from the diet. This type of diet is called a ketogenic diet because when carbohydrates are eliminated from the diet, one tends to burn fat and release ketone bodies, or broken-down fat remnants, as a waste product of fat metabolism. You might say this is great because, after all, burning fat and getting rid of it is what we want. On a ketogenic diet, however, the dieter is encouraged to eat "rich" foods, such as meats, cheeses, and sauces, along with some greens. This is one of the selling points of this diet. It is very inviting to people who are dying to find a diet that allows them to eat their favorite rich foods.

Unfortunately, the rich foods recommended on a ketogenic diet are very high in those nutrients that promote a number of chronic diseases and certain cancers. For instance, a ketogenic diet is much too high in saturated fat, cholesterol, and animal protein to be generally healthy. Also, grains and grain products—some of the healthiest foods—are not allowed on this diet because the high carbohydrate content in them would ruin the ketogenic effect. For these reasons, this type of diet has been soundly criticized in the medical literature.

*The Homocysteine Factor*

Homocysteine is a sulfur-containing amino acid that comes from the processing of other sulfur-containing amino acids in the diet. Recently, there has been substantial evidence that homocysteine may contribute to heart disease. One researcher, Dr. Kilmer McCully, had a radical new theory about atherosclerosis. He became curious about a rare disease known as homocystinuria, in which patients get excessively high levels of homocysteine in their urine. In this disease, the high levels of homocysteine result from an inborn metabolic defect, wherein the body is unable to process homocysteine and high levels therefore accumulate in the blood, forcing the body to get rid of it through the urine. Because young people who have this condition sometimes died from atherosclerotic stroke, he began to wonder if high homocysteine levels might promote atherosclerotic heart disease even in people who do not have homocysteinuria. He has now collected a body of evidence that strongly suggests it does. An accumulation of homocysteine seems to promote the oxidation of LDL, the "bad" form of cholesterol, and results in the faster deposition of cholesterol into blood vessel walls. This accumulation results in atherosclerosis and can apparently lead to both heart attacks and strokes.

The chief source of these sulfur-containing amino acids is animal protein. The body gets rid of homocysteine through enzymes that use the vitamins $B_6$, folic acid, and $B_{12}$. McCully's research indicates that high homocysteine levels result from excessive intake of animal protein, and a deficiency of $B_6$ and folic acid ($B_{12}$ deficiency is extremely rare). The way to reduce homocysteine levels is to reduce animal protein intake and to increase consumption of vegetables and leafy greens— another strong reason why people should avoid animal protein and high-protein diets.

## The Dairy Dilemma

If you examine the HawaiiDiet™ pyramid, you will notice that dairy is considered an optional food and not a required food, as suggested by the USDA pyramid. Why? Because from the ancient Hawaiian perspective of looking to the source and from the perspective of what is in balance, dairy seems to be a food that doesn't fit. No other species on earth eats dairy products in adulthood and no other species drinks the milk of another species. For years we have been told that milk is essential for bone strength, yet some Native Hawaiians grew to be seven feet tall and ate no dairy products at all. If dairy is so essential to bone growth, how is this possible?

Why is dairy recommended by many experts as a daily requirement in this country? Scientific studies are showing that dairy isn't the wonder food it was once touted to be. But there is so much money to be made that even the federal government, under the influence of commercial interests, promotes dairy. This is done despite scientific information that dairy fat promotes heart disease, that dairy protein is the leading cause of allergies in this country, and that dairy sugar cannot be digested properly by seventy percent of the adults in the world.

The main purported benefit behind daily consumption of dairy products is the prevention of osteoporosis. Many experts believe that osteoporosis is caused by calcium deficiency. Because milk is a good source of calcium, they recommend a daily intake of dairy products. The problem with this recommendation is that there is little evidence that dairy products prevent fractures from osteoporosis, and there is some evidence that dairy products may actually *promote* osteoporosis. Epidemiological studies indicate that the countries that consume the most dairy products actually have the most osteoporotic fractures. If dairy is so good for our bones, why do more people break their hips in countries where they eat the most dairy foods? In one of the most authoritative reviews of the literature, a team of experts, including experts from Harvard University, concluded that "epidemiological studies have not supported a protective role of dairy product consumption against fractures." They hypothesized that the reason dairy may not be helpful is because any animal protein, including the animal protein in dairy products, induces calcium loss through the kidneys.

The HawaiiDiet™ recommends that we obtain adequate calcium yet still avoid the potential hazards of dairy products. We can do this by relying on the HawaiiDiet™ pyramid, which recommends non-dairy calcium sources. These sources include dark leafy greens, seaweed, and other calcium-rich foods. After all, where do you suppose cows get their calcium in the first place? They get it from greens.

## THE HAWAIIDIET™ AND HORMONE BALANCE

Recently, nutritionists are beginning to pay more attention to the role of hormones in our diet and overall health. This topic is capturing the interest of people all across the country because of recent discoveries such as the hormone leptin, which seems to hold the key to obesity, at least in mice. There is also renewed interest in the fat-promoting effect of the hormone insulin, and the fat- and water-retaining power of female hormones. This is a fascinating subject, and worthy of a full book all by itself. But here, due to limitations of space, we will provide you with just enough information to let you see some of the more interesting ways in which hormones play a role in the HawaiiDiet™ and therefore in your weight, health, and general sense of well-being.

*How Hormones Work*
The human body is regulated by single and paired sets of hormones in a startling array of biomolecular control mechanisms. There are literally dozens of different types of hormones in the human body, all of them produced by various organs and glands that are governing points, or switchboard points, for various bodily functions. As we come to know more about hormones and the fascinating ways in which they influence the human body, we have also come to think of them as "messenger molecules." This is because they somehow manage to transmit vital information to various cells in the body, usually by way of the bloodstream.

Hormones are also the physical transmitters of emotion and thought. This is especially compelling when you recall the effectiveness of incorporating the ancient beliefs of the Native Hawaiians into our lifestyle. We now realize that what we think and speak can alter our physical state via hormones and other physical processes. We can see how such changes in thinking and acting can have often immediate effects on our health. Much of this connection is being explored in the field of research known as mind-body medicine—a field we have already likened to certain ancient Hawaiian methods of mental, physical, and emotional healing.

How can this work? The answer isn't simple and we are only beginning to understand the process. But suffice it to say that we are now fairly certain, at the scientific level, that for every mental process and emotion, there is an equivalent physical event that can, either immediately or over time, influence health. We also know that hormones are a key link between the mind and the body.

The immune system, the digestive system, the cardiovascular system, the nervous system—all these parts of the human body have receptors in their various cells for hormones. Hormones are a key element in the regulation of almost all body functions.

One of the body's pairs of opposing hormones is insulin and glucagon. Both hormones are created in the pancreas, which is an organ found just under and behind the stomach. Insulin keeps blood sugar from getting too high. Glucagon keeps it from getting too low. In other words, this pair of hormones keeps the human body in balance by keeping the blood sugar in balance. There are a number of diets that emphasize balance in our hormones, including in a class of hormones derived from the fatty acids known as eicosanoids, which influence a number of bodily functions, including the immune system. In fact, this or similar balancing acts are the main purpose of most of our hormones. In addition to the insulin-glucagon pair, numerous other hormone pairs have a profound impact on our health and our lives. Certain individual hormones also play a critical role.

*Insulin Balance*

One of the problems of a high-carbohydrate diet, proponents of the hormone-balance diets argue, is that high-carbohydrate diets induce an increase in the requirement for insulin, resulting in hyperinsulinemia, or too much insulin in the blood. Insulin influences the balance of the production of eicosanoid hormones. Thus, it was theorized, a high-carbohydrate diet would result in an imbalance of these important eicosanoids. It was also theorized that this would cause obesity because insulin is a lipogenic hormone, that is, a hormone that tends to promote body fat.

This is true to some extent. A diet composed of *refined* carbohydrates does indeed induce the production of insulin, and insulin influences the production of eicosanoids and body fat. However, in the studies concluding that carbohydrates cause higher insulin levels, the carbohydrate content is almost exclusively refined carbohydrates. Second, in population studies in which specific nutrients are measured, there seems to be almost no correlation between sugar intake and obesity. In addition, if the concerns about high-carbohydrate diets and insulin were universally true, there should be high rates of diabetes in populations where carbohydrate intake is high. Population studies actually show the opposite, with populations such as Japan and China, where consumption of carbohydrates is high, having the lowest rates of diabetes.

Those who express concerns about the effect of high-carbohydrate diets are at a total loss when it comes to explaining why the Hawaii-Diet™ is high in carbohydrate and yet it reduces insulin levels in nearly all our participants regardless of ethnicity. The HawaiiDiet™ actually provides the nutrients that maintain the insulin-glucagon hormone balance without adding the risks associated with a diet high in animal protein.

*Sex Hormones*

While it may seem odd to talk about sex hormones in the context of diet, we must realize that sex hormones can have a profound effect on our health, on our biological functioning, and on our feeling of well-being. I also want to emphasize that diet can have a substantial effect on these hormones, since both male and female hormones have cholesterol as a main component of their structures.

To show how profound an effect diet can have, consider the age of onset of menstrual cycles in women. In most species, the onset of fertility usually occurs at an age where the female is just about full grown, essentially an adult who can fundamentally fend for herself. This is a survival mechanism for all mammals because a female who is younger than this age and too small or too immature would be unable to protect her young. In humans, this age is about sixteen years old, and the fact that most girls have achieved practically all of their adult height by that age supports this idea.

In ancient times, girls had their first menses at about the age of sixteen. But today, in America, the age of menarche is around twelve. If a girl gets pregnant at this age, she is at an extremely high risk for complications. The size of her pelvis is smaller, the muscles around the abdomen are not fully developed, and delivery is potentially hazardous as a result. Why is this happening? In a word, our hormones are related to our diet, and in general our diet is unhealthy.

In addition to governing sexual function, sex hormones also have a profound effect on health. It is fairly clear that sex hormone levels in Americans of both sexes are too high and out of balance. In women, these elevated levels or imbalances are associated with heart disease, breast cancer, uterine cancer, ovarian cancer, osteoporosis, and menstrual dysfunction, in addition to inducing premature physical maturation.

It is more difficult to assess the impact on boys and men. Many experts feel that high levels of male hormones contribute to anger and violence, baldness, excessive sex drive, impotence, and also contribute to a number of diseases, including heart disease, prostate hypertrophy, and prostate cancer.

How are sex hormone levels affected by diet? Because sex hormones have a cholesterol nucleus, dietary changes that affect blood cholesterol also affect sex hormones. In other words, an excess of saturated fat, cholesterol, and total fat in the diet contributes to excessive sex hormone levels in both men and women. Ingestion of sex hormones and their analogs in food—such as the hormones that animals are fed to fatten them up, and the natural hormones in the flesh of the animal—also contribute to excessive sex hormone levels in the blood. To make matters worse, someone who becomes fat by eating the fat of animals has also increased his or her peripheral conversion of sex hormones because fat tissue helps to convert these hormones into their active form. This creates more of the active forms of these hormones and increases their impact on the body. Finally, it is known that vegetarians excrete more hormones in their feces due to the high fiber and high bulk of the foods in their diet, which bind the cholesterol and hormones in the gut before they can be absorbed into the body. Thus we can see that even when it comes to the balance of sexual hormones, a plant-based diet has advantages over a meat-centered one.

## OTHER NUTRIENTS

*Antioxidants*

Today, those of us who have any interest whatsoever in health are familiar with the term antioxidants, but few of us know what antioxidants really are. In short, certain internal and external factors can result in oxidation within your body—that is, in a process roughly akin to metal rusting and therefore wearing out. This occurs when oxygen molecules react adversely to molecules of certain other substances. The process of oxidation causes the release of highly dangerous and volatile oxygen atoms, also known as free radicals. Antioxidants are those substances that can interfere with oxidation by intercepting free radicals before they can do any genetic or molecular damage. They then restore the molecules to health. This is important because free radicals have been associated with many of the chronic diseases we talk about in this book, most especially with heart disease.

We find antioxidants packaged by God and nature as vitamins, minerals, and other micronutrients. Among this group are vitamins A, C, and E; the minerals selenium and zinc; and other nutrients, some known, some yet to be discovered. A large army of antioxidants are found in a class of chemical compounds known as phytonutrients, or phytochemicals. The HawaiiDiet™ is rich in both antioxidants and phytochemicals, in addition to other health-giving micronutrients.

*Other Phytochemicals*

Phytochemicals are micronutrients that have been receiving a great deal of attention in the health community. This attention is well deserved. They may be the key factors in our understanding of how foods can act as medicine. Many of these phytochemical substances are beginning to yield up their secrets. A few of the better known phytochemicals are:

- Sulforaphane, which is found in broccoli, Brussels sprouts, cauliflower, kale, carrots, and green onions and blocks tumor formation in animals
- 3-n-butyl phthalide, found in celery, which lowers blood pressure and reduces blood cholesterol in rats
- Catechin (also known as polyphenolic catechin), which is found primarily in green tea and has been used in both Japan and China since ancient times for its healing properties
- Chlorophyll, which is the substance that makes fruits, vegetables, and other growing things green
- Flavonoids, which are found in abundance in green tea and in almost all fruits and vegetables, especially citrus fruits and berries
- Lycopene, found in tomatoes, red grapefruit, and other brightly colored fruits and vegetables, which protects the cells from all types of damage
- Isoflavones, which are found in abundance in soybeans and act by stimulating the activity of certain enzymes that detoxify carcinogens. They also seem to make estrogen less potent, which means that they may act as estrogen modulators
- Retinoids, which are the pigments that make fruits and vegetables red or orange and offer great hope as disease fighters.

The HawaiiDiet's™ reliance on traditional diets as models for healthy eating and its emphasis on whole unrefined plant-based foods allow the dieter to optimize the quantity and balance of macro- and micronutrients in his or her diet. The use of the HawaiiDiet™ Pyramid also helps to ensure that there is a wide variety of plant-based foods consumed. That includes foods that are high in fiber, minerals (such as calcium), antioxidants, and other cancer-fighting phytochemicals. The pyramid also helps to keep cholesterol content low.

In addition, the use of the SMI helps to ensure that the fat content is low, the fiber content is high, hunger is satisfied, and the carbohydrates are in a form that is less likely to adversely affect blood sugar and blood insulin. The pyramid and the SMI also help to ensure that the protein intake is moderate. The combination of the two tools also helps to preserve proper hormone balance.

# SIX

# Making the HawaiiDiet™ Work for You

The HawaiiDiet™ is a powerful program that can work for you on many levels. Take a moment to carefully contemplate the following suggested steps for starting the diet. Even though these aren't all strictly dietary principles, if you integrate them into your program it will work better and you'll enjoy it more. You'll also be far more likely to make the HawaiiDiet™ a part of your lifestyle, so that you can permanently enjoy the results of weight loss and improved health.

1. If you have any health problems, or if you are taking any medication, you must check with your doctor to make sure that it's okay to follow this diet.
2. Eat foods in harmony with the seasons, your locality, and your climate. If possible, eat foods grown organically.
3. Eat in a relaxed manner, preferably with others. Take time to chew and enjoy your food—do so with gratitude.
4. Exercise at least thirty or forty minutes daily, or at least every other day.
5. Remember that optimal health involves all aspects of your being, including spiritual, mental, emotional, and physical aspects. It involves your thoughts and actions, and your relationship with the land through the food you eat. It involves

your relationship with others and your relationship with the Almighty. When all this is in harmony, stress is reduced and health is maximized.

There are a number of simple things you can do to reduce stress and contribute to your overall health. For example:

- Say a prayer daily
- Meditate daily
- Laugh daily
- Do something for someone else, with no expectation of a reward
- Be grateful for the simplest things in life

6. Always remember the source of all healing—the Great Physician, the Almighty. Therefore, say grace before each meal. Start each meal by asking the Lord to bless the food, and by being grateful for the life-giving qualities He has put into the food you eat.

There are also some subtle intangibles that surrounded the act of eating in ancient Hawaii that are part of the HawaiiDiet™. These intangibles form the source of the suggested steps I have outlined above, and, in effect, underlie many of the healing practices followed by our ancestors. For example:

- They ate together (*aloha*)
- They ate in peace (*mana*)
- They said a prayer before eating (*pono*)
- They ate foods in season (*lokahi*)
- They ate foods from their locality (*lokahi*)
- The food was prepared with love (*aloha*)
- The food was eaten with great appreciation of its source (*kumu*)

When you follow these principles and practices, you will increase the effectiveness of the HawaiiDiet™ and enhance your mental and spiritual well-being at the same time.

## WHAT TO EXPECT WHEN YOU BEGIN THE HAWAIIDIET™

The HawaiiDiet™ is not a diet at all, in the conventional sense of the word. It is actually a whole-person health program, based on the principles and practices of traditional cultures that have remained largely free of the chronic nutrition-related diseases that plague us today. There is no calorie counting or portion control on the diet. It is an "all you can eat" diet. This doesn't mean that you should stuff yourself unnaturally. However, it does mean that you can eat to your satisfaction, sometimes even more than you were eating before. The weight comes off naturally.

You may experience a slight sensation of bloating in the beginning because in general the foods are bulkier than what most Americans are accustomed to eating. This should add to a pleasant feeling of satisfaction throughout the diet, even while you are losing the pounds.

You will probably be exposed to a wider variety of foods on this diet than you have previously enjoyed. This is because the Hawaii-Diet™ embraces foods from all cultures that fit the HawaiiDiet™ model. The potential variety is limitless.

## HOW MUCH WILL I LOSE?

The weight loss is dramatic in some individuals. Some people have lost as much as thirty pounds in twenty-one days. For others, the loss is slow and steady. Your personal weight loss will depend upon your initial weight and your individual metabolism, as well as upon other factors. In general, your weight loss should be between five and thirty pounds in the first three weeks of the diet. Average weight loss has been around eleven pounds for this period of time. No one who is overweight has failed to lose weight on this program, when it is followed strictly.

## HEALTH CHANGES

For people who have health problems, the physical changes may be dramatic. I repeat: Be sure to check with your doctor if you have any health problems. People on the HawaiiDiet™ have experienced rapid and dramatic improvement in their blood sugar and blood pressure. Participants have also indicated that such symptoms as headaches, joint pains, fatigue, skin conditions, and gastrointestinal complaints have improved while they were on the HawaiiDiet™. In addition, their levels of cholesterol, triglycerides, and uric acid (a risk factor for gout) have improved.

## WHAT IS A SERVING?

As we have seen, the HawaiiDiet™ pyramid makes its dietary recommendations in terms of servings. A serving is the amount of food that an average person might consume at a single sitting. This is of course a somewhat arbitrary definition, because individual appetites vary a great deal. Nonetheless, the term provides a starting point. Here are examples of servings sizes to use as guidelines with the HawaiiDiet™ pyramid:

- Whole Grains and Other Staples
  ½ cup cooked cereal, pasta, or brown rice
  1 slice bread
  1 ounce ready-to-eat cereal, 1 medium potato
- Vegetable Group
  1 cup raw leafy greens
  ½ cup cooked, chopped, raw, or other vegetables
- Fruit Group
  1 medium whole fruit
  ½ cup chopped, cooked, or canned fruit
- Non-Dairy Calcium Group
  1 cup raw or ½ cup cooked dark leafy greens
  ½ cup sea vegetables
- No-Cholesterol Protein Group
  ½ cup cooked beans
  1½ egg whites
  3 ounces tofu
  3 ounces wheat gluten

- Optional Foods
  2–3 ounces cooked fish, chicken, or meat
  1 egg
  1 cup milk, yogurt, or ice cream
  1½ ounces fresh cheese
  2 ounces processed cheese

## Whole Grains and Other Staples

This category includes foods that are high in complex carbohydrates, like taro and poi, whole grains, and whole potatoes. Breads and pastas fit into this category, but in order to imitate the traditional Hawaiian diet as closely as possible, only unrefined (non-ground) grains and vegetables should be used. Eat 8–13 servings a day.

| | | |
|---|---|---|
| Oatmeal | Brown rice | Sweet potatoes |
| Corn | Buckwheat | Poi |
| Potatoes | Barley | Taro |

## Vegetables

You may eat vegetables cooked or raw, but remember not to use oil for dressings or for sautéeing. Vegetable broth makes a good substitute. Eat 3–5 servings a day.

| | | |
|---|---|---|
| Carrots | Lettuce | Green beans |
| Onions | Spinach | Beets |
| Squash | Cauliflower | Turnips |
| Pumpkin | Zucchini | |

## Fruit

Choose two to four pieces of whole fruit per day. Use fresh fruit instead of juices or preserves. Eat 2–4 servings a day.

| | | |
|---|---|---|
| Apples | Pears | Cherries |
| Oranges | Grapefruit | Grapes |
| Peaches | Strawberries | Pineapple |

## Non-Dairy Calcium Foods

The basic rule for this category is that dark leafy greens are a good source of calcium. Spinach is an exception because its high oxalate content makes calcium difficult to absorb. Some of these foods, such as kale, taste better if they are at least parboiled or cooked in some other way. Seaweed is a very versatile food that has a high calcium content. Eat 2–3 servings a day.

| | | |
|---|---|---|
| Broccoli | Collard greens | Turnip tops |
| Kale | Mustard greens | Chinese cabbage |
| Watercress | Seaweed | |

### No-Cholesterol Protein Foods

Nuts of all kinds are high in protein but also high in fat and can be eaten in small amounts if you are adapted to higher-fat foods. If not, use them sparingly as condiments. Eat 2–3 servings a day.

| | | |
|---|---|---|
| Lima beans | Chickpeas | Green peas |
| Kidney beans | Black beans | Lentils |
| Fava beans | Soybeans | Tofu |

### Optional Foods

Broiled, steamed, grilled, or baked low-fat fish, such as cod, perch, scrod, or tuna (not packed in oil)

Skinless chicken cooked with no oil

Ham slice (no more than ten percent of calories from fat)

Egg whites or egg substitute

Extra-virgin olive oil

Macadamia nut oil

## SAMPLE HAWAIIDIET™ MENU

- Breakfast
  Oatmeal
  Sliced bananas
  Grapefruit
- Lunch
  Baked potato with steak sauce
  Green salad with no-oil dressing
  Cooked vegetable

Soup
Pear
- Dinner
  Brown rice
  Vegetable or tofu stir-fry
  Corn on the cob
  Squash
  Two-bean chili
  Cooked greens
  Apple

## ABOUT HUNGER

If you get hungry, you can always rely upon a snack that has a moderate to high SMI value. In fact, it is okay on this diet to snack throughout the day. Often, hunger works against you. It can decrease your metabolic rate, which means it can slow down the rate at which you burn calories. But, on the other hand, a little hunger can be useful. You can learn to use your hunger in your favor, because hunger is the best flavor enhancer in the world. Try eating when you are hungry, as opposed to when you are not, and you'll see what I mean. For example, one morning, don't eat until about an hour later than you normally do. Let yourself get hungry. Then try a breakfast of oatmeal with a half a banana sliced into it, and one grapefruit—all foods that are moderate to high on the SMI scale. You will find these and many other foods much more delicious when you are a little hungry.

Once you know how this works, you can use it whenever you want. For example, if you are trying to rapidly lose weight, or you want to get a "kick start" on your eating program, you can use hunger as a tool to help you stay on your diet. It is very difficult to avoid hunger if you are trying to lose weight quickly. The best way to handle hunger is to use it in your favor.

You can also handle hunger by using it as a signal to exercise. When you get hungry, try to exercise before eating and you will find that your hunger is shut down for a while. This occurs because exercise causes a release of blood sugar into your bloodstream. This sensation of satisfaction disappears after a while, and then your hunger is sharpened a little. Then, when you eat, food will have an enhanced flavor even if it has less salt, fat, or sugar than you are used to.

## ABOUT EXERCISE

I have not discussed exercise much in this book because my focus has been on diet. However, one of the best things you can do to control your weight is to exercise. The reason any exercise is helpful, of course, is because exercise burns calories. In addition, the HawaiiDiet™ promotes the health of the whole person, and exercise is obviously one of the most important aspects of overall health. If it is approved by your doctor, you should exercise regularly, either aerobically, with activities such as jogging or cycling, or with activities designed to enhance strength, such as weight lifting.

The two types of exercise work together to keep you fit in many ways, and that includes weight control. Aerobic exercise keeps your metabolic rate up and strength, or resistance, exercise prevents loss of muscle tissue.

### Aerobic Exercise
The best type of exercise for weight control is aerobic exercise. Aerobic exercise is so called because you have to use air or oxygen to keep up the exercise. Aerobic exercise is moderate—not just strolling, and not sprinting all-out. Aerobic exercise burns calories at a moderately high rate and is the type of exercise that an average person can engage in for more than just a few minutes at a time. In addition, research indicates that regular aerobic exercise causes your metabolism—that is, the rate at which you burn calories—to rise even while you are at rest. This means that not only do you burn calories while you exercise, you also burn additional calories at other times, too. If you can build up to the point where you can jog three miles (or about forty minutes) every other day, or engage in the equivalent amount of aerobic exercise, research indicates that you will burn more calories even while you are resting.

Here are some examples of aerobic exercises:

| Exercise | Calories Burned in 15 Minutes |
|---|---|
| Walking at 20 minutes per mile | 64 |
| Jogging at 15 minutes per mile | 91 |
| Jogging at 10 minutes per mile | 183 |
| Bicycling at 10 MPH | 100 |
| Hiking | 137 |
| Playing basketball | 173 |
| Swimming | 143 |

The number of calories you burn during exercise varies with your size and how vigorously you exercise. Walking, for example, can be aerobic or it can be non-aerobic, depending on the pace. One way to determine whether an exercise is aerobic is to notice your breathing. During aerobic exercise, you should be breathing harder than normal but still able to talk. Your heart should be beating faster than normal as well. Here is how to figure out what your heart rate during exercise should be.

Subtract your age from 220 to get your maximum heart rate. For example, if you are forty-three years old, your maximum heart rate is 220 minus 43, or 177. During exercise, your heart should be beating at between sixty percent and eighty-five percent of its maximum rate. Therefore, multiply your maximum rate by .6 and .85 to get the optimal range—in this example, between 106 beats per minute (177 × .6) and 150 beats per minute (177 × .85).

I like to look at aerobic exercise as a form of play—and who says grown-ups shouldn't enjoy playing? Do what you enjoy and you'll look forward to doing it every day. You can do it with your friends, you can include your family—in fact, if you have children, engage in active games with them, run around with them, spend some energy on yourself and on them. Here, especially, you will find that the rewards will go far beyond the physical. But also remember that there are actual mood-enhancing effects inherent in exercise. We know, for instance, that exercise helps release the body's natural opiates—the endorphins—which flood us with a calm sense of well-being. And as good, glowing health returns, you'll feel better in every way.

Here are the steps you should follow before you begin any exercise program:

1. Check with your doctor.
2. Choose an activity.
3. Set aside a regular time for exercise. Make an appointment with yourself. It's funny how we'll make time for others, but when it comes to ourselves, we don't make time, as if we don't count as much. I like to exercise first thing in the morning so there's no excuse later.
4. Equip yourself properly. For example, if you can get a good pair of sports shoes, such as tennis shoes, running shoes, etc., try to do so.
5. Warm up. Once you are ready to begin your exercise, make sure you stretch—your neck, shoulders, arms, back, legs, etc.—so that you reduce the risk of injury. Don't just jump into a vigorous activity: Gradually build up the intensity of your exercise.
6. Enjoy it. As you exercise, remember how you felt when you were a child. After all, exercise is playing. And after your exercise is done, notice how you feel. You are invigorated, and you will notice that you feel a higher energy level for the rest of the day.

*Resistance Exercise*
While you don't have to lift heavy weights to be healthy, it is important that you exercise your muscles by making them push or pull against a certain amount of resistance, because that way you will retain and build muscle tissue.

Why does muscle matter? Because the lean body mass, or muscle, in our bodies is known to burn more calories—even at rest—than does fat. Fat cells are basically just along for the ride, whereas muscle cells are working, working, working—to lift that box, to move that chair, to engage in any number of other calorie-burning activities. Muscle cells, even without vigorous exercise, burn about three times as much energy as fat cells—an average of thirteen calories per kilogram per day. Fat cells burn an average of only 4.5 calories per kilogram per day. Fat cells are inherently lazy and serve no purpose except to act as depositories, while muscle cells are active even when we think we are at rest. And of course they burn much more energy when we are exercising than they do at rest. Muscle cells cause our bodies to move, to repair themselves, to grow in response to exercise, and to replenish the energy that they burn during activity. Therefore, the more muscle mass and the less fat you have on your body, the more calories you will burn at all times. This is confirmed by studies that indicate that one of the most important determinants of resting metabolic rate is body composition.

How much muscle-building, or resistance, exercise should you get? I advise you to begin with perhaps fifteen minutes per day of simple weight lifting and stretching and work to up to as much as you want to do, within reason and within your doctor's advice. If you are already reasonably fit and have an average or better-than-average muscle mass, you may want to start at a higher level. Any number of exercise videos can be used to help you get started. Or perhaps you'll want to join a gym and get individualized instruction. Maybe you'll want to start with the very best equipment, or maybe you'll just pull on your old jeans, a sweatshirt, and lift jars or bottles that have been filled with sand. However you do it, start today.

## VITAMIN AND MINERAL SUPPLEMENTS

Throughout this book, I have emphasized the health-giving properties of whole foods. Therefore, when people ask me whether or not they should take nutritional supplements while on this diet, I again emphasize that wholeness is the key to good health. In other words, the best source of vitamins and minerals is fresh, whole, natural food. This is because vitamins, minerals, phytochemicals, and other micronutrients work best as part of a synergetic whole. In most instances, we don't even understand the complex interactions among different components of our foods, much less how this complexity influences our bodies, minds, and spirits. In fact, I am especially concerned about physicians and other practitioners who prescribe individual nutrients without performing the necessary tests or understanding the whole nutritional profile of any given patient.

Be that as it may, I am practical enough to realize that few people will follow a diet strictly enough to get the maximum nutritional benefit. The most common shortfall I see in my own patients is that they don't consume enough dark leafy greens. This means that they don't get enough of certain nutrients that would enhance their health. For these patients, I recommend a daily calcium supplement of about five hundred milligrams. If you give up dairy products, as advised on this diet, but don't replace them with adequate amounts of calcium-containing foods, perhaps you should also see your own physician about supplementing your diet with calcium.

I am also concerned about people getting an adequate amount of Vitamin $B_{12}$. Those who follow this diet in full compliance will avoid the foods listed in the "optional" tip of the HawaiiDiet™ pyramid. If they do, they will be following a vegan diet, the strictest form of vegetarian diet, which includes no animal products whatsoever. A vegan diet is optimal for many people, especially those who have contracted one of America's killer diseases, like heart disease or cancer. But it is not advisable for infants, small children, or nursing mothers. It is also inadvisable for adults in the long term without supplementation of $B_{12}$.

In general, whole foods are nutritionally adequate, especially if you buy them fresh and in season. This diet is designed so that you won't require supplementation—in fact, the key to the success of this entire approach is the wholeness of your food and of your life experience. You can't have a poor diet and experience good health and a sense of well-being. And you can never effectively substitute whole food with anything processed, no matter what the manufacturer claims. If you have symptoms of nutritional deficiency, adjust your diet or visit your physician for a blood profile so that he or she can tell you what nutrients you may be lacking. Perhaps at that time you might want to consider light supplementation. But whatever you do, remember that wholeness is the key to good health: The word "health," in fact, means wholeness. Stick to whole foods, and you'll be well on your way to adequate weight control and enhanced health and well-being.

*Beginning*

Let's begin the actual process of renewing your health and revitalizing your life. And, yes, you can even improve your appearance, as that excess weight finally begins to disappear and a renewed glow comes to your face.

There can be great variety within the HawaiiDiet™. To help you enjoy this variety while still staying within the general guidelines of the diet, I have designed three basic menus that will serve as starting points. But be aware that these are not all-or-nothing styles of eating. They are, rather, parts of a continuum, with the HawaiiDiet™ Mediterranean style being at one (the higher-fat) end, the HawaiiDiet™ Hawaii/Pacific style being at the other (low-fat) end. I have also provided a Hawaii/Pacific style, "middle American" diet that includes low-fat selections from Mediterranean type dishes that still fit the low-fat criteria of the Hawaii/Pacific style diet to show you that great variety is possible within the guidelines of the whole spectrum of the Hawaii-Diet™.

How will you know which version of the diet is best for you? This will depend upon your individual genetic make-up, and your individual needs (see page 53 for the criteria). Here is a general explanation of the three menus. To help you decide which version of the diet will work best for you, let's look at them one by one.

MENU #1: HawaiiDiet™ Hawaii/Pacific style, middle American version

If you want to start with familiar dishes, start with the Hawaii-Pacific style, middle American version of the diet. This is the first menu plan, and it is a hybrid between Hawaii/Pacific style and Mediterranean style dishes, but it also includes a strong emphasis on those foods that most Americans will already find familiar. You can lose weight on this diet, because it is still low-fat, even though it allows a selection of low-fat Mediterranean dishes. (See criteria for low-fat Hawaii/Pacific style HawaiiDiet™.)

MENU #2: HawaiiDiet™ Hawaii/Pacific style

This is the actual menu plan followed by the governor of Hawaii and other community leaders in the HawaiiDiet™ program, with very good results. This diet has a distinctly Hawaiian and Asian flavor, to suit the tastes of the participants in the program and is also very low in fat. There may be some recipes that are difficult to duplicate in some parts of the United States because of the ingredients. However, most cities and towns now offer Asian groceries, assuming you cannot find what you want in your local supermarket. Some of the fish dishes are particular to the Pacific Rim, but you can easily substitute the fish that is available in your region. Substitute wherever you want, as long as the foods meet the criteria of this version of the diet. For example, you can do a great pasta with mushroom marinara (see page 210) within the Hawaii/Pacific style of eating. There are also a myriad of other multicultural dishes you can enjoy. This is an ideal diet for most people in that it adheres to the SMI and is very low in fat, but it also allows you to try some of the exotic mixes of ethnic flavors in Hawaii/Pacific regional cuisine.

MENU #3: HawaiiDiet™ Mediterranean style

The third menu plan is Mediterranean style. It includes somewhat higher fat dishes that increase the use of monounsaturated fats such as the ones found in olive oil. It also allows the use of some dairy. Because of this, it is not an ideal weight-loss diet. However, it still follows the HawaiiDiet™ Pyramid; it just includes a little more of the apex of the pyramid. This is just a one-week sampling because fewer people can follow this style of eating without causing an increase in weight and cholesterol. However, if you seem genetically adapted to this style of eating (see criteria, pages 53–54), and if you exercise adequately to keep your metabolic rate high, then this diet may work very well for you.

At this point, as you begin, I wish you *bon appétit*—and the very best of health!

# SEVEN

# The HawaiiDiet™ Three-Week Menu Plan

## MENU 1: THE PACIFIC-STYLE HAWAIIDIET™, VERSION 1

| DAY | BREAKFAST | LUNCH | DINNER |
|---|---|---|---|
| 1 | Whole Oatmeal with raisins and cinnamon (p. 165)<br>Fresh fruit | Potato and Corn Chowder (p. 154)<br>Tossed green salad with Thousand Island Dressing (p. 125)<br>Choice of vegetable*<br>Fresh fruit | Hawaiian Savory Stew (p. 230)<br>Brown rice<br>Choice of vegetable*<br>Fresh fruit |
| 2 | Whole-Grain Waffles (p. 172)<br>Fresh fruit | Barbecue Baked Beans (p. 191)<br>Brown rice<br>Tossed green salad with nonfat dressing<br>Fresh fruit | Peter Merriman's Baked Fish (p. 198)<br>Stovetop Rice Pilaf (p. 181)<br>Choice of vegetable*<br>A's Baked Apples (p. 252) |
| 3 | Shredded-wheat cereal with nonfat soy or rice milk<br>Fresh fruit | Ratatouille (p. 235)<br>Pita bread or baked potato<br>Choice of vegetable*<br>Fresh fruit | Shrimp with Snow Peas and Mushrooms (p. 202)<br>Choice of vegetable*<br>Brown rice<br>Fresh fruit |

*Vegetable suggestions: broccoli, collard greens, mustard cabbage, kale, beet greens, okra, mustard greens, turnip greens, chicory, seaweed, green soybeans, acorn squash, amaranth, butternut squash, watercress

| DAY | BREAKFAST | LUNCH | DINNER |
|-----|-----------|-------|--------|
| 4 | Whole Oatmeal with raisins and cinnamon (p. 165)<br>Fresh fruit | Mock Crabmeat over Broccoli (p. 240)<br>Brown rice<br>Choice of vegetable*<br>Fruit Compote (p. 250) | Presto Minestrone (p. 163)<br>Tomato, White Bean, and Spinach Pasta (p. 209)<br>Fresh fruit |
| 5 | Cinnamon Apple Quinoa Cereal (p. 164)<br>Fresh fruit | Southwestern Barley Salad (p. 122)<br>Fresh fruit | Cajun Chicken Jambalaya (p. 197)<br>Tossed green salad with Balsamic Vinaigrette (p. 128)<br>Choice of vegetable*<br>Kona Coffee Ice Dream (p. 256) |
| 6 | Whole-Grain Waffles (p. 172)<br>Fresh fruit | Moroccan Chicken Salad (p. 120)<br>Choice of vegetable*<br>Whole-wheat roll<br>Fresh fruit | Red Chili Lentil Stew (p. 184)<br>Brown rice<br>Confetti Slaw with Vinaigrette (p. 117)<br>Fruit Strudel (p. 254) |
| 7 | Whole Oatmeal with raisins and cinnamon (p. 165)<br>Fresh fruit | Hearty White Bean Stew (p. 185)<br>Whole-grain bread<br>Choice of vegetable*<br>Fresh fruit | Mixed Grilled Vegetables with pasta (p. 221)<br>Great Caesar Salad (p. 114)<br>Choice of vegetable*<br>Strawberry-Banana Pudding (p. 251) |
| 8 | Banana Crepes (p. 168)<br>Fresh fruit | Chicken Broccoli (p. 193)<br>Brown Basmati Rice (p. 174)<br>Sweet Potato Salad (p. 113)<br>Fresh fruit | Potato, Eggplant, and Zucchini Pie (p. 231)<br>Choice of vegetable*<br>Crusty whole-wheat bread<br>Fresh fruit |
| 9 | Whole-wheat bagel<br>Sugarless fruit preserves<br>Fresh fruit | Hawaiian Curry (p. 224)<br>Brown rice<br>Tossed green salad with nonfat dressing<br>Fresh fruit | Tofu Stir-Fry (p. 205)<br>Brown Basmati Rice (p. 174)<br>Steamed yellow squash<br>Choice of vegetable*<br>A's Poached Pears (p. 253) |
| 10 | Banana Bread (p. 170)<br>Fresh fruit | Quick Mexican Pizza (p. 139)<br>Tossed green salad with nonfat dressing<br>Fresh fruit | Baked Rice with Shiitake Mushrooms (p. 175)<br>Tossed green salad with Balsamic Vinaigrette (p. 128)<br>Choice of vegetable*<br>Fresh fruit |

| DAY | BREAKFAST | LUNCH | DINNER |
|---|---|---|---|
| 11 | Low-fat Granola (p. 166)<br>Nonfat soy or rice milk<br>Fresh fruit | Three-Bean Salad (p. 123)<br>Crusty whole-wheat bread<br>Fresh fruit | Grilled Salmon Fillet with<br>  Fresh Tomato Salsa<br>  (p. 203)<br>Brown rice<br>Choice of vegetable*<br>Mixed greens with nonfat<br>  dressing<br>Fresh fruit |
| 12 | Whole Oatmeal with<br>  raisins and sliced<br>  bananas (p. 165)<br>Nonfat soy or rice milk | Chunky Two-Bean Chili<br>  (p. 192)<br>Brown rice<br>Tossed green salad with<br>  nonfat dressing | Hula Grill's Ginger Pine-<br>  apple Chicken (p. 196)<br>Choice of vegetable*<br>Brown rice<br>Fresh fruit |
| 13 | Scrambled Tofu (p. 206)<br>Whole-wheat toast or<br>  brown rice<br>Fresh fruit | Peter Merriman's Asian<br>  Gazpacho (p. 155)<br>Simple Hummus (p. 140)<br>Pita bread<br>Choice of vegetable* | Chicken Breast in Phyllo<br>  with Tomato-Herb Sauce<br>  (p. 194)<br>Greek Salad (p. 118)<br>Choice of vegetable*<br>Fresh fruit |
| 14 | Grape Nuts cereal with<br>  nonfat soy or rice milk<br>Fresh fruit | Spicy Beanburgers (p. 190)<br>Whole-wheat roll<br>Fresh fruit | Shrimp with Snow Peas<br>  and Mushrooms (p. 202)<br>Brown rice<br>Steamed kale<br>Fresh fruit |
| 15 | Hearty Muffins (p. 167)<br>Fresh fruit | Maui Tacos' Black Bean<br>  Burrito (p. 186)<br>Tossed green salad with<br>  nonfat dressing | Sweet-and-Sour Tofu with<br>  Snow Peas and<br>  Mushrooms (p. 204)<br>Brown rice<br>Choice of vegetable*<br>Apple Bran Cake (p. 259) |
| 16 | Shredded-wheat cereal<br>  with nonfat soy or rice<br>  milk<br>Fresh fruit | Portuguese Bean Soup<br>  (p. 160)<br>Brown rice<br>Mixed greens with<br>  Balsamic Vinaigrette<br>  (p. 128)<br>Fresh fruit | Hawaiian Savory Stew<br>  (p. 230)<br>Brown rice<br>Tossed green salad with<br>  nonfat dressing<br>Choice of vegetable*<br>Pineapple Sorbet (p. 251) |
| 17 | Whole Oatmeal with<br>  raisins and cinnamon<br>  (p. 165)<br>Fresh fruit | Spicy Beanburgers (p. 190)<br>Whole-wheat roll<br>Choice of vegetable*<br>Fresh fruit | Rice-Stuffed Cabbage Rolls<br>  (p. 179)<br>Tossed green salad with<br>  nonfat dressing<br>Fresh fruit |

| DAY | BREAKFAST | LUNCH | DINNER |
|---|---|---|---|
| 18 | Bagel<br>Sugar-free fruit spread | Kabobs with Marinade of your choice (p. 226)<br>Brown rice<br>Fresh fruit | Vegetable and Whole-Wheat Couscous Paella (p. 222)<br>Mixed greens with Balsamic Vinaigrette (p. 128)<br>Choice of vegetable*<br>Fresh fruit |
| 19 | Low-fat Granola (p. 166)<br>Fresh fruit | Stuffed Baked Potato (p. 217)<br>Tossed green salad with Thousand Island Dressing (p. 125)<br>Fresh fruit | Thai Vegetable Curry (p. 225)<br>Brown rice<br>Choice of vegetable*<br>Fresh fruit |
| 20 | Scrambled Tofu (p. 206)<br>Whole-wheat toast with sugarless fruit preserves | Rasta Pasta Salad (p. 112)<br>Whole-wheat Roll<br>Fresh fruit | Rice Loaf (p. 180)<br>Savory Gravy (p. 244)<br>Choice of vegetable*<br>Tossed green salad with nonfat dressing<br>Fresh fruit |
| 21 | Whole Oatmeal with raisins and cinnamon (p. 165)<br>Nonfat soy or rice milk<br>Fresh fruit | Hearty White Bean Stew (p. 185)<br>Choice of vegetable*<br>Crusty whole-wheat bread<br>Fresh fruit | Mushroom Marinara Sauce over pasta (p. 210)<br>Choice of vegetable*<br>Great Caesar Salad (p. 114)<br>Fresh fruit |

## MENU 2: THE PACIFIC-STYLE HAWAIIDIET™, VERSION 2

| DAY | BREAKFAST | LUNCH | DINNER |
|---|---|---|---|
| 1 | Steamed Sweet Potato (p. 142) Cooked Taro (p. 143) Fresh fruit Mamaki tea | Potato and Corn Chowder (p. 154) Peter Merriman's Mixed Green Vegetable Salad with Potatoes (p. 109) Maui onions Broccoli Fresh pineapple | Chicken Laulau (p. 154) Mountain Fern Salad (p. 149) Poi Steamed Sweet Potato (p. 142) Fresh fruit Mamaki tea |
| 2 | Whole-Grain Waffles (p. 172) Fresh papaya Mamaki tea | Tofu Stir-Fry (p. 205) Spicy Szechuan Eggplant (p. 239) Brown Basmati Rice (p. 174) Fresh fruit Mamaki tea | Peter Merriman's Baked Fish (p. 198) Brown Basmati Rice (p. 174) Seaweed Vinaigrette (p. 127) Fresh fruit Green tea |
| 3 | Breakfast Miso Soup (p. 152) Brown Basmati Rice (p. 174) Fresh fruit Green tea | Pan Sushi (p. 138) Choice of vegetable* Tropical Fruit Salad (p. 121) Green tea | Shrimp with Snow Peas and Mushrooms (p. 202) Brown Basmati Rice (p. 174) Steamed Garlic Broccoli (p. 238) Fresh fruit Mamaki tea |
| 4 | Whole Oatmeal (p. 165) Fresh fruit Mamaki tea | Mock Crabmeat over Broccoli (p. 240) Brown Basmati Rice (p. 174) Fresh fruit Tea | Peking Hot and Sour Soup (p. 156) Brown Basmati Rice (p. 174) Tofu Stir-Fry (p. 205) Fresh fruit Green tea |
| 5 | Confetti Congee (p. 157) Fresh fruit Green tea | Cold Somen Salad (p. 110) Choice of vegetable* Fresh fruit Iced mamaki tea | Fish Laulau (p. 147) Steamed Sweet Potato (p. 142) Cooked Taro (p. 143) Manauwea Salad (p. 148) Fresh fruit Mamaki tea |

*Vegetable suggestions: broccoli, collard greens, mustard cabbage, kale, beet greens, okra, mustard greens, turnip greens, chicory, seaweed, green soybeans, acorn squash, amaranth, butternut squash, watercress

| DAY | BREAKFAST | LUNCH | DINNER |
|---|---|---|---|
| 6 | Pho (p. 162)<br>Brown Basmati Rice<br>(p. 174)<br>Fresh fruit<br>Green tea | Peter Merriman's Asian<br>Gazpacho (p. 155)<br>Vegetarian Eight Treasures<br>(p. 232)<br>Brown Basmati Rice<br>(p. 174)<br>Fresh fruit<br>Iced tea | Spicy Beanburgers (p. 190)<br>Choice of vegetable*<br>Fruit Compote (p. 250)<br>Iced tea |
| 7 | Cinnamon Apple Quinoa<br>Cereal (p. 164)<br>Fresh papaya<br>Mamaki tea | Thai Vegetable Curry<br>(p. 225)<br>Thai Jasmine Rice (p. 176)<br>Lomi Tomatoes (p. 141)<br>Fresh fruit<br>Mamaki tea | Wheat-Berry Vegetable<br>Soup (p. 161)<br>Chicken Broccoli (p. 193)<br>Green salad with<br>Thousand Island<br>Dressing (p. 125)<br>Fresh fruit<br>Tea |
| 8 | Hearty Muffins (p. 167)<br>Fresh fruit<br>Herb tea | Chicken Broccoli (p. 193)<br>Brown Basmati Rice<br>(p. 174)<br>Steamed Sweet Potato<br>(p. 142)<br>Fresh fruit<br>Mamaki tea | Korean Noodles (p. 214)<br>Watercress and Bean<br>Sprout Namul (p. 111)<br>Fresh fruit<br>Tea |
| 9 | Steamed Sweet Potato<br>(p. 142)<br>Cooked Taro (p. 143)<br>Tropical Fruit Salad<br>(p. 121) | Hawaiian Savory Stew<br>(p. 230)<br>Brown Basmati Rice<br>(p. 174)<br>Mixed greens with<br>Thousand Island<br>Dressing (p. 125)<br>Fresh fruit<br>Tea | Tofu Stir-Fry (p. 205)<br>Brown Basmati Rice<br>(p. 174)<br>Lomi Tomatoes (p. 141)<br>A's Poached Pears (p. 253)<br>Mamaki tea |
| 10 | Banana Bread (p. 170)<br>Fresh papaya<br>Mamaki tea | Chicken Laulau (p. 147)<br>Brown Basmati Rice<br>(p. 174)<br>Fresh fruit<br>Herb tea | Baked Rice with Shiitake<br>Mushrooms (p. 175)<br>Mixed greens with Mark<br>Ellman's Tomato Miso<br>Vinaigrette (p. 124)<br>Melt-in-Your-Mouth<br>Kabocha Squash (p. 241)<br>Fresh fruit<br>Green tea |

| DAY | BREAKFAST | LUNCH | DINNER |
|-----|-----------|-------|--------|
| 11 | Breakfast Miso Soup (p. 152) <br> Brown Basmati Rice (p. 174) <br> Fresh fruit <br> Green tea | Sweet Potato Salad (p. 113) <br> Watercress and Bean Sprout Namul (p. 111) <br> Fresh fruit <br> Iced tea | Grilled Salmon Filet with Fresh Tomato Salsa (p. 203) <br> Choice of vegetable* <br> Asparagus Artichoke Salad (p. 115) <br> Fresh fruit <br> Tea |
| 12 | Whole Oatmeal (p. 165) <br> Fresh fruit <br> Mamaki tea | Polenta with Sauteed Mushrooms and Onion (p. 171) <br> Choice of vegetable* <br> Mixed greens with Tangy Dijon Dressing (p. 126) <br> Tea | Hula Grill's Ginger Pineapple Chicken (p. 196) <br> Brown Basmati Rice (p. 174) <br> Watercress and Bean Sprout Namul (p. 111) <br> Fresh fruit <br> Iced tea |
| 13 | Scrambled Tofu (p. 206) <br> Whole-wheat toast or brown rice <br> Fresh fruit <br> Mamaki tea | Chunky Two-Bean Chili (p. 192) <br> Confetti Slaw with Vinaigrette (p. 117) <br> Fresh fruit <br> Iced tea | Roy's Blackened Ahi with Soy-Mustard Sauce (p. 200) <br> Roasted Potatoes (p. 219) <br> Fresh fruit <br> Tea |
| 14 | Low-Fat Granola (p. 166) <br> Fresh papaya <br> Herb tea | Summer Rolls with Clear and Amber Dips (p. 132) <br> Choice of vegetable* <br> Brown Basmati Rice (p. 174) <br> Fresh fruit <br> Herb tea | Shrimp with Snow Peas and Mushrooms (p. 202) <br> Brown Basmati Rice (p. 174) <br> Fresh fruit <br> Herb tea |
| 15 | Steamed Sweet Potato (p. 142) <br> Cooked Taro (p. 143) <br> Fresh fruit <br> Tea | Maui Tacos' Black Bean Burrito (p. 186) <br> Choice of vegetable* <br> Iced tea | Sweet-and-Sour Tofu with Snow Peas and Mushrooms (p. 204) <br> Apple Bran Cake (p. 259) <br> Fresh fruit <br> Tea |
| 16 | Banana Bread (p. 170) <br> Fresh fruit <br> Herb tea | Portuguese Bean Soup (p. 160) <br> Whole-wheat bread <br> Green salad with Balsamic Vinaigrette (p. 128) <br> Tea | Hawaiian Savory Stew (p. 230) <br> Choice of vegetable* <br> Brown Basmati Rice (p. 174) <br> Mixed greens with Oriental Vinaigrette (p. 127) <br> Pineapple Sorbet (p. 251) <br> Iced tea |

| DAY | BREAKFAST | LUNCH | DINNER |
|---|---|---|---|
| 17 | Confetti Congee (p. 157)<br>Fresh fruit<br>Green tea | Vegetarian Eight Treasures<br>(p. 232)<br>Brown Basmati Rice<br>(p. 174)<br>Fresh fruit<br>Iced mamaki tea | Vegetable Laulau (p. 146)<br>Manauwea Salad (p. 148)<br>Steamed Sweet Potato<br>(p. 142)<br>Poi<br>Fresh banana<br>Mamaki tea |
| 18 | Whole-wheat bagel<br>Fresh fruit<br>Tea | Greek Salad (p. 118)<br>Fresh fruit<br>Iced tea | Moo Shu Vegetables<br>(p. 229)<br>Fresh green beans<br>Tropical Fruit Salad<br>(p. 121)<br>Iced tea |
| 19 | Breakfast Miso Soup<br>(p. 152)<br>Brown Basmati Rice<br>(p. 174)<br>Fresh fruit<br>Tea | Gandule Rice (p. 177)<br>Mixed greens with<br>Balsamic Vinaigrette<br>(p. 128)<br>Fresh fruit<br>Tea | Tofu Stir-Fry (p. 205)<br>Brown Basmati Rice<br>(p. 174)<br>Spicy Szechuan Eggplant<br>(p. 239)<br>Honey Almond Fruit<br>Cocktail (p. 257)<br>Tea |
| 20 | Scrambled Tofu (p. 206)<br>Whole-wheat toast<br>Fruit preserves<br>Herb tea | Cold Somen Salad (p. 110)<br>Fresh fruit<br>Mamaki tea | Avalon's Pasta Gerry<br>(p. 208)<br>Great Caesar Salad<br>(p. 114)<br>Fresh fruit<br>Iced tea |
| 21 | Steamed Sweet Potato<br>(p. 142)<br>Cooked Taro (p. 143)<br>Fresh fruit<br>Tea | Quick Mexican Pizza<br>(p. 139)<br>Mixed greens with Tangy<br>Dijon Dressing (p. 126)<br>Iced tea | Baked Rice with Shiitake<br>Mushrooms (p. 175)<br>Mixed greens with Tomato<br>Miso Vinaigrette (p. 124)<br>Melt-in-Your-Mouth<br>Kabocha Squash (p. 241)<br>Kona Coffee Ice Dream<br>(p. 256)<br>Tea |

# MENU 3: THE MEDITERRANEAN-STYLE HAWAIIDIET™

| DAY | BREAKFAST | LUNCH | DINNER |
|---|---|---|---|
| 1 | Whole Oatmeal with raisins and cinnamon (p. 165) Fresh fruit | Polenta with Sauteed Mushrooms and Onions (p. 171) Tossed green salad with Thousand Island Dressing (p. 125) Choice of vegetable* Fresh fruit | Grilled Salmon Filet with Fresh Tomato Salsa (p. 203) Tossed green salad with nonfat dressing Brown Basmati Rice (p. 174) Choice of vegetable* Fresh fruit |
| 2 | Whole-Grain Waffles (p. 172) Fresh fruit | Hearty White Bean Stew (p. 185) Tossed green salad with nonfat dressing Choice of vegetable* Fresh fruit | Vegetable and Whole-Wheat Couscous Paella (p. 222) Stovetop Rice Pilaf (p. 181) Tossed green salad with nonfat dressing A's Baked Apples (p. 252) |
| 3 | Shredded-wheat cereal with nonfat soy or rice milk Fresh fruit | Ratatouille (p. 235) Baked potato Peter Merriman's Mixed Green Vegetable Salad with Potatoes (p. 109) Dijon Vinaigrette (p. 126) | Presto Minestrone (p. 163) Avalon's Pasta Gerry (p. 208) Tossed green salad with nonfat dressing Choice of vegetable* Fresh fruit |
| 4 | Whole Oatmeal with raisins (p. 165) Fresh fruit | Rasta Pasta Salad (p. 112) Brown Basmati Rice (p. 174) Choice of vegetable* Fruit Compote (p. 250) | Cajun Chicken Jambalaya (p. 197) Tossed green salad with Balsamic Vinaigrette (p. 128) Choice of vegetable* Crispy Apricot Turnovers (p. 258) |
| 5 | Cinnamon Apple Quinoa Cereal (p. 164) Fresh fruit | Great Caesar Salad (p. 114) Roasted Potatoes (p. 219) Fresh fruit | Tomato, White Bean, and Spinach Pasta (p. 209) Choice of vegetable* Fresh fruit |

*Vegetable suggestions: broccoli, collard greens, mustard cabbage, kale, beet greens, okra, mustard greens, turnip greens, chicory, seaweed, green soybeans, acorn squash, amaranth, butternut squash, watercress

| DAY | BREAKFAST | LUNCH | DINNER |
|---|---|---|---|
| 6 | Whole-Grain Waffles (p. 172)<br>Fresh fruit | Moroccan Chicken Salad (p. 120)<br>Whole-wheat roll<br>Choice of vegetable*<br>Fresh fruit | Red Chili Lentil Stew (p. 184)<br>Brown Basmati Rice (p. 174)<br>Confetti Slaw with Vinaigrette (p. 117)<br>Fruit Strudel (p. 254) |
| 7 | Shredded-wheat cereal with nonfat soy or rice milk<br>Fresh fruit | Peter Merriman's Asian Gazpacho (p. 155)<br>Simple Hummus (p. 140)<br>Pita bread<br>Choice of vegetable*<br>Sliced cucumbers | Chicken Breast in Phyllo with Tomato-Herb Sauce (p. 194)<br>Greek Salad (p. 118)<br>Choice of vegetable*<br>Fresh fruit |

# PART TWO

# The Recipes

# EIGHT

# Salads and Dressings

## Red Potato Salad

1½ pounds red potatoes

1 cup chopped red onion

1 cup chopped celery

2 tablespoons sliced pitted black olives

2 tablespoons chopped fresh parsley

½ cup fat-free mayonnaise

2 tablespoons prepared horseradish

1 tablespoon Dijon mustard

Salt and freshly ground black pepper to taste

Peel potatoes and cut into cubes. Boil for about 10 minutes, or until just tender. Cool in freezer for 5–10 minutes. Do not overcook. Combine potatoes with onion, celery, olives, and parsley; toss lightly. Combine mayonnaise, horseradish, mustard, salt, and pepper; blend well. Add dressing to potato salad; toss lightly. Serve chilled.

*Makes 6 servings.*

**Nutrition Information per Serving:** *127 calories; 1.3 grams (9%) fat; 8% protein; 83% carbohydrates.*

# Miso Potato Salad

*This dish combines Japanese and American cuisine into a blend that perfectly illustrates what is unique and delicious about Hawaiian food. This dish keeps well when refrigerated. You can make it at home and take it to the office to really dress up your lunch. This potato salad uses miso, a soybean paste that is full of flavor but without the high fat content of mayonnaise. A tablespoon of mayonnaise contains 99 calories and 11 grams of fat, while a tablespoon of miso has 35 calories and only 1 gram of fat.*

1 large Idaho potato
2 tablespoons red miso
1 tablespoon sweet pickle juice
2 tablespoons finely minced sweet pickles
¼ teaspoon prepared mustard

Scrub the potato and microwave it on high for about 4 minutes, or until easily pierced with a fork. Remove potato from microwave and cool in freezer for 1 minute. Meanwhile, combine remaining ingredients in a small bowl. Remove potato from freezer and cut into ½-inch cubes. Toss with dressing, mashing slightly if desired.

*Makes 1 serving.*
**Nutrition Information per Serving:** *257 calories; 2.3 grams (8%) fat; 11% protein; 81% carbohydrates.*

# Peter Merriman's Mixed Green Vegetable Salad with Potatoes

*Peter Merriman is chef and owner of Merriman's Restaurant in Kamuela, Hawaii, and the Hula Grill in Ka'anapali, Maui.*

1 pound boiling potatoes
3–4 ounces mixed salad greens
1 Maui onion, sliced
½ pound fresh broccoli, minced
1 fresh pineapple, peeled and cut into chunks
Dijon Vinaigrette to taste

Scrub potatoes and boil until tender. Soak in cold water to cool. Peel and cut into cubes. Rinse mixed greens and drain thoroughly. Place in a salad bowl. Combine potatoes, onion, broccoli, pineapple, and Dijon Vinaigrette. Arrange over greens and serve immediately.

*Makes 1 serving.*

**Nutrition Information per Serving with Dressing:** *130 calories; 1.6 grams (11%) fat; 13% protein; 76% carbohydrates.*

## Dijon Vinaigrette

10 ounces extra-firm tofu
⅓ cup Dijon mustard
⅓ cup red wine vinegar
¼ teaspoon freshly ground black pepper

Place all ingredients in a food processor and blend until smooth. Place in a covered container and store in refrigerator up to 1 week.

*Makes 8 servings.*

**Nutrition Information per Serving:** *24 calories; 1.5 grams (45%) fat; 22% protein; 33% carbohydrates.*

# Cold Somen Salad

*Somen are vermicelli-like Japanese noodles. You can use them to make a hearty soup that has virtually no fat, or in salads, with a variety of healthful vegetables.*

---

1 10-ounce package wheat somen
¼ cup rice vinegar or 2 tablespoons each rice vinegar and plum vinegar
¼ cup low-sodium soy sauce
½ cup vegetable broth
1 teaspoon sesame oil
2 tablespoons mirin (rice wine)
3 tablespoons honey, barley malt, or brown rice syrup
6–8 large fresh shiitake mushrooms, stems removed
1 carrot, thinly sliced
1 cucumber, peeled and cut into julienne strips
2 cups shredded leafy lettuce or Chinese cabbage
2 ounces radish sprouts
3 scallions, thinly sliced on the diagonal, for garnish
⅓ cup coarsely chopped fresh Chinese parsley for garnish

*Marinade*
1 tablespoon sesame seeds, toasted and crushed
½ teaspoon sesame oil
1 tablespoon low-sodium soy sauce or tamari
1 tablespoon rice vinegar
1 teaspoon honey

Cook noodles according to package directions; rinse and drain well. Arrange 8 small mounds of noodles on a large platter; cover and chill. In a small saucepan, combine rice vinegar, soy sauce, broth, sesame oil, mirin, and honey; bring to a boil. Lower heat and simmer for 2 minutes, then refrigerate until chilled. Meanwhile, bring a medium saucepan of water to boil and fill a large bowl with ice water. Blanch the shiitake mushrooms for 20 seconds, then plunge them into the ice water. Add remaining vegetables and set aside. Combine the marinade ingredients in a small bowl. Slice the mushrooms into slivers and toss with marinade. To serve, drain vegetables and pat dry. Arrange the vegetables over the chilled noodles. Garnish with scallions and Chinese parsley. Serve with chilled dressing.

*Makes 4 servings.*

**Nutrition Information per Serving:** *410 calories; 3.7 grams (8%) fat; 14% protein; 78% carbohydrates.*

# Watercress and Bean Sprout Namul

*This is a traditional Korean side dish that is high in calcium and low in fat.* Namul *means "variety of vegetables" in Korean.*

---

1 16-ounce bunch fresh watercress
1 12-ounce package fresh bean sprouts
2 tablespoons soy sauce
2 tablespoons rice vinegar
2 tablespoons sesame seeds, toasted
2 tablespoons chopped scallions
¼ teaspoon ground red pepper
⅛ teaspoon minced garlic
½ teaspoon sugar

Rinse watercress to clean; remove and discard tough stems. Chop watercress coarsely. Blanch watercress and bean sprouts, then drain well. In a large bowl, combine remaining ingredients; add blanched vegetables and mix well. Chill.

*Makes 6 servings.*

**Nutrition Information per Serving:** *44 calories; 1.6 grams (29%) fat; 26% protein; 45% carbohydrates.*

# Rasta Pasta Salad

*This salad is named for its reggae-like colors: orange, green, and
red.*

---

2 cups rotini

1½ cups sliced fresh carrots

2½ cups fresh broccoli florets

½ large red bell pepper, cut into julienne strips

¼ cup minced red onion

2 cups cherry tomatoes

1 tablespoon red wine vinegar

2 tablespoons balsamic vinegar

1 teaspoon extra-virgin olive oil

3 cloves garlic, minced

1 teaspoon dried basil

Salt and freshly ground black pepper to taste

Prepare pasta according to package directions; drain, cool, and set
aside. Steam carrots and broccoli for 5 minutes. Cool and place in a
large bowl. Add bell pepper, red onion, and cherry tomatoes; toss
lightly. Combine remaining ingredients and mix well. Add the pasta
and dressing to the vegetables; toss lightly. Serve cold.

*Makes 4 servings.*

**Nutrition Information per Serving:** *225 calories; 2.4 grams (9%) fat; 15%
protein; 76% carbohydrates.*

# Sweet Potato Salad

*In Hawaii, we use Okinawan sweet potatoes, which are purple in color, for this dish.*

1 pound sweet potatoes, cooked and cubed
1 pound purple yams, cooked and cubed
1 small Maui onion, sliced (sweet, mild onion)
½ green bell pepper, cut into julienne strips
½ red bell pepper, cut into julienne strips
½ yellow bell pepper, cut into julienne strips

*Dressing*
2 slices onion, chopped
1 teaspoon extra-virgin olive oil
2 tablespoons honey
¼ cup cider vinegar
¾ teaspoon salt
¼ teaspoon powdered mustard
Dash freshly ground black pepper
Dash Worcestershire sauce
½ bay leaf

Combine the cooked sweet potatoes, yams, onion, and bell peppers in a serving bowl; toss lightly to blend. Chill. In a small bowl, combine all the dressing ingredients; blend well and chill. Before serving, remove bay leaf from dressing and pour over salad. Toss lightly and chill for another hour.

*Makes 8 servings.*
**Nutrition Information per Serving:** *161 calories; 0.9 grams (5%) fat; 6% protein; 89% carbohydrates.*

# Great Caesar Salad

*The traditional Caesar salad can be a fine meal in itself, and is often mixed and tossed at the table in American, French, and Italian restaurants with great panache. You can serve this to guests with a flourish, or keep the secret to yourself. But whatever you do, rest assured that this version eliminates the anchovies and raw egg—two possibly problematic ingredients in the traditional version of this dish. Most of the fatty olive oil is also eliminated from the dressing. In the process, the taste is actually improved! So enjoy this traditional treat, especially on those evenings when you're too tired to cook but know you deserve something special.*

1 head Belgian endive, trimmed and separated
1 head red-leaf lettuce, torn into pieces
¼ cup shredded arugula
¼ cup shredded radicchio
½ cup oil-free croutons
Great Caesar Salad Dressing to taste
Coarsely ground black pepper to taste

In a large bowl, combine the first four ingredients; toss lightly and chill. Just before serving, add croutons, salad dressing, and pepper.

*Makes 2 servings as an entree and 4 servings as a side dish.*
**Nutrition Information per Entree Serving with Dressing:** *154 calories; 3.2 grams (23%) fat; 16% protein; 61% carbohydrates.*

## Great Caesar Salad Dressing
*There are many excellent low-fat Caesar salad dressings on the shelves of your local health-food store. If you like the addition of a splash of sherry but don't have time to make your own dressing, just add a tablespoonful to your bottled salad dressing and mix well before using.*

2 tablespoons roasted garlic, peeled and chopped

¼ cup sherry

1 teaspoon freshly squeezed lemon juice

1 teaspoon salt, or more or less to taste

1 teaspoon extra-virgin olive oil

¼ teaspoon minced fresh rosemary

1 tablespoon Dijon mustard

1 tablespoon A.1® Steak Sauce

Dash hot pepper sauce

In a medium bowl, whisk together all ingredients until well blended.

*Makes ½ cup, or 4 2-tablespoon servings.*

**Nutrition Information per Serving:** *40 calories; 1.5 grams (38%) fat; 10% protein; 52% carbohydrates.*

# *Asparagus Artichoke Salad*

½ cup marinated artichoke hearts, rinsed

1 8-ounce package frozen asparagus, thawed and well drained

½ cup chopped red onion

1 cup finely shredded Bibb lettuce

1 15-ounce can pickled beet slices, drained, juice reserved

½ cup reserved juice from pickled beets

2 tablespoons balsamic vinegar

1 teaspoon A.1® Steak Sauce

Salt and freshly ground black pepper to taste

In a large bowl, combine artichoke hearts, asparagus, red onion, lettuce, and beet slices. Toss lightly and set aside. Combine beet juice, vinegar, and steak sauce; blend well. Pour dressing over salad and toss lightly.

*Makes 4 servings.*

**Nutrition Information per Serving:** *84 calories; 1.6 grams (16%) fat; 13% protein; 71% carbohydrates.*

# Far Eastern Cole Slaw

2 cups shredded green cabbage

1 cup shredded red cabbage

1 cup shredded won bok (Chinese cabbage)

1 cup shredded carrots

½ cup chopped fresh Chinese parsley or cilantro

½ cup chopped scallions

¼ cup vegetable broth

1 tablespoon white vinegar

1 tablespoon balsamic vinegar

1 tablespoon sesame oil

1 teaspoon soy sauce

½ teaspoon powdered mustard

½ teaspoon honey

½ teaspoon grated fresh ginger

½ teaspoon minced fresh garlic

In a large bowl, combine cabbages, carrots, Chinese parsley or cilantro, and scallions; toss lightly. Whisk together remaining ingredients. Add dressing to salad and toss lightly.

*Makes 6 servings.*

**Nutrition Information per Serving:** *39 calories; 1 gram (23%) fat; 14% protein; 63% carbohydrates.*

# Confetti Slaw with Vinaigrette

2 cups shredded green cabbage

2 cups shredded red cabbage

1 cup grated carrots

1 yellow bell pepper, diced

¼ cup sliced scallions

2 tablespoons balsamic vinegar

6 tablespoons red wine vinegar

2 tablespoons Dijon mustard

1 tablespoon tamari

2 teaspoons honey

½ teaspoon celery seeds

¼ teaspoon freshly ground black pepper

In a large bowl, combine cabbages, carrots, bell pepper, and scallions; toss lightly. Whisk together remaining ingredients. Add dressing to salad and toss lightly. Chill at least 1 hour before serving.

*Makes 6 servings.*

**Nutrition Information per Serving:** *45 calories; 0.7 grams (12%) fat; 14% protein; 74% carbohydrates.*

# Greek Salad

¼ cup cider vinegar

¾-ounce package herb-and-garlic salad-dressing mix

1 teaspoon extra-virgin olive oil

½ cup water

2 cups chopped romaine lettuce

1 medium tomato, quartered

½ cup thinly sliced cucumber

2 tablespoons finely minced red onion

2 Greek olives, pitted and sliced

2 ounces low-fat feta cheese, crumbled

Pour vinegar into a container with a tight-fitting lid; add contents of dressing mix package, seal container, and shake vigorously until well blended. Add olive oil and water. Shake again until well blended. In a large bowl, combine lettuce, tomato, cucumber, red onion, and Greek olives. Top with feta cheese. Drizzle dressing over salad and toss lightly. Serve slightly chilled.

*Makes 4 servings.*

**Nutrition Information per Serving:** *69 calories; 5 grams (68%) fat; 14% protein; 18% carbohydrates.*

# Antipasto Salad

2 cups whole white button mushrooms
1 13¾-ounce can artichoke hearts, drained
1 cup nonfat Italian dressing
1 teaspoon extra-virgin olive oil
½ teaspoon freshly ground black pepper
1 head romaine lettuce, chopped
1 cucumber, thinly sliced
2 stalks celery, thinly sliced on the diagonal
4 large tomatoes, cut into eighths
1 red onion, thinly sliced
¼ cup sliced radishes

In a large bowl, combine mushrooms and artichoke hearts. Combine Italian dressing, olive oil, and black pepper; blend well. Pour over mushroom mixture; toss lightly and marinate for 30 minutes. Arrange the lettuce on a large platter. Strain the mushroom and artichoke mixture, saving marinade. Place mushrooms and artichokes in the center of the platter. Arrange the remaining vegetables around the center. Drizzle the reserved marinade over the vegetables.

*Makes 8 servings.*
**Nutrition Information per Serving:** *84 calories; 1.3 grams (12%) fat; 17% protein; 71% carbohydrates.*

# Moroccan Chicken Salad

½ chicken breast

¼ teaspoon garlic salt

⅛ teaspoon freshly ground black pepper

1½ cups instant couscous

2 tablespoons freshly squeezed lemon juice

2 tablespoons water

2 tablespoons Dijon mustard

2 cloves garlic, minced

½ cup diced scallions

2 medium tomatoes, diced

1 large cucumber, peeled and diced

1 15-ounce can chickpeas (garbanzo beans), drained

¼ cup finely chopped fresh parsley

¼ cup finely chopped fresh mint leaves

¼ cup golden raisins

Salt and freshly ground black pepper to taste

Olive oil spray

Season chicken breast with garlic salt and pepper. In a nonstick skillet, fry chicken 10 minutes on each side, or until no pink remains in the middle. Dice chicken and set aside. Cook couscous according to package directions and transfer to a serving bowl. Whisk together lemon juice, water, mustard, and garlic. Combine remaining ingredients with couscous and chicken. Add dressing and toss lightly. Serve cold.

*Makes 6–8 servings.*

**Nutrition Information per Serving:** *274 calories; 2 grams (6%) fat; 19% protein; 75% carbohydrates.*

# Tropical Fruit Salad

*This is an excellent breakfast or quick lunch dish, especially when served with cinnamon toast on the side.*

2 kiwifruit, peeled and sliced
2 bananas, cut into 1-inch slices
½ papaya, halved, seeded, peeled, and cubed
1 teaspoon freshly squeezed lime juice
2 teaspoons lime zest
1 tablespoon finely chopped fresh mint

In a large bowl, combine fruit and toss lightly. Whisk together lime juice, lime zest, and mint. Add dressing just before serving; toss lightly.

*Makes 4 servings as an entree and 6 servings as a side dish.*
**Nutrition Information per Entree Serving:** *99 calories; 0.5 grams (4%) fat; 5% protein; 91% carbohydrates.*

# Chutney Salad

*This salad tastes excellent when arranged on a bed of mixed greens and served as an accompaniment to spicy curried dishes.*

2 large green apples
2 tablespoons raisins
2 tablespoons golden raisins
6 tablespoons prepared mango chutney

Wash, peel, and core apples. Dice into ½-inch pieces. Combine with raisins and mango chutney.

*Makes 4 servings.*
**Nutrition Information per Serving:** *182 calories; 4.6 grams (21%) fat; 2% protein; 77% carbohydrates.*

# Southwestern Barley Salad

2¼ cups water

1 cup pearl barley

1 teaspoon salt

1½ cups cooked lima beans

1 red bell pepper, roasted, seeded, and sliced

4 cloves garlic, minced

⅓ cup tomato juice

1 teaspoon extra-virgin olive oil

2 tablespoons chopped fresh Chinese parsley

1 teaspoon ground cumin

1 teaspoon dried oregano

1 teaspoon seasoned salt

½ teaspoon hot pepper sauce

½ teaspoon coarsely ground black pepper

In a medium saucepan, bring water to a boil; stir in barley and salt. Return to a boil, reduce heat, and simmer for 40 minutes. Let stand for 5 minutes, then transfer to a bowl and fluff. Add lima beans and red bell pepper. Whisk together the remaining ingredients and pour over salad; toss lightly and serve.

*Makes 4 servings.*

**Nutrition Information per Serving:** *256 calories; 3 grams (9%) fat; 15% protein; 76% carbohydrates.*

# Three-Bean Salad

2 cups fresh kidney beans, cooked, or 1 15½-ounce can kidney
 beans, well drained

2 cups fresh chickpeas (garbanzo beans), cooked, or 1 15½-ounce
 can chickpeas, well drained

2 cups sliced fresh green or wax beans, cooked, or 2 cups canned
 green or wax beans, well drained, or 2 cups frozen green or
 wax beans, thawed

1 red onion, halved and thinly sliced

¼ cup diced red bell pepper

2 cloves garlic, pressed

1 teaspoon Dijon mustard

¼ cup freshly squeezed lemon juice

¼ cup red wine vinegar

¼ cup honey or brown rice syrup

½ teaspoon salt, or more or less to taste

¼ teaspoon freshly ground black pepper, or more or less to taste

If using canned beans, rinse well under cold water, drain, and pat
dry. In a large bowl, combine beans, red onion, and bell pepper.
Whisk together remaining ingredients. Add dressing to bean mixture; toss lightly, cover, and marinate in refrigerator for several
hours or overnight.

*Makes 6 servings.*
**Nutrition Information per Serving:** *240 calories; 2 grams (7%) fat; 18% protein; 75% carbohydrates.*

# Mark Ellman's Tomato Miso Vinaigrette

*Mark Ellman is one of Hawaii's premier chefs. He owns Avalon restaurant in Lahaina, Maui, and is a partner in six Maui Tacos restaurants throughout Hawaii. Tomato miso vinaigrette was probably the favorite dressing on the Hawaii Health Program. You will enjoy its Pacific Rim flavors.*

2 tablespoons chopped onion
½ teaspoon chopped garlic
1 cup white wine
1 cup rice vinegar
1 cup tomato puree
2 sprigs fresh tarragon
½ cup red miso
1 tablespoon extra-virgin olive oil
1 teaspoon sesame oil

Saute onion and garlic in wine until wine has evaporated and pan is just glazed. Add vinegar and saute until liquid is reduced by half. Add tomato puree and tarragon. Cook until liquid is reduced by half again and add miso. Bring to a boil and remove from heat. Cool. Transfer to the bowl of a food processor or blender and blend with olive oil and sesame oil. Add water if too thick.

*Makes 4 cups, or 32 2-tablespoon servings.*
**Nutrition Information per Serving:** *31 calories; 1 gram (37%) fat; 14% protein; 49% carbohydrates.*

# Thousand Island Dressing

*No, this is not the usual high-fat version! This one is so good that many people believe that it is "illegal" on this diet, but when you see that the fat content is less than 1 gram per serving you'll want to use it more often.*

1 cup crumbled soft tofu
2 tablespoons ketchup
¼ cup water
⅛ teaspoon salt
⅛ teaspoon freshly ground black pepper
1 teaspoon seasoned salt
4 sprigs fresh parsley (optional)
1 tablespoon finely chopped cucumber
1 tablespoon finely chopped celery

In a blender, combine all ingredients except cucumber and celery; blend until smooth. Stir in cucumber and celery. Chill.

*Makes 1½ cups, or 12 2-tablespoon servings.*
**Nutrition Information per Serving:** *18 calories; 0.8 grams (40%) fat; 34% protein; 26% carbohydrates.*

# Tangy Dijon Dressing

*Even the most finicky eaters will come back for more of this delicious salad dressing.*

1 tablespoon canola oil

⅔ cup water

4½ tablespoons white wine vinegar

2–3 cloves garlic, minced

4 teaspoons Dijon mustard

¼ teaspoon dried thyme

½ teaspoon salt

¼ teaspoon freshly ground black pepper

2 teaspoons sugar or honey

Combine all ingredients in a jar; shake well. Chill.

*Makes 1 cup, or 8 2-tablespoon servings.*

**Nutrition Information per Serving:** *24 calories; 1.8 grams (67%) fat; 2% protein; 31% carbohydrates.*

# Oriental Vinaigrette

*For an Oriental flair, add this dressing to vegetables such as wong
bok, water chestnuts, bean sprouts, or jicama.*

¼ cup rice vinegar

¼ cup soy sauce

2 tablespoons water

1 tablespoon prepared mustard

2 tablespoons sugar or honey

1 teaspoon sesame oil

1 teaspoon olive oil

Combine all ingredients in a jar; shake well. Chill.

*Makes approximately 1 cup, or 8 2-tablespoon servings.*

**Nutrition Information per Serving:** *39 calories; 1.6 grams (34%) fat; 11%
protein; 55% carbohydrates.*

# Balsamic Vinaigrette

*The secret ingredient to this dressing is the balsamic vinegar. Like all vinegars, it has no fat or cholesterol, and it has a savory, tangy taste without the sour smell of some vinegars.*

⅓ cup balsamic vinegar

¼ cup cider vinegar

¼ cup water

1 tablespoon minced garlic

1 tablespoon olive oil

1 tablespoon minced fresh parsley

2 tablespoons frozen apple juice concentrate

Combine all ingredients in a small bowl. Whisk together and let sit for at least 15 minutes to allow flavors to meld.

*Makes 1 cup, or 8 2-tablespoon servings.*

**Nutrition Information per Serving:** *25 calories; 1.7 grams (56%) fat; 1% protein; 43% carbohydrates.*

# Tofu Mayonnaise

*Tofu spoils easily, so if you want to keep this dressing for more than one day, steam the tofu for three minutes before blending and refrigerate the dressing immediately. You can use this as you would regular mayonnaise.*

5 ounces soft tofu or 10 ounces extra-firm silken tofu
1 clove garlic
1 tablespoon dried parsley
1 tablespoon freshly squeezed lemon juice
¾ teaspoon ground coriander
2 tablespoons low-sodium soy sauce

Place all ingredients in a blender or food processor and blend until smooth. Add a little water if the texture is too firm.

*Makes 1 cup, or 8 2-tablespoon servings.*
**Nutrition Information per Serving:** *204 calories; 0.77 grams (34%) fat; 42% protein; 24% carbohydrates.*

# NINE

# Appetizers and Snacks

## Pot Stickers

*Pot stickers, a favorite at parties, are typically laden with pork fat and oil. This version has most of the fat and all of the cholesterol removed. And the sauce makes it lip-smacking good.*

¾ pound won bok (Chinese cabbage), blanched
8 ounces extra-firm frozen tofu, thawed
2 teaspoons cornstarch
1 teaspoon sesame oil
½ teaspoon salt
1 tablespoon sherry
1 tablespoon tamari or soy sauce
¼ cup minced scallions or green onions
¼ cup minced fresh Chinese parsley or cilantro
3 cloves garlic, finely minced or pressed
1 12-ounce package mun doo or gyoza wrappers
1 cup vegetable broth, or more if needed
Cooking spray
Dipping Sauce

Chop won bok very fine; squeeze the liquid out with your hands and drain. Press tofu with your hands to remove excess liquid and cut or break it into ½-inch pieces. In a large bowl, combine tofu and won bok with remaining ingredients except wrappers and broth; mix well. Put 1 tablespoon of cabbage mixture in the center of each wrapper. Dampen edges slightly with water, fold in half, and seal edges by forming 2 or 3 pleats on each side and pinching them to meet the opposite side, or use a gyoza press to seal. Spray a non-stick skillet with cooking spray and heat over medium-high heat. Arrange dumplings in skillet; cook until bottoms are brown. Pour in ½ cup vegetable broth and cover immediately. Cook on low heat for about 10 minutes, or until most of the liquid is absorbed. Check after 5 or 6 minutes. Add 1 or 2 tablespoons more broth or water if liquid dries out too quickly. Replace cover. After 10 minutes, uncover and continue cooking until liquid is completely absorbed. Repeat until all dumplings are cooked. Serve with Dipping Sauce.

*Makes 6 servings (12 dumplings).*

*Dipping Sauce*
>    2 tablespoons tamari or soy sauce
>    1 tablespoon rice vinegar
>    ½ teaspoon sesame oil

Combine all ingredients and blend well.

*Makes ¼ cup.*

**Nutrition Information per Serving with Sauce:** *113 calories; 3.6 grams (27%) fat; 21% protein; 52% carbohydrates.*

# Summer Rolls with Clear and Amber Dips

1 cup rice sticks

1 12-ounce package rice paper (20 sheets)

1 head romaine lettuce, shredded

1 cup fresh mint leaves

⅛ cup fresh basil (optional)

⅛ cup fresh Chinese parsley (cilantro)

1 cup fresh bean sprouts

1 cup shredded carrots

8 ounces extra-firm tofu, cut into 20 strips

Clear Dip

Amber Dip

Cook rice sticks according to package directions. Dip rice paper sheets in water and place them on paper towels to soften. Combine noodles with remaining ingredients and place a mound of this mixture in the middle of each sheet of rice paper. Roll each sheet of rice paper from the long end to form a cigar-like shape. Place rolls seam side down on a serving tray. Serve with Clear Dip and Amber Dip.

*Makes 20 servings.*

**Nutrition Information per Serving with Dip:** *131 calories; 1.2 grams (8%) fat; 8% protein; 84% carbohydrates.*

### Clear Dip

2 cloves garlic, crushed

6 tablespoons barley malt, brown rice syrup, or sugar

1 tablespoon freshly squeezed lemon juice

1 tablespoon rice vinegar

¼ cup water

Chopped fresh chili peppers to taste

Combine all ingredients; blend well.

*Makes ¾ cup, or 24 ½-tablespoon servings.*
**Nutrition Information per Serving:** *14 calories; 0 fat; 1% protein; 99% carbohydrates.*

### Amber Dip

1 cup Chinese bean sauce

¼ cup barley malt, brown rice syrup, or sugar

2 cloves garlic, minced

½ cup water

1 tablespoon cornstarch (optional)

1 teaspoon ground peanuts (optional)

In a skillet over medium heat, cook bean sauce, barley malt, and garlic together for 3–4 minutes, stirring constantly. Add water and stir. Thicken with a paste made of cornstarch and water, if desired. Add ground peanuts if desired.

*Makes 2 cups, or 32 1-tablespoon servings.*
**Nutrition Information per Serving:** *19 calories; 0.3 grams (15%) fat; 12% protein; 73% carbohydrates.*

# Thai Dipping Sauce

*This is a great dip for Summer Rolls and Pot Stickers.*

¼ cup sugar

½ cup water

½ cup red wine vinegar

1–2 tablespoons fish sauce or ½–1 teaspoon salt

1–2 teaspoons ground red pepper

½ carrot or daikon, shredded

¼ cup coarsely chopped peanuts or macadamia nuts

In a small saucepan, combine sugar and water; bring to a boil. Reduce heat and simmer for about 5 minutes, or until sugar is dissolved. Remove from heat. Stir in red wine vinegar, fish sauce, and pepper. Pour sauce into a serving bowl. Chill, then top with carrots and sprinkle with nuts before serving.

*Makes 2 cups, or 32 1-tablespoon servings.*

**Nutrition Information per Serving:** *13 calories; 0.6 grams (35%) fat; 9% protein; 56% carbohydrates.*

# Eggplant Spread

*Serve this with fat-free crackers or toasted baguette slices for a delicious appetizer or snack.*

---

4 oriental eggplants or 2 regular eggplants

1 cup chopped red onion

2 tablespoons chopped fresh parsley

1 small red bell pepper, seeded and chopped

4 cloves garlic, minced

1 large tomato, seeded and coarsely chopped

1 tablespoon chopped fresh basil

¼ cup red wine vinegar

1 teaspoon dried oregano

Salt and freshly ground black pepper to taste

Roast whole eggplants at 400°F. for 15 minutes, or until soft. Place in plastic bag while still warm and refrigerate. Chop cooled eggplant and combine with remaining ingredients. Refrigerate overnight to allow flavors to blend.

*Makes 6 servings.*

**Nutrition Information per Serving:** *126 calories; 1 gram (6%) fat; 11% protein; 83% carbohydrates.*

# Vegetables with Garden Dip

*Using dips with vegetables makes eating raw or cooked vegetables more fun.*

---

4 large carrots
4 stalks celery
1 green bell pepper
2 cups broccoli florets
2 cups cauliflower florets
Garden Dip

Peel carrots and cut into sticks. Cut celery similarly. Remove seeds from pepper and cut into strips. Place all vegetables on a serving tray and place a bowl of Garden Dip in the center.

*Makes 8 servings.*
**Nutrition Information per Serving with Dip:** *49 calories; 1 gram (19%) fat; 14% protein; 67% carbohydrates.*

*Garden Dip*
1 cup frozen green peas, thawed
¼ cup avocado
¼ cup finely chopped green onions
1 clove garlic, minced
Salt and freshly ground black pepper to taste
Pimientos for garnish

Combine all ingredients except pimientos; blend until creamy. Garnish with pimientos.

*Makes 1 cup, or 8 2-tablespoon servings.*
**Nutrition Information per Serving:** *35 calories; 1.2 grams (30%) fat; 18% protein; 52% carbohydrates.*

# Stuffed Portobello Mushrooms

1 teaspoon olive oil

2 tablespoons low-sodium soy sauce

1 tablespoon vegetable broth or water

6 large portobello mushrooms, stems removed (finely chop ½ cup stems and reserve)

2 tablespoons white wine

2 medium onions, diced

3 cloves garlic, minced

3 tablespoons chopped fresh rosemary or 2 teaspoons dried rosemary

2 tablespoons chopped fresh thyme or 2 teaspoons dried thyme

1 medium red bell pepper, diced

1 medium yellow bell pepper, diced

1 tablespoon balsamic vinegar, or more or less to taste

Salt and freshly ground black pepper to taste

Preheat oven to 350°F. In a small bowl, combine olive oil, soy sauce, and broth. Brush mushrooms with this mixture. Place mushrooms on baking sheet coated lightly with cooking spray and bake for 15 minutes. Set aside. Reduce oven temperature to 300°F. Heat large nonstick skillet coated with cooking spray over medium-high heat. Add wine, onions, garlic, rosemary, and thyme. Cook and stir until onions are soft, about 3–5 minutes. Add reserved mushroom stems and bell peppers and cook about 3 minutes. Stir in vinegar, salt, and pepper. Reduce heat to low and cook 2–3 minutes more. Remove from heat and let cool slightly. Fill mushroom caps with mixture and place on baking sheet. Just before serving, return to oven and bake until heated, about 10 minutes.

*Makes 4–6 servings.*

**Nutrition Information per Serving:** *74 calories; 1 gram (11%) fat; 28% protein; 61% carbohydrates.*

# Pan Sushi

½ cup shredded carrots
½ cup shredded lotus root
½ cup chopped mushrooms
½ cup chopped watercress
½ cup chopped cooked konbu (kelp)
¼ cup water
1 tablespoon soy sauce
1 tablespoon mirin
½ cup sugar or honey
½ cup rice vinegar
5 cups cooked and cooled brown rice

Line a 13 × 9-inch pan with wax paper and set aside. In a medium skillet, combine vegetables, water, soy sauce, and mirin. Saute vegetables for 3–5 minutes and set aside. Dissolve sugar in vinegar. In a medium bowl, toss brown rice with vinegar mixture. Spread half the rice in the lined pan, then top with half the vegetables. Top with the remaining rice and sprinkle with the remaining vegetables. Cover with wax paper. Using another pan or cutting board, press the mixture firmly into the pan. Slice into thirds vertically and thirds horizontally.

*Makes 9 servings.*

**Nutrition Information per Serving:** *172 calories; 1 gram (5%) fat; 8% protein; 87% carbohydrates.*

# Quick Mexican Pizza

4 8-inch whole-wheat-flour tortillas or 4 6-inch corn tortillas
1 16-ounce can low-fat refried beans
½ medium onion, finely chopped
½ small green or red bell pepper, chopped
1 large tomato, diced
½ cup thick, chunky prepared salsa
¼ cup finely chopped scallions
¼ cup chopped fresh cilantro

Preheat oven to 400°F. Place tortillas on baking sheet and bake until crisp, about 4 minutes. Meanwhile, combine beans, onion, and bell pepper; mix well. Spread an equal amount of the bean mixture over each tortilla. Return tortillas to oven for about 2 minutes. Remove from oven and layer remaining ingredients on warm tortillas, starting with tomatoes, then salsa, then scallions, and finishing with the cilantro. Cut each pizza into 4 wedges and serve.

*Makes 4 servings.*

**Nutrition Information per Serving:** *213 calories; 2 grams (1%) fat; 17% protein; 82% carbohydrates.*

# Simple Hummus

1 cup canned chickpeas (garbanzo beans)
2–3 tablespoons freshly squeezed lemon juice
1 tablespoon minced onion
1 clove garlic, crushed
1 teaspoon ground cumin
Low-sodium soy sauce to taste
Freshly ground black pepper to taste

Mash the chickpeas and combine with remaining ingredients.

*Makes 4 servings.*
**Nutrition Information per Serving:** *35 calories; 0.49 grams (12%) fat; 22% protein; 66% carbohydrates.*

# Potato Garlic Dip

2 large Idaho potatoes
5–6 cloves garlic, pressed
1 teaspoon extra-virgin olive oil
1 cup fresh parsley leaves
2 tablespoons red wine vinegar
2 tablespoons balsamic vinegar
2 tablespoons red onion, chopped
Salt and freshly ground black pepper to taste

Peel potatoes and cut into cubes. Boil 5–10 minutes, or until tender. Cool. Place potatoes, garlic, olive oil, parsley, vinegars, and onion in food processor. Add salt and pepper to taste. Process for 3–5 minutes and adjust seasonings. Blend until smooth. Chill overnight.

*Makes 2 servings.*
**Nutrition Information per Serving:** *330 calories; 2.9 grams (8%) fat; 8% protein; 84% carbohydrates.*

# TEN

# Traditional Hawaiian Foods

## Lomi Tomato

*This is a vegetarian version of* lomi *salmon, which is a standard modern Hawaiian lu'au food. People are surprised how good this is without the salmon, but they shouldn't be.*

5 tomatoes, diced
8 scallions, thinly sliced
1 medium onion, finely chopped
1–2 tablespoons cider vinegar
1 teaspoon sea salt
3–5 drops hot pepper sauce

Combine all ingredients; blend well. Chill thoroughly.

*Makes 8 servings.*
**Nutrition Information per Serving:** *23 calories; 0.2 grams (7%) fat; 15% protein; 78% carbohydrates.*

# Sweet Potato

*Also known as 'uala in Hawaiian, sweet potato is an excellent high-bulk food, high on the SMI index, that has the versatility of being a dessert as well as a main dish or side dish. As a delicious semisweet snack, it curbs the craving for sweets.*

### Steamed
Scrub sweet potatoes, pour 1 inch of water into a pot or steamer. Place sweet potatoes on a steamer rack and cover. Make sure water does not touch rack. Bring to a boil and steam for 25–30 minutes, or until fork-tender. This method also works well in a rice cooker. When the machine turns itself off, the sweet potatoes are done.

### Boiled
In a saucepan, bring enough water to cover sweet potatoes to a boil. Add scrubbed sweet potatoes, cover, and cook for 30–45 minutes, or until fork-tender.

### Baked
Preheat oven to 350°F. Wrap scrubbed sweet potatoes in foil for extra moistness and prick the skin through the foil with a fork. Bake for 45–60 minutes.

**Nutrition Information per 4-ounce Serving:** *118 calories; 0.1 grams (1%) fat; 7% protein; 92% carbohydrates.*

# Taro

*Although many people are familiar with poi (the mashed or pounded form of taro), most people are unfamiliar with cooked whole taro—that is, taro meant to be cooked and eaten in chunks rather than as poi. It is really important to get high-quality taro if you are going to eat it whole. My favorite is a type called moi, and a close second is lehua, which is the type used to make poi.*

*Do not eat taro or taro leaves raw. Taro must be cooked properly. Taro has a high concentration of calcium oxalate in the form of needle-like crystals found throughout the entire plant. If it is eaten raw or half cooked, it may cause itching in the throat.*

*Do not peel the taro prior to boiling or steaming. It is easier and less irritating to the skin to cook it unpeeled and peel it after it is cooked. If your skin gets itchy after contact with raw taro or taro leaves, make a paste out of baking soda and water, then spread it on the affected area. Leave it on until the itching disappears, then wash it off.*

### Steamed

Pour 1 inch of water into a pot or steamer. Place whole scrubbed taro on a steamer rack and cover. Make sure water does not touch rack. Bring to a boil and steam for 2 hours, or until fork-tender. This method also works well in a pressure cooker. Set timer for 1 hour and follow manufacturer's directions. Cool taro under cold tap water. Remove outer skin by scraping with a dull knife or spoon. Cut into slices or cubes. Serve warm or cold.

### Boiled

Place whole scrubbed taro in a large pot. Add water to cover half the taro. Cover pot and boil 2 hours, or until fork-tender. Cool under cold tap water. Remove outer skin by scraping with a dull knife or spoon. Cut into slices or cubes. Serve warm or cold.

**Nutrition Information per 4-ounce Serving:** *93.5 calories; .075 grams (0.07%) fat; 1% protein; 98% carbohydrates.*

# *Breadfruit*

*Like taro, breadfruit was another staple food in the traditional Hawaiian diet. Its nutritional profile includes starch, fiber, and B vitamins.*

### Steamed

Pour 1 inch of water into a pot or steamer. Peel the breadfruit and remove the stem and core. Cut into bite-size pieces and place on a steamer rack. Make sure water does not touch rack. Cover and bring to a boil. Steam for 2 hours, or until tender. This method also works well in a pressure cooker. Set timer for 1 hour and follow manufacturer's directions.

### Baked

Wash a ripe unpeeled breadfruit and place in a roasting pan with a small amount of water (to keep the pan from burning). Bake in a preheated 400°F. oven for 1 hour. Test to see if breadfruit is soft by poking it with a bamboo skewer. When soft, remove from oven, twist off the stem, and core. Peel and slice into bite-size pieces.

**Nutrition Information per 1-cup Serving:** *226 calories; .51 grams (2%) fat; 4% protein; 94% carbohydrates.*

# 'Ono Taro Tops

'Ono *means "delicious" in Hawaiian, and simple cooked taro tops are indeed quite delicious. Taro (lu'au) leaves are very high in calcium, iron, and vitamins. They are one of the most nutritious of Hawaiian foods.*

1 whole taro
1 1-pound package precooked thawed taro leaves
1 small onion, chopped
1-inch piece fresh ginger, minced
1 clove garlic, minced
2–3 tablespoons coconut milk
¼ tablespoon soy milk
1 teaspoon sea salt
Dash freshly ground black pepper

Cook taro and cut into bite-size pieces. In a medium saucepan, saute onion, ginger, and garlic in a small amount of water. Add coconut milk, soy milk, taro leaves, taro, salt, and pepper. Bring to a boil and remove from heat immediately. Serve warm.

*Makes 4 servings.*
**Nutrition Information per Serving:** *239 calories; 3.2 grams (11%) fat; 8% protein; 81% carbohydrates.*

# Vegetable Laulau

*This meatless variation of the typical pork laulau was used in the last week of the Hawaiian Health Program, which was a vegetarian week. You can cook other vegetables in this manner, such as carrots, white potatoes, squash, etc. The ti leaf is the traditional laulau wrapper, but is itself inedible.*

1 pound taro leaves or spinach leaves
1 pound taro
1 pound sweet potatoes
Salt to taste
8–12 ti leaves

Cut stems from taro leaves and rinse well. Separate into four portions. Scrub taro and sweet potatoes thoroughly. Peel and cut into ½-inch cubes. Divide cubes among taro leaves; add salt to taste and wrap taro leaves to cover the vegetables. Wrap in ti leaves and steam in a pressure cooker for 20–25 minutes, or until tender. (See page 143 for cautions in handling and cooking taro.)

*Makes 4 servings.*
**Nutrition Information per Serving:** *264 calories; 0.8 grams (2%) fat; 10% protein; 88% carbohydrates.*

# Chicken or Fish Laulau

*This is chicken or fish steamed in the traditional Hawaiian way. Steaming is a great way to prepare food without any added oil. You can also try adding cubes of steamed sweet potato or taro to the bundles before cooking.*

5–7 taro leaves or spinach leaves

3 ounces boned and skinless chicken or fish

2 pinches salt (optional)

2 medium ti leaves

Cut the stems from taro leaves and rinse well. Stack taro leaves on top of each other. Place chicken or fish in the center of taro leaves. Add salt, if desired, and wrap taro leaves to cover the chicken or fish. Wrap in ti leaves and place on a steamer rack. Add 1 inch of water and bring to a boil; steam for approximately 2 hours. (See page 143 for cautions in handling taro leaves.)

*Makes 1 serving.*
**Nutrition Information per Serving of Chicken:** *194 calories; 3.4 grams (15%) fat; 64% protein; 21% carbohydrates.*
**Nutrition Information per Serving of Fish:** *138 calories; 1.5 grams (9%) fat; 63% protein; 28% carbohydrates.*

# Squid or Fish Lu'au

*This is another traditional Hawaiian dish that is prepared without oil. Precooked taro leaves can often be found in the frozen-food section of the health-food store.*

4 cups precooked frozen taro (*lu'au*) leaves, thawed
3 ounces fresh or frozen squid or fish, such as salmon, butterfish, or albacore tuna, cut into bite-size pieces
Salt to taste

Heat taro leaves in medium saucepan. Add squid and simmer 30 minutes, or until tender. If you use fish, simmer 10 minutes. Stir occasionally. Add salt to taste.

*Makes 3 servings.*
**Nutrition Information per Serving:** *171 calories; 2.2 grams (10%) fat; 39% protein; 51% carbohydrates.*

# Manauwea Salad

*This seaweed salad, a cross between Hawaiian and Japanese, is a great source of calcium.*

1 pound fresh manauwea or ogo (seaweed)
1 large tomato, cut into thin wedges
½ large onion, cut into julienne strips
3 tablespoons cider vinegar
3 tablespoons sugar
1 teaspoon grated fresh ginger

Rinse and clean seaweed to remove sand and coral. Transfer to a colander and blanch with boiling water (seaweed will turn color). Rinse immediately with cold water and chop into 2-inch pieces. Transfer to a large bowl and add tomatoes and onion; toss lightly. Combine vinegar, sugar, and ginger; blend well. Pour dressing over vegetables and toss. Refrigerate at least 1 hour.

*Makes 6 servings.*

**Nutrition Information per Serving:** *11 calories; 0.1 grams (7%) fat; 16% protein; 77% carbohydrates.*

# Mountain Fern Salad

*This salad is made of the tender fern shoots (ho'i'o) that are used in the traditional diets of many cultures. Fiddlehead ferns are native to Hawaii.*

5 bunches fiddlehead ferns, cleaned and cut into 1-inch pieces
5 large tomatoes, cut into quarters
2 large Maui onions, cut into julienne strips
¼ cup cider vinegar
¼ cup sugar
1-inch piece fresh ginger, grated

Combine ferns, tomatoes, and onions; toss lightly. In a separate bowl, combine vinegar, sugar, and ginger. Pour over vegetables; toss lightly. Refrigerate at least 1 hour.

*Makes 10 servings.*

**Nutrition Information per Serving:** *56 calories; 0.6 grams (8%) fat; 27% protein; 65% carbohydrates.*

# Chickenless Long Rice

*This is a variation on the lu'au-style "long rice," or cellophane noodles, which are traditionally served with chicken. Everyone should try this at least once to see that the dish can be tasty with or without meat.*

½ cup dried shiitake mushrooms

8 ounces cellophane noodles

1 large onion, diced

3 cloves garlic, crushed

½ teaspoon sesame oil

2 quarts water

3 tablespoons instant powdered chicken-flavored vegetable broth

1-inch piece fresh ginger, peeled and crushed

½ cup chopped scallions

Soak shiitake mushrooms in warm water to cover for 10–15 minutes. Drain, slice, and set aside. Soak noodles in warm water to cover for 10–15 minutes. Saute onion and garlic in sesame oil until onions are slightly browned. Add water, broth, and ginger; simmer together at least 10 minutes. Drain noodles and cut into 3-inch lengths. Add to broth and cook until noodles are done, approximately 5 minutes. Add mushrooms and stir. Garnish with scallions and serve.

*Makes 6 servings.*

**Nutrition Information per Serving:** *173 calories; 0.5 grams (3%) fat; 7% protein; 90% carbohydrates.*

# *Haupia*

*Islanders have enjoyed this local treat for generations. By reducing the quantity of coconut milk from the amount called for in the traditional version, this recipe keeps the fat to a minimum.*

2¼ cups rice milk or soy milk
¼ cup maple syrup
¼ cup coconut milk
⅔ cup cornstarch
½ teaspoon coconut extract (optional)

Combine 1½ cups of the rice milk and the maple syrup in a saucepan. Bring to a simmer. Add coconut milk. In a small bowl, combine the remaining 1 cup rice milk and cornstarch; blend well. Add cornstarch mixture to mixture in saucepan, then add the coconut extract if desired. Cook, stirring constantly, until mixture thickens. Pour into an 8-inch square pan. Cool to room temperature, then cover with plastic wrap. Refrigerate until firm, about 30 minutes, and cut into squares.

*Makes 12 servings.*
**Nutrition Information per Serving:** *76 calories; 1.4 grams (16%) fat; 2% protein; 82% carbohydrates.*

# ELEVEN

# Soups

## Breakfast Miso Soup

*Miso soup for breakfast may sound a little odd, but believe me, on a cold day this is a delicious treat. Miso soup with rice, which contains no cholesterol, is commonly eaten for breakfast in Japan, where the heart-disease rate is very low.*

2½ cups water
1 3-inch strip dried wakame (seaweed)
1 scallion, finely chopped
1–2 tablespoons barley miso
2½ ounces extra-firm tofu, cut into ½-inch cubes

Bring water to a boil and add wakame and half the scallion. Simmer 5 minutes, then remove from heat. In a small bowl, ladle ½ cup wakame broth and add miso. Mash and stir the miso into the broth, then return it to the pot. Pour soup into a serving bowl and add tofu. Garnish with remaining scallion and serve steaming hot.

*Makes 4–6 servings.*
**Nutrition Information per Serving:** *18 calories; 0.8 grams (35%) fat; 30% protein; 35% carbohydrates.*

# Mushroom-Broccoli Noodle Soup

1 medium bunch broccoli

2 ounces dried mushrooms

1 medium onion, cut into thin crescents

1 8-ounce can water chestnuts, drained and sliced

6 cups boiling water

2 cups vegetable broth

¼ teaspoon sea salt

2 cups soba (buckwheat noodles)

2 tablespoons sesame seeds, lightly toasted

2–3 tablespoons low-sodium soy sauce or tamari

Cut broccoli stems into ¼-inch rounds and florets into 2-inch pieces. Cover mushrooms with boiling water and allow to soak for 10 minutes. Drain and slice into thin slices. In a skillet, saute onions in a small amount of water until transparent. If they stick to the pan, add more water as necessary. Add broccoli stems and saute briefly, then add mushrooms, water chestnuts, boiling water, vegetable broth, and salt. Cover and bring to a boil, then lower heat and simmer for 10 minutes. Add soba and simmer for a few minutes until tender. Add broccoli florets and cook until they turn bright green, about 1 minute. Sprinkle with sesame seeds. Stir in soy sauce and heat, without boiling, until ready to serve.

*Makes 10 servings.*

**Nutrition Information per Serving:** *78 calories; 1.1 grams (12%) fat; 20% protein; 68% carbohydrates.*

# Potato and Corn Chowder

*This was probably the best-liked soup on the Hawaii Health Program.*

---

2 teaspoons dry sherry

1¼ cups finely chopped sweet yellow onion

2 cloves garlic, crushed

2 cups cubed red potatoes

1 14¼-ounce can vegetable broth

1 teaspoon dried basil

¼ teaspoon dried thyme

¼ teaspoon paprika

1 bay leaf

1 cup fresh or frozen corn

1 cup soy milk

Salt and freshly ground black pepper to taste

Olive oil cooking spray

Spray a large skillet with cooking spray. Add sherry and heat over medium heat. Add onion and garlic and saute for 5 minutes, stirring frequently to prevent browning. Add water as needed. Add potatoes, broth, basil, thyme, paprika, and bay leaf. Cover pan, bring to a boil, and cook over medium heat for 10–15 minutes. When potatoes are tender, add corn and milk. Simmer until the corn is tender, about 3 minutes. Discard the bay leaf. Puree a cup of soup in a blender or food processor, then return it to the pot. This will give your soup a creamy texture. Season with salt and pepper to taste.

*Makes 6–8 servings.*

**Nutrition Information per Serving:** *117 calories; 1.3 grams (10%) fat; 18% protein; 72% carbohydrates.*

# Peter Merriman's Asian Gazpacho

*Asian gazpacho is a zesty cold soup with an international flavor—
great on hot days.*

½ Maui onion, peeled
5 plum tomatoes
1 cucumber, peeled and seeded
1 tablespoon chopped garlic
1 tablespoon grated fresh ginger
1 green bell pepper, seeded
¼ teaspoon hot pepper sauce
¼ cup rice wine vinegar
1 tablespoon soy sauce
1 cup tomato juice
½ cup chicken stock
Fresh Chinese parsley for garnish

Puree the first nine ingredients in a food processor until smooth.
Add the tomato juice and chicken stock and puree 1 minute longer.
Chill until ready to serve, then garnish with Chinese parsley leaves.

*Makes 6 servings.*
**Nutrition Information per Serving:** *39 calories; 0.4 grams (8%) fat; 18% protein; 74% carbohydrates.*

# Peking Hot and Sour Soup

*This and other thickened soups are a snap to make if you have a hand blender, which you can use to partially blend the soup right in the pot. Just wait until it's almost done, then do your blending, leaving enough chunky ingredients to give the soup texture. Watch out for spattering, though, if the soup is really hot.*

¼ cup dried Chinese wood ears (mushrooms)
¼ cup dried golden needles (tiger lily buds)
1 14½-ounce can vegetable broth
½ cup water
2 tablespoons cider vinegar
1 tablespoon low-sodium soy sauce
½ teaspoon sea salt
¼ teaspoon ground white pepper
¼ cup cubed extra-firm tofu
2 teaspoons cornstarch dissolved in 2 tablespoons water
1 tablespoon thinly sliced scallions

Soak wood ears and golden needles in separate bowls of boiling water for about 15 minutes. Break off any hard pieces from the wood ears and any hard stems from the golden needles. Cut golden needles in half and snap the large wood ears into smaller pieces. Rinse and drain. In a large saucepan, combine vegetable broth, water, vinegar, soy sauce, salt, and white pepper. Bring to a boil and add wood ears and golden needles. Boil 1 minute. Add tofu. As soup boils, stir in the cornstarch until the mixture thickens. Garnish with scallions. Serve hot, with extra vinegar and pepper on the side.

*Makes 4–6 servings.*
**Nutrition Information per Serving:** *47 calories; 1.2 grams (21%) fat; 30% protein; 49% carbohydrates.*

# Confetti Congee

*Congee, also known as jook, is Chinese rice porridge. This dish could also be called rainbow congee because of the colors added to the otherwise plain rice. It is surprisingly enjoyable for breakfast.*

3 cups long-grain or short-grain white or jasmine rice
3 dried Chinese wood ears (mushrooms) or any dried mushrooms
1 teaspoon peanut oil
4–5 shallots, minced
3 carrots, peeled and chopped
12 cups chicken-flavored vegetable broth
2 tablespoons tamari
2 cups fresh peas
Shredded lettuce for garnish
Thinly sliced scallions for garnish
Chinese pickled cucumber for garnish

Wash rice until water runs clear. Drain and set aside. Cover dried mushrooms with hot water and let stand for approximately 20 minutes. Remove mushrooms from water and discard stems. Dice mushrooms in ¼-inch pieces. In a large stock pot or wok, heat peanut oil and saute shallots until transparent. Add mushrooms and carrots and simmer for about 1 minute. (At this point, the dish may be transferred to a crock pot.) Stir in rice, broth, and tamari and bring to a boil. Cook about 2 minutes over high heat, stirring occasionally. Reduce heat to low. Cover and simmer for about an hour (2 hours in a crock pot), or until the mixture reaches the consistency of porridge. Stir in peas. Serve garnished with lettuce, scallions, and pickled cucumber.

*Makes 6 servings.*

**Nutrition Information per Serving:** *421 calories; 5.7 grams (11%) fat; 13% protein; 76% carbohydrates.*

# Miso Soup with Daikon

¼ cup dried wakame (seaweed)
1 small onion, diced
½ cup diced daikon
4 cups water
1 handful daikon greens, chopped
1–2 tablespoons miso

Place wakame, onion, and daikon in a saucepan and add water. Bring to a boil, reduce heat, and simmer for 20 minutes. Add the greens about 5 minutes before serving so that they can retain their bright green color. Place miso in a small bowl and add ½ cup of the broth. Mash and smooth out the miso, stirring until the mixture is smooth. Return mixture to the soup pot and simmer for about 2 minutes.

*Makes 4 servings.*
**Nutrition Information per Serving:** *15 calories; 0.3 grams (18%) fat; 23% protein; 59% carbohydrates.*

# Corn Soup

*This corn soup is especially delicious, and a variation of it was served at one of the follow-up sessions of participants in the Hawaii Health Program. People liked it so much that they were getting seconds from the kitchen before it ran out.*

6 ears fresh corn, husked, silk removed
2 medium tomatoes, peeled and coarsely chopped
1 tablespoon water
1 medium onion, finely chopped
1 tablespoon ground cumin

3 cloves garlic, minced

1 green bell pepper, seeded and coarsely chopped

1 red bell pepper, seeded and coarsely chopped

1 teaspoon salt or salt substitute (optional)

4 cups vegetable broth

1 tablespoon cornstarch dissolved in 3 tablespoons water
(optional)

Fresh cilantro leaves, strips of roasted pimiento, and minced
jalapeno peppers for garnish

Cut the kernels from the ears of corn over a bowl to catch any corn milk. Then scrape the ears with the back of a knife to extract the remaining milk. The milk will act as a natural thickener for the soup. Set the bowl of milk aside. In a heavy casserole over low heat, cook tomatoes, water, onion, and cumin, stirring until the onion is softened but not brown. Add garlic and cook for about 2 minutes. Add bell peppers and salt, if desired. Continue stirring until the peppers are slightly limp. Stir in the vegetable broth and corn milk and bring to a simmer. Cook 5 minutes (the corn should still be crunchy). If a thicker consistency is desired, add cornstarch and water. When ready to serve, garnish with cilantro, pimiento, and a sprinkling of jalapeno peppers.

*Makes 8 servings.*

**Nutrition Information per Serving:** *106 calories; 1.1 grams (9%) fat; 17% protein; 74% carbohydrates.*

# Portuguese Bean Soup

*This version of the traditional Portuguese favorite is low in fat, has no cholesterol, and is filling and hearty despite the absence of meat. Spices give the dish its distinctive flavor.*

6 cloves garlic, crushed

1½ onions, chopped

2 stalks celery, chopped

4 carrots, diced

2 cans (1 pound, 13 ounces each) whole tomatoes, undrained and cut into chunks

1 14½-ounce can vegetable broth

4 cups water

½ head cabbage, chopped

3 Idaho potatoes, cubed

3 cups cooked kidney beans

1 cup cooked macaroni

Saute garlic and onions in a small amount of water until transparent. Add celery and carrots and continue cooking 5 minutes. Add tomatoes, vegetable broth, and water. Cook 15 minutes, then add cabbage and potatoes. Bring to a boil, then reduce heat to low and cook 30 minutes. Add beans and simmer for 30 minutes more. Add macaroni a few minutes before serving.

*Makes 8 servings.*

**Nutrition Information per Serving:** *231 calories; 1 gram (4%) fat; 20% protein; 76% carbohydrates.*

# Wheat-Berry Vegetable Soup

*Wheat berries are whole kernels of wheat that are slightly plump and cook well enough so that they can be eaten in a similar fashion to brown rice. This soup also freezes well.*

---

3 cups water
1 cup dried kidney beans, soaked overnight in water and drained
2 teaspoons olive oil
1 large onion, chopped
1 large leek, rinsed well and chopped
1 stalk celery, chopped
1 cup wheat berries, soaked overnight in water and drained
1 medium Idaho potato, peeled and diced
1 14½-ounce can tomatoes, chopped
3 sprigs fresh rosemary, about 3 inches long, tied in cheesecloth

In a medium saucepan, bring water to a boil; add beans and cover. Lower heat and simmer until beans are tender, between 40 minutes and 1 hour. Do not drain. Heat oil in a large saucepan and saute onion, leek, and celery, stirring frequently, until vegetables are soft, about 10 minutes. Stir in beans and the water they were cooked in. Add wheat berries, potato, tomatoes, and rosemary sprigs. Cover and simmer gently over low heat until wheat berries are swollen and tender, about 40 minutes. Stir occasionally to keep vegetables from sticking. Remove rosemary and discard. Serve hot or cold.

*Makes 6 servings.*
**Nutrition Information per Serving:** *224 calories; 2.5 grams (9%) fat; 16% protein; 75% carbohydrates.*

# Pho

*Vietnamese food is the rage in Honolulu's Chinatown. Pho (pro-nounced "fa") is a traditional Vietnamese noodle soup that was served on the Hawaii Health Program, sometimes for breakfast.*

½ pound rice sticks (rice-flour noodles)
1 2½-inch piece fresh ginger
1 medium onion, peeled
3 quarts chicken-flavored vegetable broth
1½ teaspoons salt
2 whole star anise
4 whole cloves
½ stick cinnamon
1 stalk sugarcane, sliced lengthwise into 4 strips
2 tablespoons fish sauce

*Garnishes*
2 scallions, thinly sliced
¼ bunch fresh Chinese parsley, chopped
½ pound fresh bean sprouts
12 sprigs fresh basil
1 lime, cut into wedges
Chili paste with garlic

Soak rice sticks in hot water for 20 minutes, then drain and set aside. Dry roast ginger and onion by placing them in a skillet over medium-high heat. Cook 20 minutes on each side without charring skins. Set aside. Pour broth into a large stock pot. Add salt, ginger, onion, star anise, cloves, cinnamon, sugarcane, and fish sauce. Simmer about 2 hours. Arrange the garnishes on a platter and set aside. Divide the drained noodles among 4 serving bowls and pour broth over noodles. Garnish as desired.

*Makes 4 servings.*

**Nutrition Information per Serving:** *244 calories; 0.5 grams (2%) fat; 6% protein; 92% carbohydrates.*

# Presto Minestrone

4 cloves garlic, minced
1 medium onion, minced
1 carrot, cut into ½-inch slices
1 stalk celery, thinly sliced
1 Idaho potato, cut into ½-inch pieces
1 cup frozen peas, thawed
2 14½-ounce cans Italian stewed tomatoes
3 cups water
½ cup whole-wheat elbow macaroni

In a large saucepan, saute garlic and onion in 2–4 tablespoons water. Add remaining ingredients except macaroni and simmer for 30 minutes. Add macaroni and boil until macaroni is tender, about 10 minutes.

*Makes 8 servings.*

**Nutrition Information per Serving:** *97 calories; 0.4 grams (4%) fat; 14% protein; 82% carbohydrates.*

# TWELVE

# Whole Grains and Breads

## Cinnamon Apple Quinoa Cereal

1 cup quinoa, thoroughly rinsed and drained
1 cup apple juice
1 cup water
1 medium cooking apple (such as Cortland or Winesap), peeled
   and thinly sliced
¼ cup raisins
½ teaspoon cinnamon
Rice milk or soy milk to taste
Honey to taste

In a 1½-quart saucepan, combine quinoa, apple juice, and water. Bring to a boil. Reduce heat to low and simmer, covered, for 5 minutes. Add apple, raisins, and cinnamon and simmer until liquid is absorbed, about 10–15 minutes. Serve with milk and sweeten with honey.

*Makes 4 servings.*
**Nutrition Information per Serving:** *236 calories; 2.7 grams (10%) fat; 10% protein; 80% carbohydrates.*

# Whole Oatmeal

*This is a simple breakfast that can be enhanced greatly by pan-roasting the oatmeal before cooking. Simply toss the oatmeal in a skillet over medium heat until slightly brown before adding it to the water. The amount of water used will determine the texture of the oatmeal. For a thicker oatmeal, use less water; for a thinner consistency, use more water to taste. Hawaii's governor apparently found this dish delicious, and his chef liked it so much that he said he once had it for lunch. For variety, add a sprinkle of cinnamon, raisins, sliced bananas, or other fresh fruit before serving.*

4 cups water
1 cup rolled oats
1 teaspoon vanilla extract
1 teaspoon salt

Bring water to a boil. Add oatmeal and whisk over medium heat until oatmeal is tender but still coarse, about 10–15 minutes. Add vanilla and salt. Drain, scoop into bowls, and serve.

*Makes 4 servings.*
**Nutrition Information per Serving:** *155 calories; 2.7 grams (15%) fat; 17% protein; 68% carbohydrates.*

# Low-Fat Granola

4 cups rolled oats

¼ cup brown sugar, firmly packed

¼ cup sunflower or pumpkin seeds

2 teaspoons cinnamon

½ cup frozen apple juice concentrate, thawed

2–3 tablespoons honey

2 tablespoons vanilla extract

½ cup dried cranberries or dried blueberries

⅓ cup raisins

1 cup dried apricots, thinly sliced

Preheat oven to 400°F. In a large bowl, combine oats, brown sugar, seeds, and cinnamon; mix lightly. In a small bowl, combine apple juice concentrate, honey, and vanilla. Drizzle over cereal and stir to coat. Spread the mixture onto a large baking sheet. Bake for 20–25 minutes, stirring every 5–7 minutes, until the granola is crisp and golden. Cool. Stir in dried fruit, then store in an airtight container.

*Makes 5 servings.*

**Nutrition Information per Serving:** *483 calories; 7.9 grams (14%) fat; 11% protein; 75% carbohydrates.*

# Hearty Muffins

2 cups whole-wheat pastry flour

2 teaspoons baking powder

1 teaspoon salt

1 teaspoon cinnamon

½ cup brown sugar, firmly packed, or ⅓ cup maple syrup

1 cup rolled oats

1 cup applesauce

1 cup fat-free soy milk

1 teaspoon vanilla extract

½ cup raisins

Cooking spray

Preheat oven to 400°F. Lightly coat a nonstick muffin tin with cooking spray. In a large bowl, combine flour, baking powder, salt, cinnamon, brown sugar, and oats; mix lightly. In a smaller bowl, combine applesauce, soy milk, and vanilla; blend well. Add liquid ingredients to dry ones, then add raisins and stir just until mixed. Spoon into muffin tin and bake for 30 minutes.

*Makes 18 servings.*

**Nutrition Information per Serving:** *166 calories; 0.8 grams (4%) fat; 11% protein; 85% carbohydrates.*

# Banana Crepes

*Banana crepes were one of the favorite breakfasts on the Hawaii Health Program. You can wrap your favorite fruits in these light crepes—not just bananas.*

½ cup plus 1 teaspoon egg substitute
1 cup water
3 tablespoons honey
1 cup whole-wheat pastry flour
⅔ cup applesauce
1 teaspoon vanilla extract
3 cups sliced bananas
⅛ teaspoon freshly squeezed lemon juice
Confectioners' sugar for garnish
Cooking spray

In a food processor or blender, combine egg substitute, water, and 1 tablespoon honey; process until smooth. Transfer to a large bowl and beat in flour, applesauce, and vanilla. Let batter stand for 5 minutes. In a medium saucepan, combine bananas, remaining honey, and lemon juice. Cook over medium heat for 3–5 minutes. (This sauce can be made ahead of time and stored, tightly covered, in the refrigerator.) Lightly spray an 8-inch crepe pan with cooking spray and heat over medium-high heat. Pour ¼ cup of the batter into the hot pan. Lift pan off heat and tilt until the batter covers the bottom of the pan evenly. Return to heat and cook 15–20 seconds, until the top is dry and the bottom a golden brown. Flip crepe over and cook the other side. Turn the crepes out onto a dinner plate and repeat the procedure until you have used up all the batter. (The crepes can be made ahead of time and stored, tightly covered, in the refrigerator.) Preheat the oven to 325°F. Place 2 tablespoons of filling in the crepes and roll them closed. Place rolled crepes on a cookie sheet, cover with aluminum foil, and heat in preheated oven for 10 minutes. Remove from oven and sprinkle with confectioners' sugar.

*Makes 6 servings.*

**Nutrition Information per Serving:** *264 calories; 1.3 grams (4%) fat; 6% protein; 90% carbohydrates.*

# Simple Whole-Wheat Bread

5 cups whole-wheat flour
2 cups warm water
1 teaspoon sea salt
1 tablespoon active dry yeast

Mix ingredients together thoroughly and let rise. If mixed well, kneading may be unnecessary. Place in floured bread pan and bake at 400°F. for 30 minutes.

*Makes 2 loaves, 24–30 servings.*

**Nutrition Information per Serving:** *76.7 calories; 0.4 gram (5%) fat; 16% protein; 80% carbohydrates.*

# *Banana Bread*

*Banana bread was another favorite on the Hawaii Health Program. This recipe has no oil, unlike most banana bread recipes.*

---

3 very ripe large bananas, mashed
¼ cup egg substitute
2 tablespoons applesauce
⅓ cup honey
¼ cup rice milk or skim milk
½ teaspoon salt
1 teaspoon baking soda
1 teaspoon baking powder
1½ cups whole-wheat pastry flour
Cooking spray

Preheat oven to 350°F. In a food processor, combine bananas, egg substitute, applesauce, honey, rice milk, and salt; process until smooth. Add baking soda, baking powder, and flour and gently blend for about 20 seconds, or until dry ingredients are just moistened. Spray a 7½ × 3-inch loaf pan with cooking spray and pour batter into pan. Bake for 45 minutes, or until a toothpick inserted in the center comes out clean.

*Makes 8 servings.*
**Nutrition Information per Serving:** *158 calories; 1 gram (5%) fat; 11% protein; 84% carbohydrates.*

# Polenta with Sauteed Mushrooms and Onion

2 cups water

½ teaspoon salt

1 cup yellow cornmeal

1 cup sliced fresh mushrooms

2 cloves garlic, sliced

1 large sweet onion, thinly sliced

Salt and freshly ground black pepper to taste

2 tablespoons balsamic vinegar

1 tablespoon finely chopped fresh parsley

Garlic-flavored cooking spray

Place water in a heavy saucepan and bring it to a full boil. Add salt and gradually sprinkle cornmeal into the water, stirring constantly with a wooden spoon. Cook over low heat, stirring frequently, for 10–15 minutes, or until mixture is thick and spoon is able to stand alone. Add small amounts of water if the cornmeal is not cooked and too much liquid has evaporated. Once it is cooked, transfer polenta to a baking dish or cookie sheet and smooth it to a uniform height—about ½ inch. Spray a skillet with garlic-flavored cooking spray. Saute mushrooms, garlic, and onion until onion begins to brown. Lower heat and season mixture with salt and pepper. Continue to saute until onions are limp. Add balsamic vinegar; stir and pour over prepared polenta. Sprinkle with chopped parsley and serve.

*Makes 4 servings.*

**Nutrition Information per Serving:** *151 calories; 3.6 grams (7%) fat; 13% protein; 80% carbohydrates.*

# Whole-Grain Waffles

1 cup whole-grain pancake mix
1 cup water
1½ teaspoons egg substitute mixed with 2 tablespoons water
1 teaspoon canola oil
Sliced strawberries for garnish
Non-dairy whipped topping for garnish

Stir together pancake mix, water, egg substitute, and oil until lumps disappear. Cook in a waffle iron according to manufacturer's directions. Garnish as desired.

*Makes 2–7 servings.*
**Nutrition Information per Serving:** *377 calories; 8 grams (18%) fat; 18% protein; 64% carbohydrates.*

# THIRTEEN

# Rice

## Rice Cooker Brown Rice

*Everyone who is in a hurry should own a rice cooker and learn how to make rice in it. You just measure out the water—usually 2 cups of water for each cup of rice—add a pinch of coarse salt, then just press the button and forget it until the bell goes off and it's done!*

---

1 cup brown rice
2 cups water
Pinch of coarse salt

Rinse rice until water runs clear and drain. Place rice, water, and salt in a rice cooker. Follow directions provided by the manufacturer.

*Makes 3 servings.*

**Nutrition Information per Serving:** *216 calories; 1.8 grams (7%) fat; 9% protein; 84% carbohydrates.*

# Pressure-Cooked Brown Rice

*This is my preferred method of cooking brown rice.*

---

1 cup brown rice
1⅓–1¾ cups water
Pinch of coarse salt

Rinse rice until water runs clear. If possible, soak rice in clean water for 2–6 hours. (Rice will take a little longer to cook if it is not pre-soaked.) Place rice and water into a pressure cooker (stainless steel, if possible). Add salt and cover. Bring to pressure on high heat, then reduce heat to low and cook for 30–40 minutes. Let pressure come down, then let stand for 5–10 minutes. Stir and serve.

*Makes 3 servings.*
**Nutrition Information per Serving:** *216 calories; 1.8 grams (7%) fat; 9% protein; 84% carbohydrates.*

# Brown Basmati Rice

*This is an excellent brown rice for people who are accustomed to white rice. I like basmati because it has a rich, nutty aroma and takes on a character of its own even without added spices.*

---

2 cups brown basmati rice
3½–4 cups water
2 pinches of coarse salt

Gently wash rice until water runs clear. If possible, soak rice in clean water for 2–6 hours. (Rice will take a little longer to cook if it is not presoaked.) Place rice in a 2-quart pot (stainless steel, if possible). Cover with water and add salt. Cover, bring to a boil, reduce heat, then simmer 45–60 minutes. (Do not uncover rice while cooking.) When done, remove from heat and let sit for 10 minutes before serving.

*Makes 6 servings.*

**Nutrition Information per Serving:** *216 calories; 1.8 grams (7%) fat; 9% protein; 84% carbohydrates.*

# Baked Rice with Shiitake Mushrooms

*This is another dish that always runs out at parties because of its popularity. It was served at the governor's mansion during a celebration of the Hawaii Health Program. I like to prepare it with wild rice as a special Thanksgiving treat.*

---

2 cups brown rice
4–5 dried shiitake mushrooms
2 pinches of coarse salt
2 tablespoons tamari

Preheat oven to 350°F. Rinse brown rice until the water runs clear, then drain. Soak mushrooms in ½ cup very hot water until soft. Drain, reserving soaking water, and slice into thin slices. In a 13 × 9-inch baking dish, combine the rice, mushrooms, salt, and tamari. Mix together so that the mushrooms are evenly distributed. Add mushroom soaking water and enough clean water to make 3½ cups of liquid. Cover the baking dish and bake for 50–60 minutes. Remove from the oven and allow to stand, covered, for 10–15 minutes before serving.

*Makes 4 servings.*

**Nutrition Information per Serving:** *357 calories; 2.6 grams (7%) fat; 8% protein; 85% carbohydrates.*

# Thai Jasmine Rice

2 cups brown basmati rice

3 tablespoons brewed jasmine tea

1 tablespoon fish sauce

1 stalk fresh lemon grass, ground in a blender

¼ cup chopped sweet yellow onion

2 tablespoons finely grated lime peel

2 tablespoons freshly squeezed lime juice

2 tablespoons chopped fresh parsley stems

3 sprigs fresh mint, finely chopped

¼ cup golden raisins

Lime wedges, fresh mint sprigs, and fresh Chinese parsley for
garnish

Cook basmati rice until soft and fluffy. In a large skillet, combine jasmine tea, fish sauce, lemon grass, onion, lime peel, lime juice, and parsley stems; mix well. Stir in rice and heat through. Remove from heat and fold in chopped mint and golden raisins. Place in a serving dish and garnish with lime wedges, mint, and Chinese parsley.

*Makes 4 servings.*

**Nutrition Information per Serving:** *384 calories; 2.8 grams (7%) fat; 8% protein; 85% carbohydrates.*

# Gandule Rice

*This is a dish that everyone should try at least once. It is a Puerto Rican specialty that is very low in fat and has a zesty flavor. It was probably the best-liked recipe in our cooking classes. Gandule beans, also known as pigeon peas, are a tropical legume.*

1 green bell pepper, chopped

1 large onion, diced

2–3 stalks celery, diced

2 bunches fresh cilantro, chopped

3–4 cloves garlic

1–2 teaspoons extra-virgin olive oil

1 teaspoon ground cumin

1 teaspoon dried oregano

1 18-ounce envelope goya powder

Salt to taste

2 cups dried gandule beans or 1 15-ounce can gandule beans, drained

3 cups chicken-flavored vegetable broth

1 8-ounce can tomato sauce

4 cups white rice, rinsed and drained

Fresh cilantro for garnish

In a large saucepan, saute bell pepper, onion, celery, cilantro, and garlic in olive oil. Add cumin, oregano, goya powder, and salt. Add gandules and saute for another 5 minutes. Add broth and tomato sauce and bring to a boil. Stir in rice and return to a boil. Cook for about 2 minutes over high heat, stirring occasionally. Reduce heat to low. (At this point, the dish may be transferred to a crock pot.) Cover and simmer for about an hour (2 hours in a crock pot), stirring every 30 minutes. The mixture should be the consistency of porridge. Garnish with cilantro.

*Makes 6 servings.*

**Nutrition Information per Serving:** *478 calories; 4.1 grams (8%) fat; 13% protein; 79% carbohydrates.*

# Rice-Stuffed Acorn Squash

3 acorn squash, halved, seeds left in
1 small yellow onion, minced
½ cup chopped celery
¼ teaspoon dried basil
½ teaspoon dried oregano
½ teaspoon ground sage
¼ teaspoon dried thyme
1 cup brown rice, cooked in vegetable broth
½ cup currants
⅛ cup sunflower seeds
1 tablespoon tamari
Cooking spray

Preheat oven to 375°F. Spray a shallow baking pan with cooking spray. Place squash cut side down in pan and bake for 45 minutes. Meanwhile, saute onion and celery in a small amount of water for 2–4 minutes. Add basil, oregano, sage, and thyme. Cook for 2 minutes. Add rice, currants, sunflower seeds, and tamari and mix thoroughly. Remove squash from oven and scoop out seeds. Discard seeds and fill squash evenly with the rice mixture. Increase oven temperature to 400°F. and bake, uncovered, for 20 minutes. Serve immediately.

*Makes 6 servings.*
**Nutrition Information per Serving:** *156 calories; 2.1 grams (11%) fat; 9% protein; 80% carbohydrates.*

# Rice-Stuffed Cabbage Rolls

1 medium head cabbage

1 cup plus 6 tablespoons chopped onion

4 cloves garlic, minced

¼ cup finely chopped fresh parsley

1 teaspoon dried thyme

1 teaspoon salt

Dash cayenne pepper

1 teaspoon extra-virgin olive oil

2 12-ounce packages ground vegetable patties

1 cup cooked brown rice

2 15-ounce cans tomato sauce

¼ cup cider vinegar

3 tablespoons brown sugar, firmly packed

2 teaspoons capers

Cooking spray

Rinse cabbage and place in a large pot of cold water. Bring it slowly to a boil, uncovered, and boil for 5 minutes. Drain and plunge cabbage quickly into cold water. Drain again and separate the leaves, drying them on paper towels. In a large saucepan, saute 1 cup onion, garlic, parsley, thyme, salt, and cayenne pepper in olive oil. Add vegetable patties and rice. Stir, breaking up patties, until well mixed. Divide this mixture into 8 portions. Put 1 portion in the center of each of 8 well-dried cabbage leaves. Fold the sides of the leaves over the center, envelope fashion, and secure with toothpicks. Spray a baking dish with cooking spray. Place rolls close together in baking dish. Preheat oven to 375°F. Combine tomato sauce, vinegar, brown sugar, capers, and 6 tablespoons onion in a small saucepan. Simmer for 5 minutes. Pour sauce over cabbage rolls. Cover baking dish with aluminum foil and bake for 50 minutes.

*Makes 8 servings.*

**Nutrition Information per Serving:** *223 calories; 4.3 grams (16%) fat; 30% protein; 54% carbohydrates.*

# Rice Loaf

½ cup dried garbanzo beans, soaked in water to cover for 1 hour
½ cup water at room temperature
1 cup hot water
1 cup seasoned bread crumbs
1 cup cooked brown rice
1 8-ounce can water chestnuts, chopped
½ cup chopped celery
1 medium onion, chopped
1 teaspoon dried marjoram
1 teaspoon dried thyme
1 teaspoon salt, or more or less to taste
Savory Gravy (page 244)
Cooking spray

Preheat oven to 350°F. Combine garbanzo beans and room-temperature water in a blender or food processor and blend until smooth. In a large bowl, combine remaining ingredients except gravy and let stand for 5 minutes. Stir in garbanzo beans mixture. Press into a 5½ × 9½-inch loaf pan sprayed with cooking spray. Bake for 45 minutes. Transfer to a serving dish and serve with Savory Gravy.

*Makes 4 servings.*
**Nutrition Information per Serving:** *212 calories; 2 grams (8%) fat; 17% protein; 75% carbohydrates.*

# Stovetop Rice Pilaf

⅛ cup finely chopped mild yellow onion

½ cup vegetable broth

⅛ cup finely chopped scallions

1 small carrot, cut into julienne strips

1 cup cooked brown rice

½ cup cooked wheat berries

⅛ cup chopped celery

⅛ teaspoon freshly ground black pepper

In a large nonstick skillet, saute the onion in 2 tablespoons of the vegetable broth until tender. Add remaining vegetable broth, heat, then add scallions and carrots. Saute, stirring constantly, until carrots are heated through and slightly tender, about 5 minutes. Add rice and wheat berries and mix well. Add celery and pepper. Cook 1–2 more minutes to blend the flavors. Fluff and serve.

*Makes 5 servings.*

**Nutrition Information per Serving:** *76 calories; 0.5 grams (5%) fat; 12% protein; 83% carbohydrates.*

# FOURTEEN

# Beans

## Maui Tacos' Black Beans

1 pound dried black beans
¼ medium onion, chopped
1 teaspoon salt
1 tablespoon garlic powder

Wash beans thoroughly in three changes of clean water. In a large pot, combine beans, onion, salt, garlic powder, and enough water to cover beans while cooking. Bring to a boil, then reduce heat to low. Cook for 4 hours, or until beans are tender. Remove from heat and cool.

*Makes 5 servings.*
**Nutrition Information per Serving:** *125 calories; 0.5 grams (4%) fat; 25% protein; 71% carbohydrates.*

# Peter Merriman's Black Bean Sauce

*Use this sauce to add spice to broiled fish or chicken. Or jazz up a*
*veggie stir-fry by adding this sauce in the last minute of cooking.*

½ cup Chinese fermented black beans
½ cup sugar
⅜ cup soy sauce
¼ cup mirin
2 tablespoons minced garlic
1½ tablespoons grated fresh ginger

Rinse black beans thoroughly. Place beans in a medium saucepan and add water to a level of ½ inch above the beans. Combine sugar, soy sauce, mirin, garlic, and ginger. Add this mixture to the beans and water. Bring to a boil, then reduce heat. Simmer for 5 minutes. Remove from heat and divide mixture in half. Place one half in a blender or food processor and puree until smooth. Combine puree with the remaining half of the bean mixture in the pan and blend well.

*Makes 2 cups, or 16 2-tablespoon servings.*
**Nutrition Information per Serving:** *42 calories; 0.1 grams (1%) fat; 12% protein; 87% carbohydrates.*

# Red Chili Lentil Stew

*Chef Roy Yamaguchi of Roy's restaurants contributed this spicy, versatile recipe. It can be served as a hot, hearty soup, as a side dish, or as a condiment for broiled fish. To prepare it as a side dish or condiment, cut the quantities in half and omit the vinaigrette. Cook as directed, then strain the lentils and reserve the liquid. Spread the lentils on a baking sheet, then refrigerate. Serve cold, or you may warm the lentils in a saucepan along with a little of the reserved liquid. I have modified the recipe slightly in order to reduce the fat content.*

1 cup red or brown lentils
3 teaspoons olive oil
1 onion, finely diced
1½ tablespoons minced garlic
2 tablespoons finely diced carrots
2 tablespoons finely diced celery
3 bay leaves
1 teaspoon dried red pepper flakes, crushed
1 pound fresh tomatoes, peeled, seeded, and diced
2 cups chicken-flavored vegetable broth
1½ cups tomato juice
2 teaspoons fresh basil cut into julienne strips
1 teaspoon minced fresh thyme
1 teaspoon minced fresh tarragon
1 tablespoon salt
½ teaspoon sugar
½ teaspoon freshly ground black pepper
½ tablespoon sherry vinegar

In a colander, wash lentils under running water. Then soak in a bowl of water for half an hour, drain, and set aside. Heat 2 teaspoons of the olive oil in a large stock pot and saute onion, garlic, carrots, and celery over high heat about 1–2 minutes, or until lightly browned. Stir in all remaining ingredients except the lentils, sherry vinegar, and remaining olive oil. Continue to stir for about a minute, and then add the lentils. Cook over medium heat for about 30 minutes, or until the lentils are just tender. Do not let the lentils get mushy. Just before serving, whisk together sherry vinegar and 1 teaspoon olive oil and stir it into the lentil stew.

*Makes 6 servings.*

**Nutrition Information per Entree Serving:** *127 calories; 3.4 grams (22%) fat; 20% protein; 58% carbohydrates.*

# Hearty White Bean Stew

- 1 teaspoon extra-virgin olive oil
- 1 medium onion, diced
- 3 cloves garlic, crushed
- 3 cups cooked dried cannellini beans or 3 cups canned cannellini beans, drained and rinsed
- 1 14-ounce can whole peeled tomatoes, drained and chopped
- ½ teaspoon dried rosemary
- 1 teaspoon salt, or more or less to taste
- ½ teaspoon freshly ground black pepper
- 6 cups vegetable broth
- ¼ cup pearl barley
- ¼ cup finely chopped fresh flat-leaf parsley

In a large pot, heat olive oil. Add onion and garlic and cook over medium-high heat until onions soften, about 5 minutes. Stir in beans, tomatoes, rosemary, salt, and pepper. Add broth and bring to a boil over high heat. Add barley and simmer until barley is cooked and stew is slightly thickened, about 1 minute. Stir in chopped parsley and serve.

*Makes 6 servings.*

**Nutrition Information per Serving:** *228 calories; 3 grams (13%) fat; 18% protein; 69% carbohydrates.*

# Maui Tacos' Black Bean Burrito

*One of my assistants asserts that caffeine and newsprint make a complete protein. This is not so. However, rice and beans, the daily fare of Latin Americans, do make a healthy combination. Add some potatoes and enjoy this hearty burrito recipe contributed by chef Mark Ellman of Avalon and Maui Tacos restaurants. The Pineapple-Tomatillo Salsa and the guacamole can also be enjoyed on their own with your favorite low-fat tortilla chips. (Avocados are high in fat, so enjoy the guacamole in moderation.) Store-bought avocados usually need two or three days to ripen before they are ready to be eaten, so this is a dish you will want to plan in advance. If you want this recipe made for you, go to one of the Maui Tacos locations in Napili, Lahaina, Kihei, Kahului, Hilo, or Honolulu.*

5 small boiling potatoes

1 teaspoon salt

½ onion, chopped

1 tablespoon garlic powder

1 16-ounce can black beans

12 ounces cooked brown rice or Spanish rice

5 12-inch whole-wheat-flour tortillas

8 ounces shredded lettuce

1 cup Maui Tacos' Pineapple-Tomatillo Salsa

½ cup Maui Tacos' Guacamole

Wash and peel potatoes. Place in a saucepan and add water to cover. Add salt. Boil potatoes for 35–40 minutes, or until tender. Drain and cut into ½-inch cubes and set aside. Saute onion and garlic powder in a small amount of water until translucent. Add black beans, potatoes, and rice. Gently mix together until combined. Lay out tortillas on a flat surface. Layer an equal amount of fillings on each tortilla in the following order: bean mixture, lettuce, salsa, and guacamole. Fold the edges of the tortillas over the fillings in the center, envelope fashion.

*Makes 5 servings.*

**Nutrition Information per Serving with Sauces:** *440 calories; 4.9 grams (10%) fat; 13% protein; 77% carbohydrates.*

## Maui Tacos' Pineapple-Tomatillo Salsa

24 ounces canned crushed pineapple or 1 whole fresh pineapple, peeled and chopped

1 12-ounce can tomatillos

2 fresh jalapeno peppers

1 tablespoon chopped fresh cilantro

¼ onion, sliced

3 cloves garlic

3 cups water

1 tablespoon salt

In a blender, combine all ingredients and blend to desired consistency.

*Makes 8 cups, or 32 ¼-cup servings.*

**Nutrition Information per Serving:** *14 calories; 0.1 grams (7%) fat; 6% protein; 87% carbohydrates.*

## Maui Tacos' Guacamole

½ pound avocado flesh (about 2 ripe avocados, pitted and peeled)

2 tablespoons finely chopped fresh cilantro

3 tablespoons finely chopped onion

2 teaspoons freshly squeezed lime juice

1 teaspoon jalapeno juice from canned jalapeno peppers

1 teaspoon salt, or more or less to taste

1 fresh tomato, finely diced

Mash avocado flesh to a chunky consistency. Add cilantro, onion, lime juice, and jalapeno juice. Season to taste with salt. Add tomato and stir gently.

*Makes 2 cups, or 8 ¼-cup servings.*

**Nutrition Information per Serving:** *55 calories; 4.9 grams (74%) fat; 5% protein; 21% carbohydrates.*

# Dick Allgire's Lazy Enchiladas

*Television newsman Dick Allgire, of Honolulu's channel 4 (KITV), who contributed this recipe, says: "I call these Lazy Enchiladas because the sauce and filling are cooked in the same pot and there is no baking time. With tomatoes on the inside, it has a nice creamy texture that I missed when I gave up cheese. The spices are approximate because I don't measure; I just taste until it's right."*

1 medium onion, chopped

½ medium red or green bell pepper, chopped

2 cloves garlic, minced

½ teaspoon cinnamon

½ teaspoon dried oregano, or more or less to taste

2 tablespoons chili powder, or more or less to taste

1–2 teaspoons ground cumin, or more or less to taste

Pinch of cayenne pepper

9–10 medium fresh mushrooms, thinly sliced

1 15-ounce can stewed tomatoes, with juice

½ cup frozen corn, thawed

1 15-ounce can black beans, rinsed

4 medium whole-wheat-flour tortillas

Saute onion, pepper, and garlic in a small amount of water until onion is translucent. Add spices and let them coat the onion mixture. Add mushrooms and cook briefly for 1–2 minutes. Add stewed tomatoes and bring to a boil, then reduce heat and simmer for 10 minutes. Add corn and simmer for 10 more minutes. Add beans and simmer for 5 minutes. Mixture should be soupy. Warm tortillas in the oven so they are pliable and, with a slotted spoon, scoop ¼ of the bean-and-vegetable mixture into each tortilla, roll the tortillas closed, and place them on a serving plate. Pour remaining liquid in the skillet over the tortillas.

*Makes 4 servings.*
**Nutrition Information per Serving:** *316 calories; 3.5 grams (10%) fat; 18% protein; 72% carbohydrates.*

# Tuscan Beans

1 tablespoon extra-virgin olive oil
6 cloves garlic, minced
6 fresh sage leaves
2 16-ounce cans cannellini beans
3 cups canned crushed tomatoes, with juice
1 teaspoon chopped fresh Chinese parsley
Salt and freshly ground black pepper to taste

In a large saucepan, combine oil, garlic, and sage. Cover and cook over medium-high heat for 1 minute. Add beans, tomatoes, Chinese parsley, salt, and pepper, stirring constantly. Reduce heat to medium-low and cover. Simmer for 10 minutes, stirring occasionally.

*Makes 10 servings.*
**Nutrition Information per Serving:** *121 calories; 1.9 grams (14%) fat; 21% protein; 65% carbohydrates.*

# Spicy Beanburgers

¼ cup chopped onion

¼ cup chopped red or green bell pepper

1 15-ounce can kidney beans, drained

1 cup cooked brown rice

3 cloves garlic, minced

2 teaspoons egg substitute

1 teaspoon Cajun seasoning

1 teaspoon chili powder

1 teaspoon hot pepper sauce

¼ teaspoon dried oregano

¼ teaspoon dried thyme

2 tablespoons flour

¼ cup chopped scallions

4 whole-grain hamburger rolls

4 lettuce leaves for garnish

4 fresh tomato slices for garnish

*Sauce*

¼ cup nonfat mayonnaise

½ teaspoon capers

1 tablespoon minced dill pickle

1 teaspoon spicy prepared mustard

In a small skillet, saute onion and pepper in a small amount of water until limp. In a food processor, combine sauteed onion and pepper, kidney beans, ½ cup brown rice, garlic, egg substitute, and seasonings. Process until thoroughly mixed but beans are still chunky. Pour into a bowl and add remaining ½ cup brown rice, flour, and scallions. Mix together and shape into 4 patties. Spray a nonstick pan with cooking spray and fry patties until browned.

Place patties on rolls and garnish with lettuce leaves and tomato slices. Combine sauce ingredients in a small bowl and serve alongside the patties.

*Makes 4 servings.*

**Nutrition Information per Serving:** *360 calories; 4 grams (9%) fat; 16% protein; 75% carbohydrates.*

# Barbecue Baked Beans

1 cup diced onion

3 cans (14–16 ounces each) beans (choose one or more from the following varieties: kidney, black, navy, pinto, great Northern, or lima)

2 tablespoons blackstrap molasses

2 tablespoons cider vinegar

1 tablespoon powdered mustard

½ teaspoon garlic powder

½ cup ketchup

Cooking spray

Preheat oven to 350°F. Spray a skillet with cooking spray and saute onions until translucent. Discard half the liquid from each can of beans. Combine half-drained beans and their juice with remaining ingredients in a large bowl and add sauteed onion. Mix thoroughly. Transfer to a 2-quart casserole and bake, uncovered, for 1½ hours, stirring after 1 hour.

*Makes 4 servings.*

**Nutrition Information per Serving:** *279 calories; 1.6 grams (5%) fat; 18% protein; 77% carbohydrates.*

# Chunky Two-Bean Chili

*This recipe is best when made the day before serving.*

---

1 cup TVP (textured vegetable protein)

⅓ cup vegetable broth

3 cloves garlic, chopped

½ medium onion, chopped

1 stalk celery, chopped

1 green bell pepper, chopped

1 sprig fresh Chinese parsley, chopped

1–2 tablespoons chili powder

½ teaspoon dried red pepper flakes

1 teaspoon ground cumin

Freshly ground black pepper to taste

2 cups canned black beans, drained and rinsed

2 cups canned kidney beans, drained and rinsed

2 bay leaves

1 cup canned tomato sauce

½ cup tomato paste

½ cup water

1 teaspoon freshly squeezed lime juice

Soak TVP in heated vegetable broth for 10 minutes. Saute garlic, onion, celery, green pepper, and Chinese parsley in a small amount of water until onions are translucent. Add the soaked TVP and all remaining ingredients; simmer for 20 minutes. Remove bay leaves before serving.

*Makes 8 servings.*

**Nutrition Information per Serving:** *186 calories; 0.9 grams (4%) fat; 39% protein; 57% carbohydrates.*

# FIFTEEN

# Chicken and Seafood

## Chicken Broccoli

2 cups water

1-inch piece fresh ginger, peeled and crushed

3 cloves garlic, crushed

2 medium onions, sliced and quartered

1 pound boneless and skinless chicken breast, cut into small
strips

3 tablespoons soy sauce

½ teaspoon freshly ground black pepper

1 pound fresh broccoli, chopped

1 small carrot, cut into julienne strips

In a saucepan, combine ½ cup of the water, ginger, garlic, and onions. Cook 3–5 minutes over high heat until tender. Stir in chicken and cook for 5 minutes, or until meat turns white. Add the remaining 1½ cups water, soy sauce, and pepper. Cover pan and let simmer for 10 minutes. Add broccoli and carrots. Stir, cover, and simmer for another 5 minutes.

*Makes 6 servings.*

**Nutrition Information per Serving:** *132 calories; 2.4 grams (16%) fat; 61% protein; 23% carbohydrates.*

# Chicken Breast in Phyllo
# with Tomato-Herb Sauce

*This was a dish served on the Mediterranean portion of the HawaiiDiet™ study. It is much lower in fat than most dishes of this type because we cut down on the oils and dairy products. Even so, go easy on the feta cheese, as it is the main source of fat in this recipe.*

1 pound skinless and boneless chicken breast
½ cup minced onion
1 clove garlic, minced
2 tablespoons minced fresh oregano
1 pound fresh mushrooms, minced
¼ cup minced fresh parsley
1 tablespoon whole-wheat pastry flour
½ cup dry white wine
Salt and freshly ground black pepper to taste
2 cups whole-wheat bread crumbs
¼ pound reduced-fat feta cheese, crumbled
1 1-pound box frozen phyllo dough, thawed
Tomato-Herb Sauce
Garlic-flavored cooking spray

Spray a large skillet with garlic-flavored cooking spray. Add chicken and saute until golden brown. Slice chicken in ½-inch diagonal slices. Divide chicken into 8 portions and set aside on a platter. Saute onion, garlic, and oregano in a small amount of water for 5–7 minutes. Add mushrooms and parsley and cook until all liquid evaporates. Add flour and stir until it is completely incorporated and mixture is smooth. Add wine and stir over moderate heat until mixture is thickened. Season with salt and pepper to taste. Cool. Divide this mixture into 8 portions in the skillet. Place bread crumbs on a plate and divide them into 8 portions. Divide feta into 8 portions. Preheat oven to 350°F. Remove 1 sheet of phyllo from the wrapper (cover remaining sheets with plastic wrap and a damp towel until you are ready to work with them). Lay the phyllo sheet on a flat surface and spray with garlic-flavored cooking spray. Sprinkle evenly with 1 portion of bread crumbs. Place a second sheet of phyllo over the bread crumbs. Spray with cooking spray. Place a portion of chicken about ½ inch from the shorter end of the phyllo layers. Spoon a portion of the mushroom mixture over the chicken. Sprinkle a portion of the feta cheese over the mushroom mixture. Fold the sides of the phyllo over the chicken as if it were an envelope. Repeat with the remaining sheets of phyllo and fillings. Spray filled rolls lightly with cooking spray and place them seam side down on an ungreased baking sheet. Bake for 50 minutes, or until golden brown. Transfer to a serving platter, drizzle Tomato-Herb Sauce around rolls, and serve.

*Makes 8 servings.*

*Tomato-Herb Sauce*
    ½ cup chopped Maui onion
    3 cloves garlic, minced
    1 teaspoon extra-virgin olive oil
    ½ cup sliced fresh mushrooms
    1 fresh tomato, peeled, seeded, and chopped
    1 teaspoon dried oregano
    ½ cup dry white wine

Saute onion and garlic in olive oil for 3 minutes. Add mushrooms, tomato, oregano, and wine and cook no more than 10 minutes.

*Makes 1 cup, or 8 2-tablespoon servings.*
**Nutrition Information per Serving with Sauce:** *360 calories; 8.8 grams (24%) fat; 36% protein; 40% carbohydrates.*

# Hula Grill's Ginger Pineapple Chicken

*This is a creation of the Hula Grill's chef, Peter Merriman. The sauce can be used in any stir-fry or entree, with or without chicken.*

½ medium onion, sliced on the diagonal
1½ teaspoons chopped garlic
1½ teaspoons minced fresh ginger
4 ounces boneless and skinless chicken breast
1 medium carrot, sliced on the diagonal
1 stalk celery, sliced on the diagonal
½ cup broccoli florets
½ cup sliced water chestnuts
Stir-Fry Sauce
2 ounces fresh pineapple, diced

In a wok or skillet, saute onion, garlic, and ginger in a small amount of water until vegetables are light brown. Add chicken and cook until golden brown, adding water if necessary. Add carrot, celery, and broccoli and cook until vegetables are tender yet still crisp. Add water chestnuts and Stir-Fry Sauce and cook until the mixture thickens. Add pineapple and serve immediately.

*Makes 4 servings.*

*Stir-Fry Sauce*
2 tablespoons hoi sin sauce
2 tablespoons sweet soy sauce
2 tablespoons soy sauce
2 tablespoons pineapple juice or pureed pinapple
1 tablespoon cornstarch

In a small bowl, combine the first 4 ingredients, then add cornstarch and mix thoroughly.

*Makes ½ cup, or 8 1-tablespoon servings.*
**Nutrition Information per Serving with Sauce:** *112 calories; 2.4 grams (19%) fat; 38% protein; 43% carbohydrates.*

# Cajun Chicken Jambalaya

1 large onion, chopped
1 medium green bell pepper, seeded and chopped
½ cup chopped celery
1 tablespoon chopped scallions
8 ounces boneless and skinless chicken breast, cut in ¾-inch
    strips
1 14½-ounce can tomato sauce
1 teaspoon dried basil, crushed
½ teaspoon dried thyme
½ teaspoon Poultry Magic®
½ teaspoon garlic powder
¼ teaspoon salt
1 bay leaf
¼–½ teaspoon hot red pepper sauce
1 cup cooked brown rice
Garlic-flavored cooking spray

Saute onion in a large nonstick skillet coated with garlic-flavored cooking spray, then add bell pepper, celery, and scallions. Cook for several minutes, or until vegetables are tender. Add chicken and cook for 5 minutes. Stir in tomato sauce and all spices. Add rice; bring to a boil, then reduce heat, cover, and simmer about 10 minutes. Remove bay leaf before serving.

*Makes 8 servings.*
**Nutrition Information per Serving:** *83 calories; 2 grams (8%) fat; 39% protein; 53% carbohydrates.*

# Peter Merriman's Baked Fish

*This is another tasty recipe contributed by one of Hawaii's great regional chefs. The sauce used in this dish is versatile and can be used on vegetables or other entrees as well.*

15 ounces wahoo ono fillets

2 tablespoons freshly squeezed lime juice

½ teaspoon minced garlic

2 teaspoons minced shallots

½ tablespoon chopped fresh rosemary

½ tablespoon chopped fresh thyme

½ cup sliced fresh shiitake mushrooms

1-inch piece fresh ginger, cut into julienne strips

Dash of white pepper

⅛ cup chopped fresh Chinese parsley

1 small carrot, cut into julienne strips

⅓ cup water

3 tablespoons chopped scallions

Preheat oven to 350°F. Place wahoo fillets in a baking dish. Combine lime juice, garlic, shallots, herbs, mushrooms, ginger, white pepper, Chinese parsley, and carrot; pour over fillets. Add water and cover with foil. Bake for 15–20 minutes, or until fillets are tender. Garnish with scallions and serve.

*Makes 4 servings.*

**Nutrition Information per Serving:** *101 calories; 1.5 grams (17%) fat; 53% protein; 30% carbohydrates.*

# Roy's Blackened Hawaiian Swordfish in Miso

*Chef Roy Yamaguchi shares some of his secrets here. This recipe is fancy enough for any dinner guest, yet low enough in fat for everyday meals. The marinade "cooks" the fish to a certain degree, so keep the grilling time to a bare minimum to ensure that the fish will not dry out.*

## Marinade

⅓ cup white miso
1½ tablespoons sake
2 teaspoons brown sugar, firmly packed
⅔ cup hoi sin sauce
1½ tablespoons minced fresh ginger
1½ tablespoons minced garlic
1½ tablespoons freshly squeezed orange juice
1 tablespoon chili paste with garlic

## Fish

4 swordfish steaks, about 6 ounces each
1 cup red pickled ginger
1 pound unpeeled cucumber, seeded and chopped

## Garnishes

2 ounces radish sprouts
1 teaspoon black sesame seeds
1 teaspoon white sesame seeds, toasted
Guacamole (optional)

In a large bowl, combine all the ingredients for the marinade and mix well. Add swordfish steaks and let sit in the refrigerator for 4 hours. Preheat the grill or broiler. Puree the pickled ginger in a food processor until smooth. Drain in a sieve. Puree the cucumbers in a food processor and drain in a sieve. Set ginger and cucumbers aside. Grill or broil swordfish pieces for 45–60 seconds on each side (for medium rare). On each serving plate, lay out a circle of pureed cucumber and a small circle of pickled ginger within it. Place the swordfish steak on the pureed ginger. Garnish with sprouts and sesame seeds and serve with a little guacamole, if desired.

*Makes 8 servings.*
**Nutrition Information per Serving:** *217 calories; 6 grams (25%) fat; 45% protein; 30% carbohydrates.*

# Roy's Blackened Ahi with Soy-Mustard Sauce

*Hawaii is proud of chef Roy Yamaguchi. This is one of his signature dishes, a Pacific version of a Cajun classic. I have modified it slightly to reduce the fat content. Roy notes that the sandalwood in the blackening spice is optional but that it gives the dish a reddish color and an intriguing flavor. If you prefer, you can substitute ¼ cup of any Cajun spice blend for the blackening spice recipe given here.*

*Soy-Mustard Sauce*
    ¼ cup powdered mustard
    2 tablespoons hot water
    2 tablespoons rice vinegar
    ¼ cup soy sauce

*Blackening Spice*
    1½ tablespoons paprika
    ½ tablespoon cayenne pepper
    ½ tablespoon chili powder
    ¼ teaspoon white pepper
    ½ tablespoon ground sandalwood (optional)

*Fish*

> 1 yellowfin tuna (ahi) fillet, about 2 inches thick and 5 inches long
> (approximately 8 ounces)

*Garnishes*

> 2–3 tablespoons red pickled ginger
>
> ½ teaspoon black sesame seeds
>
> 1 ounce sunflower sprouts (top 2 inches only)
>
> 1 tablespoon diced yellow bell pepper
>
> 1-inch slice cucumber, cut into julienne strips

Make the sauce by combining the mustard and hot water and blending them into a paste. Let the mixture sit for a few minutes to develop its flavor. Add rice vinegar and soy sauce, then strain through a fine sieve and chill in the refrigerator. Meanwhile, make the blackening spice by mixing paprika, cayenne, chili powder, white pepper, and sandalwood on a plate. Dredge the tuna in this mixture on both sides. Heat a lightly oiled cast-iron skillet and sear tuna on high heat for 15 seconds per side for rare or 60 seconds per side for medium rare. Cut tuna into 16 thin strips. On each serving plate, lay out 4 strips of fish in a pinwheel or cross shape. Put a little Soy-Mustard Sauce in the spaces between the fish. To garnish, put a small mount of red pickled ginger on two of the Soy-Mustard Sauce pools and sprinkle the sesame seeds over the other two pools. Arrange the sprouts, bell pepper, and cucumber at the center of the pinwheel.

*Makes 4 servings.*

**Nutrition Information per Serving:** *139 calories; 4.3 grams (26%) fat; 49% protein; 25% carbohydrates.*

# Shrimp with Snow Peas and Mushrooms

*This was a dish used in the HawaiiDiet™ study to demonstrate how a traditional Asian-style meal uses a small amount of meat and a large amount of vegetables.*

---

2 tablespoons soy sauce

1 tablespoon rice vinegar

¼ teaspoon five-spice powder (cloves, fennel, cinnamon, star anise, and szechuan pepper)

6 ounces shrimp, peeled and deveined

¾ cup vegetable broth

¼ cup dry white wine

1 tablespoon minced garlic

1 tablespoon minced fresh ginger

6 ounces snow peas (about 2 cups), stems and strings removed

6 ounces fresh mushrooms, sliced

1 tablespoon cornstarch dissolved in 2 tablespoons cold water

Cooking spray

In a large bowl, combine 1 tablespoon soy sauce, rice vinegar, and five-spice powder. Add shrimp and marinate 20–30 minutes. Combine vegetable broth, white wine, and remaining soy sauce in a bowl. Heat a nonstick wok or skillet over high heat for 2 minutes. Spray with cooking spray and add garlic and ginger; stir-fry 15 seconds. Add snow peas and mushrooms. Cook for 2 minutes more. Add shrimp and marinade and stir until mixture boils. Add cornstarch and stir 1 minute until thick.

*Makes 3 servings.*

**Nutrition Information per Serving:** *181 calories; 1.7 grams (10%) fat; 46% protein; 44% carbohydrates.*

# Salmon Fillet with Fresh Tomato Salsa

1 12–14-ounce salmon fillet
Salt and freshly ground black pepper to taste
1 teaspoon olive oil
Fresh Tomato Salsa

Sprinkle the salmon with salt and pepper to taste. Heat a large non-stick skillet and coat it with the olive oil. Saute the salmon fillet, skin side up, until lightly browned, about 3 minutes. Turn fillet, cover, and cook over medium heat until it is opaque throughout, about 5 minutes. Cut fillet diagonally into 4 slices. Serve with Fresh Tomato Salsa.

*Makes 4 servings.*

*Fresh Tomato Salsa*
    2 medium fresh tomatoes, diced
    ½ medium sweet onion, finely chopped
    6–8 scallions, thinly sliced (about ⅓ cup)
    2 tablespoons chopped fresh cilantro
    1½ tablespoons freshly squeezed lime or lemon juice
    2 tablespoons low-sodium soy sauce or tamari
    4–5 drops hot pepper sauce
    ⅛ teaspoon freshly ground black pepper

Combine all ingredients and chill thoroughly.

*Makes 2 cups, or 16 2-tablespoon servings.*
**Nutrition Information per Serving:** *155 calories; 5 grams (28%) fat; 57% protein; 15% carbohydrates.*

# SIXTEEN

# Tofu

## Sweet-and-Sour Tofu
## with Snow Peas and Mushrooms

1 medium onion, sliced

2 cloves garlic, minced

2 dried shiitake mushrooms, soaked in water for 5 minutes and
    thinly sliced

1 cup snow peas

1 8½-ounce can bamboo shoots

2 slices canned pineapple in heavy syrup, cut into eighths
    (reserve syrup for sauce)

12 ounces tofu, cut into ½-inch cubes

Sweet-and-Sour Sauce

In a large skillet, saute onion and garlic in a small amount of water
for 3–5 minutes. Add mushrooms, snow peas, bamboo shoots,
pineapple, and tofu. Stir-fry over medium-high heat for approximately 2 minutes. Pour Sweet-and-Sour Sauce over vegetables and
toss lightly.

*Makes 6 servings.*

*Sweet-and-Sour Sauce*
- 1 tablespoon ketchup
- 2 tablespoons tamari
- ½ cup reserved syrup from canned pineapple
- 3 tablespoons cider vinegar
- ¼ cup brown sugar, firmly packed
- 1 tablespoon cornstarch dissolved in ¼ cup water

In a small saucepan, combine all ingredients and blend well. Simmer, stirring occasionally, for 2–3 minutes.

*Makes 1⅛ cups, or 6 2-tablespoon servings.*
**Nutrition Information per Serving:** *207 calories; 2.6 grams (11%) fat; 13% protein; 76% carbohydrates.*

# Tofu Stir-Fry

- 3 chicken-flavored vegetable bouillon cubes
- 1½ cups water
- ¾ cup dry sherry
- 3 tablespoons cornstarch
- ¼ cup Stir-Fry Sauce (page 196)
- 5 tablespoons soy sauce
- 6 cloves garlic, minced
- 1 tablespoon minced fresh ginger
- 3 cups sliced carrots
- 9 cups broccoli, cut into bite-size pieces
- 16 ounces extra-firm tofu, cut into 1-inch cubes
- 3 tablespoons sesame seeds, toasted
- Fresh Chinese parsley sprigs for garnish

Dissolve bouillon cubes in water. Add sherry, cornstarch, Stir-Fry Sauce, and soy sauce; set aside. Saute garlic and ginger in a small amount of water for 2 minutes. Add carrots and cook for 4 minutes, then add broccoli and cook until tender. Push vegetables to the side and add sauce mixture; stir until it thickens, then combine with vegetables. Add tofu and cook for 3 minutes, stirring constantly. Place on a serving platter and garnish with sesame seeds and fresh Chinese parsley.

*Makes 8 servings.*
**Nutrition Information per Serving:** *189 calories; 4.8 grams (24%) fat; 27% protein; 49% carbohydrates.*

# Scrambled Tofu

*Scrambled tofu is a delicious substitute for scrambled eggs. The best reason to replace eggs for breakfast is the amount of cholesterol found in two eggs (more than the amount of cholesterol in an eight-ounce steak). Tofu, of course, like any plant product, has no cholesterol.*

¼ cup minced onion
1 teaspoon poultry seasoning
½ teaspoon turmeric
¼ teaspoon sea salt
¼ teaspoon onion powder
¼ teaspoon garlic powder
16 ounces extra-firm tofu, drained
Cooking spray

Lightly spray a large nonstick skillet with cooking spray. Saute onion, adding a slight amount of water if it starts to stick. As the onion cooks, add seasonings and mix well. Break tofu into small chunks and add it to the mixture. Cook until the mixture is thoroughly heated and resembles scrambled eggs.

*Makes 5 servings.*
**Nutrition Information per Serving:** *95 calories; 4.2 grams (38%) fat; 38% protein; 24% carbohydrates.*

# Chinese Stir-Fry Supreme

*Serve this dish with buckwheat noodles, whole-wheat noodles, or brown rice.*

---

- 1 medium onion, cut into eighths
- 3 stalks celery
- 4 dried shiitake mushrooms
- 1 teaspoon sesame oil
- ½ pound extra-firm tofu, cut into 1-inch cubes
- 3 tablespoons low-sodium soy sauce or tamari
- 2 cups finely shredded won bok (Chinese cabbage)
- 3 cups fresh bean sprouts
- 3 tablespoons arrowroot, dissolved in ¼ cup cool water

Slice onion into wedges. Cut celery diagonally into ½-inch pieces. Soak mushrooms in warm water for 15 minutes, then slice. Heat oil over low heat in a nonstick skillet. Add tofu and brown on all sides, until it slides around in the pan. Add mushrooms and 1 tablespoon of the soy sauce and saute a minute or two longer. Set aside. In a separate large skillet or wok, saute onion, celery, won bok, and sprouts. Add enough water to cover. When it boils, add arrowroot. Let cook 3–4 minutes. Add remaining soy sauce, mix in tofu and mushrooms, and pour immediately into a serving dish.

*Makes 6 servings.*
**Nutrition Information per Serving:** *94 calories; 2.8 grams (24%) fat; 25% protein; 51% carbohydrates.*

# SEVENTEEN

# Pasta and Noodles

## Avalon's Pasta Gerry

*Chef Mark Ellman shares a recipe from his Avalon restaurant in Lahaina, Maui. This pasta has an interesting combination of flavors and is easy to prepare.*

1 teaspoon chopped fresh ginger

1 teaspoon chopped garlic

1 teaspoon chopped onion

1 teaspoon extra-virgin olive oil

½ teaspoon sesame oil

½ teaspoon chopped fermented black beans

⅛ cup sliced fresh shiitake mushrooms

1 teaspoon chopped fresh mint

1 teaspoon chopped fresh basil

1 teaspoon chopped fresh cilantro

1 cup chopped fresh or high-quality canned tomatoes

½ cup white wine or vegetable broth

32 ounces cooked pasta

In a saucepan, saute all ingredients except tomatoes, wine, and pasta for 5 minutes. Add tomatoes and wine and cook for 5 more minutes. Serve over hot pasta.

*Makes 8 servings.*

**Nutrition Information per Serving:** *200 calories; 3 grams (16%) fat; 14% protein; 70% carbohydrates.*

# Tomato, White Bean, and Spinach Pasta

¼ cup coarsely minced garlic

¼ cup finely shredded fresh basil leaves or 2 teaspoons dried basil

1 teaspoon freshly ground black pepper or ¼ teaspoon dried red pepper flakes, crushed

1 teaspoon olive oil

2 large fresh plum tomatoes or 1 large fresh beefsteak tomato, chopped

1 15-ounce can crushed tomatoes (no salt added)

1 cup cooked dried white beans or 1 cup canned white beans (great Northern or cannellini), rinsed and drained

1 16-ounce package penne or mostaccioli

1 cup finely shredded fresh spinach leaves, thoroughly rinsed

In a large nonstick saucepan over medium heat, saute garlic, basil, and black pepper in the olive oil. Cook about 2 minutes, stirring constantly, to make sure garlic doesn't burn. Add fresh and canned tomatoes. Cover and bring to a boil; reduce heat and simmer for 8–10 minutes. Add beans and cook, stirring constantly, for 2 minutes. Add 1–2 tablespoons water if sauce is too thick. Cook the pasta according to package directions and drain. Immediately toss pasta with sauce and spinach.

*Makes 8 servings.*

**Nutrition Information per Serving:** *97 calories; 1.3 grams (11%) fat; 18% protein; 71% carbohydrates.*

# Mushroom Marinara Sauce for Pasta

*Instead of chopping the herbs with a knife, try to twist the leaves or stems into ⅛-inch or slightly smaller pieces. This is the best way to release their full flavor.*

2 ounces dried mushrooms (any type)

1 cup hot water

2 cloves garlic, pressed

1 large onion, thinly sliced

2 tablespoons chopped fresh basil

1 tablespoon chopped fresh rosemary

5 tablespoons chopped fresh parsley

2 teaspoons chopped fresh oregano

3 cups canned plum tomatoes, with juice

¼ cup red wine

Salt and freshly ground black pepper to taste

Soak dried mushrooms in hot water for 15–20 minutes. Drain mushrooms, reserving the soaking liquid. Rinse and chop the mushrooms. Heat a large nonstick skillet and saute garlic and onion in a small amount of water, then quickly add basil, rosemary, parsley, and oregano. When the herbs begin to wilt, add tomatoes and juice, mushrooms, soaking water, and wine. Bring to a boil, then reduce heat. Add salt and pepper to taste and let simmer for about 10 minutes.

*Makes 6 servings.*

**Nutrition Information per Serving:** *69 calories; 0.6 grams (7%) fat; 16% protein; 77% carbohydrates.*

# Baked Rigatoni

1 pound rigatoni
1 zucchini, cut into ½-inch dice
1 oriental eggplant, cut into ½-inch dice
1 red bell pepper, cut into ½-inch dice
Salt and freshly ground black pepper to taste
1 medium red onion, cut into ½-inch dice
4 cloves garlic, minced
2 tablespoons flour
¼ cup port
1 28-ounce can tomatoes, coarsely chopped
2 egg whites or 4 teaspoons egg substitute mixed with 4 tablespoons water

Preheat oven to 350°F. Cook pasta according to package directions. Heat a nonstick skillet and spray with garlic-flavored cooking spray. Saute zucchini, eggplant, and bell pepper until they are tender yet still crisp. Add salt and pepper to taste. Remove vegetables from pan and set aside. Spray the pan again and saute onion and garlic until they "sweat." Add flour and saute until lightly brown. Add port and tomatoes and simmer for 10 minutes. Mix egg whites with rigatoni. Combine with vegetables and sauce and pour into casserole that has been sprayed with cooking spray. Top with rice parmesan cheese and bake for about 30 minutes.

*Makes 6 servings.*
**Nutrition Information per Serving:** *157 calories; 2.3 grams; (13%) fat; 21% protein; 66% carbohydrates.*

# Basic Buckwheat Noodles

*Buckwheat noodles are a favorite of mine because they are commonly available, even in restaurants. In Japanese restaurants, they are served hot or cold. Buckwheat noodles make an excellent base around which to plan a meal.*

8 ounces soba (buckwheat noodles)
Pinch of sea salt (optional)
Nori (seaweed) flakes for garnish
Thinly sliced scallions for garnish
Soba Dipping Sauce

In a stock pot, boil enough water to fully cover the noodles, then add the noodles. As the noodles boil, they will foam. Before the pot overflows, pour a small amount of cool water into it and the foaming will stop for a short while before it builds up again. You'll have to do this about three times before the noodles are cooked. If the noodles already contain salt, do not salt the cooking water. If they do not contain salt, add a pinch of sea salt to the cooking water. After the noodles are cooked, drain and rinse in cool water and drain again. Garnish with nori flakes and scallions. Serve cold with Soba Dipping Sauce in individual bowls on the side.

*Makes 4 servings.*

**Nutrition Information per Serving without Sauce:** *190 calories; 0.4 grams (2%) fat; 16% protein; 82% carbohydrates.*

*Soba Dipping Sauce*
>    2 cups water
>    1 piece konbu (kelp), about 3 × 2 inches
>    ¼ cup low-sodium soy sauce
>    1 teaspoon grated fresh ginger
>    1 teaspoon wasabi (optional)
>    1–2 teaspoons freshly squeezed lemon juice (optional)
>    1 clove garlic, crushed (optional)

Boil konbu in water for 5 minutes, remove it, and reserve for another use (it can be sliced and eaten with other vegetables). Add the remaining ingredients to the water in which it was boiled and serve.

*Makes ½ cup, or 8 1-tablespoon servings.*

**Nutrition Information per Serving:** *10 calories; 0 fat; 21% protein; 79% carbohydrates.*

# Garlic Noodles

>    1 6-ounce package whole-wheat noodles
>    ¼ teaspoon salt (optional)
>    2–3 medium cloves garlic, diced
>    ½ teaspoon sesame oil

Cook noodles according to package directions. If noodles do not already contain salt, add salt to the cooking water. When noodles are ready, drain and rinse with cool water, then drain again. Saute garlic in the sesame oil. Add the cooked noodles, heat through, and serve.

*Makes 4 servings.*

**Nutrition Information per Serving:** *269 calories; 1.4 grams (5%) fat; 15% protein; 80% carbohydrates.*

# Korean Noodles

*This dish, which Koreans call chop chae, uses seasonings that give it a golden, amber-brown appearance.*

---

3½ ounces cellophane noodles

3 tablespoons soy sauce

1 tablespoon ko choo jung (Korean sauce made of cooked mochi [rice], miso, and chili peppers)

2 teaspoons honey

1 teaspoon sea salt

¼ teaspoon freshly ground black pepper

1 small onion, sliced

1 medium carrot, cut into julienne strips

1 tablespoon minced garlic

½ teaspoon grated fresh ginger

½ bunch watercress, cut into 2-inch lengths

6 ounces fresh bean sprouts

½ cup vegetable broth

Cooking spray

Soak noodles in water for 15 minutes. Drain and cut into 2-inch lengths. Drop into 1 quart boiling water, turn heat off, and let stand for 5 minutes, then drain. Combine soy sauce, ko choo jung, honey, salt, and pepper and blend well. Spray a nonstick skillet with cooking spray and saute onion, carrot, garlic, and ginger until onions are just limp. Add watercress and cook until crisp yet tender. Add the soy sauce mixture, then the bean sprouts and vegetable broth. Stir in the noodles and serve immediately.

*Makes 6 servings.*

**Nutrition Information per Serving:** *145 calories; 0.5 grams (3%) fat; 12% protein; 85% carbohydrates.*

# EIGHTEEN

# Potatoes

## All-American Fries

4 medium Idaho potatoes
1 small sweet yellow onion
Water or vegetable broth
Salt and spices, such as freshly ground black pepper, garlic powder, curry powder, or paprika, to taste

Preheat the oven to 350°F. Pierce potatoes with a fork and bake for
20 minutes, or until they are almost done but still firm. Heat a
medium nonstick skillet over very high heat. While the skillet is
heating, slice the potatoes and onion into thin slices. Put enough
water or broth into the skillet to lightly cover the bottom, add the
onions, and cook until they turn golden brown and aromatic. Add
the potatoes and small amounts of water or broth as needed to prevent the vegetables from sticking. Add salt and seasonings, if
desired. Cook until the potatoes are well browned, but watch the
skillet carefully: The vegetables will burn very easily.

*Makes 4 servings.*

**Nutrition Information per Serving:** *230 calories; 0.3 grams (1%) fat; 8% protein; 91% carbohydrates.*

# Garlic 'n Onion Potatoes

2 pounds (about 6 medium) Idaho potatoes, scrubbed and thinly
  sliced

10 cloves garlic, minced

2 large onions, halved and thinly sliced

1 tablespoon finely chopped fresh rosemary or 1 teaspoon dried
  rosemary

2 tablespoons flour

⅛ teaspoon freshly ground black pepper, or more or less to taste

2–3 cups vegetable broth, or more or less as needed

Preheat oven to 400°F. Place sliced potatoes in a bowl of cold water until ready to use. In a nonstick skillet coated with cooking spray, saute garlic until golden brown, about 3–4 minutes. Remove garlic from pan and set aside. In the same pan, saute onions until softened and lightly brown, then set aside. Drain potato slices well and dry on paper towels. Place one-third of potatoes in a 2-quart casserole coated with cooking spray. Cover with half the onions. Sprinkle with half the garlic and half the rosemary, then add 1 tablespoon flour and half the pepper. Repeat, ending with a layer of potatoes on top. Pour enough broth over potatoes to barely cover them, pressing potatoes down so broth comes to top layer. Bake, uncovered, for 1–1½ hours, or until tender. Turn top layer of potatoes over after 40 minutes to keep them from drying out. Check after 1 hour, and if there is still liquid that has not been absorbed, raise the temperature to 425°F. and continue baking until broth is absorbed.

*Makes 6 servings.*
**Nutrition Information per Serving:** *175 calories; 0.8 grams (4%) fat; 11% protein; 85% carbohydrates.*

# Stuffed Baked Potatoes

4 large Idaho potatoes, scrubbed

¾ cup chopped red onion

4 cloves garlic, minced

½ cup vegetable broth

½ cup frozen corn, thawed

1 cup chopped fresh broccoli

¾ ounce nondairy mozzarella cheese

4–6 tablespoons finely chopped fresh chives

Pierce potatoes with a fork. Microwave on high power for 15–20 minutes, turning once halfway through cooking time. Leave cooked potatoes in microwave. Meanwhile, in a nonstick skillet, saute onion and garlic in vegetable broth. Add corn, cook for 1–2 minutes, add broccoli and cook 5 minutes longer, then set aside. Preheat broiler. Remove potatoes from microwave and allow them to cool. Split tops open lengthwise. Transfer split potatoes to a baking dish. Scoop out potato flesh from cooked potatoes and mix with the vegetables. Spoon potato-vegetable mixture into potatoes. Top with mozzarella and chopped chives and broil until cheese melts, about 2 minutes.

*Makes 4 servings.*

**Nutrition Information per Serving:** *351 calories; 3.8 grams (9%) fat; 17% protein; 74% carbohydrates.*

# Topped Baked Potatoes

*One of the simplest, most inexpensive substitutes for taro is the familiar Idaho potato. It has a slightly higher SMI value than poi and is easy to prepare. When I mention that I do not recommend topping potatoes with butter or sour cream because of their fat content, I usually hear groans and complaints. My answer to those complaints is that I'm taking away two condiments but I'm giving back ten.*

---

1 Idaho potato

**Toppings**
    Steak sauce
    Barbecue sauce
    Marinara sauce
    Salsa
    Old Bay® seasoning
    Creamed corn
    Chili
    Horseradish
    Ratatouille (page 235)
    Low-fat gravy

Preheat the oven to 375°F. Scrub the potato and puncture it with a fork several times. Place potato on a cooking sheet and bake for approximately 1 hour. If you use a microwave oven, scrub and puncture the potato as above and microwave on high power for approximately 5–7 minutes. Remove potato from oven and allow to cool. Split top open lengthwise and top as desired.

*Makes 1 serving.*

# Roasted Potatoes

*This dish brings out the full flavor of potatoes yet limits the fat to less than two grams, as compared to typical fried potatoes, which contain about eight grams of fat (48% of the total calories) per serving.*

1 bulb garlic, unpeeled
1½ pounds red potatoes, unpeeled
¼ cup chopped fresh rosemary
Salt and freshly ground black pepper to taste

Preheat the oven to 375°F. Roast the garlic by spraying the whole bulb with cooking spray and placing it in the oven for 20 minutes. Cut potatoes in half and place them cut side up in a baking pan. Cut off ends of garlic cloves and squeeze pulp over potatoes. Spray with cooking spray and sprinkle with rosemary. Cover pan with foil and bake for 20 minutes. Remove cover and roast for 10–15 minutes. Season with salt and pepper.

*Makes 3 servings.*
**Nutrition Information per Serving:** *273 calories; 1 gram (4%) fat; 9% protein; 87% carbohydrates.*

# Teriyaki Potatoes

*For a change of pace in potatoes, try this East-West variation that combines the great tastes of two worlds.*

---

½ cup soy sauce

3 tablespoons brown sugar, firmly packed

3 cloves garlic, mashed

1-inch piece fresh ginger, mashed

2 scallions, chopped

1 teaspoon sesame oil

Freshly ground black pepper to taste

2 pounds red potatoes, peeled and quartered

Preheat oven to 375°F. In a bowl, combine soy sauce, brown sugar, garlic, ginger, scallions, sesame oil, and pepper; mix well. Add the potatoes and marinate overnight. Line a baking pan with aluminum foil and place the marinated potatoes in the middle of the pan. Bake for 15–20 minutes, basting occasionally with the marinade. Remove pan from the oven and preheat the broiler. When hot, transfer pan to the broiler and broil for 10 minutes, or until potatoes are crispy.

*Makes 8 servings.*

**Nutrition Information per Serving:** *136 calories; 0.7 grams (5%) fat; 10% protein; 85% carbohydrates.*

# NINETEEN

# Vegetables

## Mixed Grilled Vegetables

½ small eggplant, cut into bite-size chunks
½ medium zucchini, cut into bite-size chunks
2 ounces medium-size fresh mushrooms
Salt and freshly ground black pepper to taste
2 romaine lettuce leaves
2 tablespoons Mark Ellman's Tomato Miso Vinaigrette (page 124)
Fresh basil leaves for garnish
Garlic-flavored cooking spray

Preheat grill. Spray eggplant, zucchini, and mushrooms with garlic-flavored cooking spray. Season with salt and pepper. Thread vegetables onto skewers or place in grilling baskets, and grill until golden brown, about 5 minutes. Place romaine leaves on serving plates. Top with grilled vegetables and drizzle with Tomato Miso Vinaigrette. Garnish with basil.

*Makes 2 servings.*

**Nutrition Information per Serving:** *20 calories; 0.2 grams (9%) fat; 23% protein; 68% carbohydrates.*

# Vegetable and Whole-Wheat Couscous Paella

1 small red onion, chopped

2 large garlic cloves, minced or pressed

1 9-ounce package frozen baby lima beans, thawed (about
   1½ cups)

½ teaspoon turmeric

⅛ teaspoon ground red pepper

1 14½-ounce can Italian tomatoes, with liquid

1 cup low-sodium vegetable broth

1 small yellow summer squash or zucchini, cut into ½-inch dice

1 cup instant whole-wheat couscous

1 cup frozen peas, thawed

½ teaspoon dried oregano, crushed

¼ cup chopped scallions

¼ cup chopped fresh Chinese parsley

Spray a large nonstick pan with cooking spray and heat over medium-high heat. Add onion and garlic; cook until onion is soft and lightly browned. Add lima beans, turmeric, and pepper. Stir in tomatoes and broth. Cover and bring to a boil; lower heat and simmer 5 minutes. Stir in squash, cover, and cook 5 minutes more. Stir in couscous and peas; boil again, lower heat, and cook 2 minutes. Remove from heat and add oregano, scallions, and Chinese parsley. Cover and let stand for 10 minutes before serving.

*Makes 4 servings.*

**Nutrition Information per Serving:** *325 calories; 6 grams (16%) fat; 17% protein; 67% carbohydrates.*

# Nishime

*This is a traditional Japanese stew-like dish that is low in fat and was one of the favorites on both the HawaiiDiet™ study and our program. The Japanese taro (arimo) used in this dish is 1½–2 inches in length, much smaller than Hawaiian or Samoan taro.*

2 strips (½ inch × 36 inches each) dried konbu (kelp)
4 dried shiitake mushrooms
5 whole arimo (Japanese taro)
2 konyaku, sliced
3 pieces aburage
1 whole turnip
1 cup canned bamboo shoots
1 whole burdock
1 teaspoon peanut oil
1½ cups vegetable broth
1 cup sliced carrots
¼ cup tamari
⅓ cup sugar

Soak konbu and mushrooms in water until soft, about 10 minutes. Wash and scrub taro thoroughly, then peel and cut into 1½-inch pieces. Cut konyaku, aburage, turnip, and bamboo shoots into 2-inch pieces. Cut burdock into ¼-inch diagonal slices and soak in water until ready to use. Tie konbu into knots, leaving 1 inch between knots. Cut between knots. Drain and slice mushrooms. In a large saucepan, heat peanut oil, vegetable broth, mushrooms, konbu, konyaku, and bamboo shoots. Cover and cook for 10 minutes. Add tamari and sugar; cook for 5 minutes. Add turnip, carrots, and burdock and cook for 15 minutes. Add taro and cook until taro is fork-tender, about 30 minutes. Toss in aburage and serve.

*Makes 4 servings.*

**Nutrition Information per Serving:** *241 calories; 3.9 grams (14%) fat; 10% protein; 76% carbohydrates.*

# Hawaiian Curry

3 tablespoons water

1 large onion, chopped

2 cloves garlic, minced

1-inch piece fresh ginger, mashed

1–2 teaspoons soy sauce

1 teaspoon honey

1–3 tablespoons curry powder

2 large carrots, peeled and cut into 1-inch chunks

2 stalks celery, cut into 1-inch chunks

3 red potatoes, quartered

3 cups cauliflower florets

½ cup lima beans

2 cups vegetable broth

Salt to taste

1 tablespoon cornstarch or arrowroot dissolved in 1 tablespoon
   water

Saute onion and garlic in water. Add ginger, soy sauce, honey, curry powder, carrots, celery, potatoes, cauliflower, lima beans, vegetable broth, and salt. Pour in enough water to cover. Cook for 20 minutes, or until carrots become tender. Add cornstarch and stir until mixture is thickened.

*Makes 6 servings.*

**Nutrition Information per Serving:** *118 calories; 0.6 grams (4%) fat; 15% protein; 81% carbohydrates.*

# Thai Vegetable Curry

1 teaspoon canola oil

2 shallots, minced

2 cloves garlic, minced

2–3 tablespoons curry powder

½ teaspoon turmeric

1 teaspoon chili paste

2 tablespoons soy sauce

1 stalk lemon grass, chopped in a blender

1-inch piece fresh ginger

2¾ cups rice milk

¼ cup low-fat coconut milk

1 tablespoon coconut extract

½ teaspoon salt

3 tablespoons brown sugar, firmly packed

2 carrots, peeled and cut into ½-inch slices

1 pound Idaho potatoes, peeled and cut into 1-inch cubes

½ onion, chopped

½ head cauliflower, cut into 1-inch pieces

2 cups fresh green beans, sliced diagonally

2 fresh tomatoes, cut into thin wedges

3 kaffir lime leaves, finely shredded

10 fresh basil leaves

In a large saucepan, heat canola oil and saute shallots, garlic, curry powder, turmeric, and chili paste for 1–2 minutes. Add soy sauce, lemon grass, and ginger and stir-fry for 30 seconds. Add rice milk, coconut milk, coconut extract, salt, and brown sugar. Bring to a boil. Add carrots, potatoes, onion, and cauliflower; cook until almost tender. Add green beans and tomatoes and cook for 3 minutes. Stir in lime leaves and basil leaves before serving.

*Makes 5 servings.*

**Nutrition Information per Serving:** *246 calories; 7.4 grams (26%) fat; 14% protein; 60% carbohydrates.*

# Kabobs with Marinades

*Kabobs can be a festive treat and relatively easy to prepare. I got interested in kabobs when a patient of mine said that she had to go to a potluck dinner where all the guests were making kabobs and she didn't know what to bring. I told her she could easily bring delicious vegetable kabobs. The secret, I told her, was in the marinade. The happy ending was that everyone liked her kabobs best. You can either steam the kabobs as directed, and use the marinades as a sauce, or marinate the kabobs in any one of the marinades and then cook them over a grill.*

---

8 ounces extra-firm tofu or tempeh, cut into cubes
2 carrots, cut into 1-inch pieces
3 stalks celery, cut into 1-inch pieces
10 green beans, halved, or 1 small head broccoli, cut into florets
1 small head cauliflower, cut into florets
Sea salt to taste
Marinade

Bring 2–3 inches of water to a boil in a pot or steamer. Place tofu and vegetables on a steamer rack. Make sure water does not touch rack. Cover and steam until just tender, about 10 minutes for a crunchy texture or 15 minutes for a softer texture. On each of 4 skewers, place pieces of tofu, carrot, celery, beans or broccoli, and cauliflower. Place the cauliflower on last so it will look like a flower on the end of the skewer. Top kabobs with one of the following marinades.

*Makes 4 servings.*
**Nutrition Information per Serving without Marinade:** *160 calories; 4.6 grams (24%) fat; 30% protein; 46% carbohydrates.*

### Dijon Marinade
2 tablespoons Dijon mustard
3 tablespoons low-sodium soy sauce or tamari

3 tablespoons freshly squeezed lemon juice

2 cloves garlic, crushed

Combine all ingredients and blend well.

*Makes ½ cup, or 4 2-tablespoon servings.*
**Nutrition Information per Serving:** *15 calories; 0.1 grams (3%) fat; 33% protein; 64% carbohydrates.*

### Teriyaki Marinade

⅓ cup low-sodium soy sauce or tamari

2 tablespoons blackstrap molasses or honey

1 tablespoon grated fresh ginger

1 clove garlic, crushed

2 teaspoons arrowroot or cornstarch dissolved in 2 teaspoons
  water

1 tablespoon sake or white wine (optional)

1 tablespoon freshly squeezed lemon juice (optional)

2 tablespoons water

Combine all ingredients in a saucepan and blend well. Bring to a boil and let cool.

*Makes ¾ cup, or 5 2-tablespoon servings.*
**Nutrition Information per Serving:** *47 calories; 0 fat; 20% protein; 80% carbohydrates.*

### Korean Barbecue Marinade

⅓ cup low-sodium soy sauce

2 tablespoons blackstrap molasses or honey

3 cloves garlic, crushed

2 teaspoons arrowroot or cornstarch dissolved in 2 teaspoons
  water

½ teaspoon sesame oil

1 tablespoon sake or white wine (optional)

1 tablespoon freshly squeezed lemon juice (optional)

2 tablespoons water

Combine all ingredients in a saucepan and blend well. Bring to a boil and let cool.

*Makes ¾ cup, or 5 2-tablespoon servings.*
**Nutrition Information per Serving:** *51 calories; 0.6 grams (11%) fat; 17% protein; 72% carbohydrates.*

## White Wine Marinade

½ cup white wine
2 tablespoons freshly squeezed lemon juice
2–3 bay leaves
¾ teaspoon dried thyme
Freshly ground black pepper to taste

Combine all ingredients and blend well.

*Makes ½ cup, or 4 2-tablespoon servings.*
**Nutrition Information per Serving:** *23 calories; 0 fat; 7% protein; 93% carbohydrates.*

## Barbecue Marinade

¾ cup ketchup
¼ cup freshly squeezed lemon juice
3 tablespoons blackstrap molasses or honey
¼ cup steak sauce
½ teaspoon sea salt
Freshly ground black pepper to taste

Combine all ingredients in a saucepan and bring to a boil. Cover and simmer 4–5 minutes.

*Makes 1½ cups, or 12 2-tablespoon servings.*
**Nutrition Information per Serving:** *36 calories; 0.3 grams (2%) fat; 3% protein; 95% carbohydrates.*

# Mu Shu Vegetables

*This is a delicious dish that is often offered in Szechuan Chinese restaurants with a pork or meat filling. My version dispenses with the pork and eggs. Mu shu is actually a Chinese delicacy, a crinkly dark brown fungus, that is difficult to find but not necessary for this dish.*

¼ head won bok (Chinese cabbage)
½ medium onion
4 dried shiitake mushrooms, soaked in warm water
½ carrot
1 1¾-ounce bundle cellophane noodles (optional)
Dash of sesame oil
6 pieces mu shu (optional)
Water and soy sauce to taste
6 teaspoons hoi sin sauce
12 10-inch whole-wheat-flour tortillas

Slice cabbage into thin strips and slice onion into thin wedges. Drain and chop mushrooms and grate or cut carrot into julienne strips. Soak cellophane noodles in water until soft. In a small skillet or wok, saute onion in a small amount of water and sesame oil until slightly translucent. Cut each piece of mu shu in half. In a second skillet, saute the mushrooms, carrots, and mu shu in water and soy sauce. Spread ½ teaspoon hoi sin sauce on each tortilla. Arrange an equal portion of sauteed mushroom mixture and onions down the middle of each tortilla. Arrange cellophane noodles and cabbage on top of vegetables. Roll the tortillas closed.

*Makes 12 servings.*
**Nutrition Information per Serving:** *145 calories; 2 grams (12%) fat; 8% protein; 80% carbohydrates.*

# Hawaiian Savory Stew

*This dish was so well liked on the HawaiiDiet™ program, despite the fact that it has no meat in it, that the recipe was published in the newspaper. You'll be pleasantly surprised at its authentic island flavor.*

1 large onion, chopped

2 cloves garlic, minced

3 tablespoons water

1 8-ounce box seitan (wheat gluten), cut in 1-inch pieces, or 1 cup fresh mushrooms, cut in half

1-inch piece fresh ginger, mashed

1 tablespoon soy sauce

2 large carrots, cut in 1-inch chunks

2 stalks celery, cut in 1-inch chunks

3 red potatoes, quartered

1 15-ounce can whole tomatoes

2 cups vegetable broth

Salt and freshly ground black pepper to taste

3 bay leaves

2 tablespoons whole-wheat flour dissolved in ¼ cup water

Hot pepper sauce to taste (optional)

In a large saucepan, saute onion and garlic in water. Add seitan, ginger, soy sauce, carrots, celery, potatoes, tomatoes, vegetable broth, salt, pepper, bay leaves, and water to cover. Cook until vegetables are tender. Stir in whole-wheat flour and continue to cook until mixture thickens. Add hot pepper sauce if desired.

*Makes 6–8 servings.*

**Nutrition Information per Serving:** *With seitan: 256 calories; 1.2 grams (4%) fat; 32% protein; 64% carbohydrates. With mushrooms: 132 calories; 0.5 grams (3%) fat; 17% protein; 80% carbohydrates.*

# Potato, Eggplant, and Zucchini Pie

1 large onion, thinly sliced

2 cloves garlic, chopped

1 14-ounce can stewed tomatoes

¼ cup finely chopped fresh parsley

2 tablespoons minced fresh basil or 2 teaspoons dried basil

1 teaspoon dried oregano

½ teaspoon salt

½ teaspoon freshly ground black pepper

3 red potatoes, peeled

2 small zucchini

½ pound oriental eggplant

Garlic powder to taste

Cooking spray

In a medium saucepan coated with cooking spray, saute onion and garlic in a small amount of water until onion is translucent. Add tomatoes, parsley, basil, oregano, salt, and pepper. Simmer until sauce thickens, about 30 minutes. Cook potatoes in water for 20 minutes. Drain, cool, and slice into ⅛-inch slices. Trim the ends of the zucchini and slice lengthwise into ¼-inch slices. Peel and cut eggplant into ¼-inch slices. Preheat the oven to 400°F. Spray a baking sheet with cooking spray. Arrange zucchini and eggplant slices on sheet, sprinkle with garlic powder, and bake for 10 minutes, turning once. Spray an 8-inch square baking pan with cooking spray. Arrange potatoes on bottom. Top with some of the sauce. Add a layer of eggplant and top with more sauce. Finish with zucchini and remaining sauce. Lower heat to 350°F. and bake for 30–40 minutes.

*Makes 10 servings.*

**Nutrition Information per Serving:** *60 calories; 0.4 grams (6%) fat; 10% protein; 84% carbohydrates.*

# Vegetarian Eight Treasures

*This is a great traditional Chinese dish that has been a staple of all our HawaiiDiet™ programs because of its popularity.*

2 16-ounce blocks extra-firm tofu

1 medium cucumber

1 medium carrot

1 8-ounce can water chestnuts

½ pound snow peas, stems and strings removed

1 teaspoon peanut oil

2 teaspoons chili paste

2 tablespoons hoi sin sauce

3 tablespoons soy sauce

1½ tablespoons sugar

1 tablespoon rice wine

1½ tablespoons water

¼ cup unsalted dry roasted peanuts

Soak tofu in hot water for 1 hour. Drain by wrapping tofu with paper towels and placing it in a colander over a bowl. Place two unopened soup cans, or an equivalent weight, on top of wrapped tofu for 1 hour. Cut tofu into ½-inch pieces. Dice the cucumber and carrot into ½-inch cubes. Steam for 8 minutes. Drain and dice water chestnuts. In a skillet or wok, saute cucumber, carrot, water chestnuts, snow peas, and tofu for 1–2 minutes in a small amount of water. Remove from skillet and set aside. In the same pan, heat peanut oil and chili paste for about 10 seconds. Add hoi sin sauce, soy sauce, sugar, rice wine, and water. Stir until sauce begins to thicken. Add the cooked vegetables and peanuts and toss lightly until mixed.

*Makes 6 servings.*

**Nutrition Information per Serving:** *142 calories; 5.6 grams (34%) fat; 21% protein; 45% carbohydrates.*

# Vegetarian Chop Suey

*This is a Chinese-style stir-fry that is usually high in fat. In this version, however, we keep the oil to a minimum and use a mixture of water, soy sauce, and arrowroot as the saute medium.*

1 teaspoon peanut oil

¼ cup water

½ teaspoon salt

¼ teaspoon freshly ground black pepper

½ onion, thinly sliced

1 cup thinly sliced celery

2 cups fresh chop suey mix (bean sprouts, carrots, and watercress)

1 cup thinly sliced water chestnuts

½ cup snow peas, stems and strings removed

1 teaspoon tamari

1½ teaspoons arrowroot dissolved in 6 teaspoons water

In a wok or skillet, heat peanut oil, water, salt, and pepper. Add onion, celery, chop suey mix, and water chestnuts. Cover and cook over medium heat for 10–15 minutes. During the last 5 minutes, add the snow peas. Drain sauce from vegetables into a bowl and add enough water so that you have 1¼ cups of liquid. Place liquid in a saucepan and add tamari. Cook over medium heat, stirring occasionally. When mixture is thickened, pour sauce back over vegetables, toss lightly, and serve.

*Makes 4 servings.*

**Nutrition Information per Serving:** *84 calories; 1.4 grams (14%) fat; 13% protein; 73% carbohydrates.*

# Stuffed Zucchini

6 small zucchini

1 teaspoon extra-virgin olive oil

1 cup minced red onion

6 cloves garlic, minced

2 teaspoons capers

4 cups bread crumbs

2 tablespoons freshly grated nondairy Parmesan cheese

½ teaspoon dried oregano

Salt and freshly ground black pepper to taste

Garlic-flavored cooking spray

Preheat oven to 375°F. Spray the bottom of a 13 × 9-inch glass baking dish with garlic-flavored cooking spray. Cut zucchini in half lengthwise and remove the pulp from each one, reserving pulp. Arrange the cored zucchini in a single layer in the baking dish and finely chop the pulp. Heat a skillet over medium-high heat and add olive oil. Saute zucchini pulp, onion, garlic, and capers for 3–5 minutes. Turn off the heat and stir in bread crumbs, cheese, oregano, salt, and pepper. With a teaspoon, loosely fill the cored zucchini with bread-crumb mixture; do not pack. Pour about ½ cup water into the bottom of the baking dish. Bake for 25–30 minutes, or until bread crumbs are lightly browned.

*Makes 6 servings.*

**Nutrition Information per Serving:** *302 calories; 5.5 grams (16%) fat; 15% protein; 69% carbohydrates.*

# Ratatouille

*This ratatouille is crunchy, colorful, and brightly flavored because the cooking time is held to a minimum—only a few minutes. It can be served by itself, or you can spoon it over baked potatoes, arborio rice, brown basmati rice, or millet; ladle it over fresh-cooked pasta; or heap it on slices of toasted whole-wheat French bread, which you could then top with grated fat-free Monterey Jack cheese and broil.*

2 teaspoons olive oil

1 small onion, chopped

2 large cloves garlic, minced or pressed

1 pound eggplant, cut into ½-inch cubes

1 carrot, peeled and sliced

¼ pound fresh mushrooms, sliced

2 fresh plum tomatoes, cut into ½-inch cubes

1 teaspoon each dried basil and dried oregano

Salt and freshly ground black pepper to taste

1 medium zucchini, sliced

½ medium yellow bell pepper, seeded and cut into ¼-inch cubes

1 15-ounce can tomato sauce or crushed tomatoes (no salt added)

Heat oil in a large nonstick skillet over medium heat. Add onion and garlic and saute until onion is limp. Add eggplant, carrot, mushrooms, fresh tomatoes, basil, oregano, salt, and pepper. Reduce heat, cover, and cook, stirring occasionally, until vegetables are tender, about 8 minutes. Add zucchini and bell pepper, cover, and cook about 3 minutes. Stir in tomato sauce, bring to a simmer, and cook, uncovered, about 5 minutes longer, or until mixture thickens.

*Makes 4 servings.*

**Nutrition Information per Serving:** *113 calories; 3 grams (21%) fat; 13% protein; 66% carbohydrates.*

# Wakame Vinaigrette

*You can prepare this recipe with just about any raw vegetable for a tasty no-fat salad or side dish. Wakame lends itself well to the dish and is also high in calcium.*

1 carrot
½ teaspoon salt
1 ounce dried wakame (seaweed)
¼ cup rice vinegar
3 tablespoons honey
½ teaspoon grated fresh ginger
Juice of ½ lemon or lime

Cut carrot into julienne strips and sprinkle with salt. Let stand for about 30 minutes. Rinse and squeeze water from carrot. Soak wakame in cold water just until hydrated. Squeeze out excess water. Combine wakame, carrot, vinegar, honey, ginger, and citrus juice and transfer to a serving bowl.

*Makes 4 servings.*
**Nutrition Information per Serving:** *64 calories; 0.1 grams (1%) fat; 3% protein; 96% carbohydrates.*

# Ginger Mustard Cabbage with Konbu

*Mustard cabbage and konbu are both excellent sources of calcium. This versatile side dish complements most entrees.*

2 pounds mustard cabbage

1 tablespoon sea salt

1 ½-inch × 36-inch strip dried konbu (kelp)

⅓ cup barley malt

¼ cup low-sodium soy sauce

¼ cup rice vinegar

1 tablespoon toasted sesame seeds

1 tablespoon minced fresh ginger

Chop cabbage, add salt, and let stand for 30 minutes. Soak konbu in water just until hydrated. Squeeze out excess water, then cut into ½-inch lengths. In a saucepan, combine barley malt and soy sauce. Heat until barley malt dissolves, then remove from heat. Add rice vinegar and konbu while still hot. Cool the sauce a little, then mix in the cabbage, sesame seeds, and ginger. Transfer to a bowl, cover, and let sit overnight in the refrigerator so flavors can blend.

*Makes 4 servings.*

**Nutrition Information per Serving:** *85 calories; 1.6 grams (10%) fat; 15% protein; 75% carbohydrates.*

# Steamed Garlic Broccoli

*This is a simple, high-calcium dish that can be served as a side dish with just about any entree. In addition to being high in calcium, broccoli is a cruciferous vegetable, which means it is loaded with anti-cancer elements, such as beta carotene, indole amines, and fiber.*

1 bunch broccoli
½ cup water
1 clove garlic, minced
Toasted sesame seeds to taste

Rinse the broccoli, separating the stems and florets. Chop the stems and florets separately. Place the water in a 1½-quart saucepan and bring to a boil. Place the broccoli stems and garlic in a steamer basket and set in saucepan. Cover and steam for 4 minutes. Uncover and stir. Arrange the florets on top of the stems, then cover and steam for another 4 minutes. Serve with a sprinkling of toasted sesame seeds.

*Makes 4 servings.*

**Nutrition Information per Serving:** *28 calories; 0.3 grams (8%) fat; 33% protein; 59% carbohydrates.*

# Spicy Szechuan Eggplant

¼ cup soy sauce

1 tablespoon honey

1 tablespoon white vinegar

1 tablespoon cornstarch

2 fresh red chili peppers, minced

2 slices fresh ginger, minced

2 cloves garlic, minced

1½ pounds eggplant, peeled and cut into 3-inch strips

1 cup dried Chinese wood ears (mushrooms), soaked in water for
    10 minutes and sliced into strips

Combine soy sauce, honey, vinegar, cornstarch, chili peppers, ginger, and garlic; mix well and set aside. In a wok or skillet sprayed with cooking spray, saute eggplant over medium heat until golden brown, about 5 minutes. Add sauce and wood ears. Cook for 1 minute, or until sauce thickens.

*Makes 4 servings.*

**Nutrition Information per Serving:** *97 calories; 1 gram (5%) fat; 15% protein; 80% carbohydrates.*

# Mock Crabmeat over Broccoli

1½ pounds broccoli

1 16-ounce block firm tofu

1 teaspoon sesame oil

1 teaspoon peanut oil

1½ teaspoons minced fresh garlic

2 teaspoons minced fresh ginger

5 tablespoons white wine

2 teaspoons salt

½ cup water

½ teaspoon sugar

¼ teaspoon white pepper

2 egg whites, beaten

1½ teaspoons cornstarch dissolved in 1 tablespoon water

3 tablespoons minced carrot

Wash and cut broccoli into florets. Cut stems into 1-inch diagonal pieces. Steam broccoli in a steamer for 3 minutes. Mash tofu with a fork and add ½ teaspoon of the sesame oil. Heat a wok or skillet on high heat and add peanut oil. Add garlic and ginger and cook for 10 seconds. Add broccoli, 3½ tablespoons of the wine, 1½ teaspoons of the salt, and the remaining ½ teaspoon sesame oil and stir-fry for 1 minute. Transfer to a platter and set aside. Clean the wok or skillet, reheat over high heat, add mashed tofu, and stir-fry for 30 seconds. Add water, the remaining 1½ tablespoons wine, the remaining ½ teaspoon salt, sugar, white pepper, and egg whites. Cook for 20 seconds. Slowly add cornstarch mixture, stirring constantly, until sauce thickens. Pour over broccoli and sprinkle with minced carrot. Serve immediately.

*Makes 4 servings.*

**Nutrition Information per Serving:** *120 calories; 4.1 grams (30%) fat; 30% protein; 40% carbohydrates.*

# Melt-in-Your-Mouth Kabocha Squash

*Kabocha squash is a delicious and beautiful vegetable that can be eaten with its skin. For variety, try mixing a tablespoon of miso and a tablespoon of sweetener, such as honey or barley malt, and drizzling it over the squash before baking.*

Carefully wash 1 kabocha squash and cut into 4-inch squares. Place on a baking pan with a tiny bit of water and bake at 350°F. until tender, about 1 hour.

*Makes 2 servings.*

**Nutrition Information per Serving:** *115 calories; 0.3 grams (2%) fat; 7% protein; 92% carbohydrates.*

# TWENTY

# Sauces

## Cremini Mushroom Sauce

½ tablespoon olive oil

1 medium onion, chopped

2–3 cloves garlic, minced

1½ cups chopped fresh cremini mushrooms

2 tablespoons white wine

2 cups water

3 tablespoons soy sauce

1 teaspoon powdered vegetable bouillon

1 teaspoon cornstarch dissolved in 2 tablespoons water

Salt and freshly ground black pepper to taste

In a medium saucepan, heat oil over medium heat. Add onion and garlic; cook and stir until onion is soft, about 5 minutes. Add mushrooms and wine; cook and stir until mushrooms release their juices. Add water, soy sauce, bouillon, and cornstarch; stir well. Simmer until slightly thickened, about 8–10 minutes. Season with salt and pepper.

*Makes 4 cups, or 16 ¼-cup servings.*

**Nutrition Information per Serving:** *86 calories; 2.6 grams (31%) fat; 19% protein; 50% carbohydrates.*

# Mushroom Teriyaki Sauce

*This sauce makes an excellent topping for vegetables, tofu, beans, or noodles. It can also make a great sandwich spread.*

---

½ cup chopped fresh mushrooms
1 teaspoon grated fresh ginger
2 tablespoons low-sodium soy sauce or tamari
1 teaspoon honey or blackstrap molasses
1 teaspoon arrowroot or cornstarch dissolved in 2 tablespoons
    cool water

In a skillet, saute mushrooms, ginger, soy sauce, and honey. Add arrowroot and additional water if necessary until the mixture achieves the desired consistency. Continue to saute for a minute or so until the ingredients are blended.

*Makes ¾ cup, or 3 ¼-cup servings.*
**Nutrition Information per Serving:** *59 calories; 0.2 grams (2%) fat; 29% protein; 69% carbohydrates.*

# Savory Gravy

½ cup whole-wheat flour

3 cups vegetable broth

½ cup water

1 teaspoon Old Bay® seasoning

¼ teaspoon freshly ground black pepper, or more or less to taste

¼ teaspoon garlic powder

Preheat oven to 300°F. Sprinkle flour in a baking pan and place in oven for 10–15 minutes, or until lightly brown. Combine flour and all remaining ingredients in a blender to make a smooth sauce. Pour into a saucepan and cook over medium heat, stirring frequently, until thickened. Cover and simmer for about 10 minutes.

*Makes 4 cups, or 8 ½-cup servings.*

**Nutrition Information per Serving:** *55 calories; 0.8 grams (12%) fat; 18% protein; 70% carbohydrates.*

# Ginger Miso Sauce

*This sauce is a great choice for vegetables or as a dipping sauce.
It also makes a good base for any stir-fry recipe.*

¼ cup white miso
1 tablespoon fresh ginger juice
1 tablespoon grated fresh ginger
1 large clove garlic, minced
Juice of 1 lemon
½ teaspoon cornstarch
1 cup water

Combine all ingredients; blend well, then heat gently in a saucepan.
Stir until thickened.

*Makes 1½ cups, or 8 3-tablespoon servings.*
**Nutrition Information per Serving:** *23 calories; 0.6 grams (21%) fat; 19%
protein; 60% carbohydrates.*

# Roasted Garlic and Red Bell Pepper Sauce

1 red bell pepper
6 cloves garlic, unpeeled
½ teaspoon olive oil
1 cup low-fat soy milk
¼ cup finely chopped onion
2 tablespoons white wine
1 tablespoon arrowroot
Salt and freshly ground black pepper to taste
Cooking spray

Preheat oven to 375°F. Place pepper and garlic cloves in a small baking pan. Spray with cooking spray. Roast in oven until pepper blisters and starts to blacken and garlic is soft, about 30 minutes. Transfer pepper to a paper or plastic bag. Close bag tightly and let pepper steam for 20 minutes. Peel off skin with your fingers, scraping off any stubborn pieces with a small knife. Cut roasted pepper in half and remove seeds and veins. Cut halves into bite-size pieces and puree in a food processor. Add ½ cup of the soy milk and blend until smooth. Squeeze pulp from skins of roasted garlic cloves, add to red pepper puree, and blend well. In a saucepan, cook onion in remaining ½ teaspoon olive oil until translucent. Add white wine and cook until liquid is reduced by half. Dissolve arrowroot in the remaining ½ cup soy milk. Add red pepper-garlic puree and arrowroot mixture to the saucepan and stir vigorously until it makes a smooth, creamy sauce. Add salt and pepper to taste.

*Makes 1 cup, or 8 2-tablespoon servings.*
**Nutrition Information per Serving:** *55 calories; 1.3 grams (22%) fat; 17% protein; 61% carbohydrates.*

# Simple Curry Sauce

4 teaspoons whole-wheat flour

2 teaspoons curry powder

1 cup vegetable broth

1 cup water

2 teaspoons finely chopped fresh ginger

1 medium onion, chopped

1 bay leaf

1 clove garlic, crushed

Combine all ingredients; blend well, then cook over medium heat until thickened. Simmer 10 minutes. Remove bay leaf before serving.

*Makes 2 cups, or 16 2-tablespoon servings.*

**Nutrition Information per Serving:** *6 calories; 0.1 grams (7%) fat; 19% protein; 74% carbohydrates.*

# Honey-Mustard Sauce

2 tablespoons minced onion
1 tablespoon minced garlic
1 tablespoon whole-wheat flour
1 cup vegetable broth
1 tablespoon Dijon mustard
1 teaspoon honey
Cooking spray

In a saucepan sprayed with cooking spray, saute onion and garlic in a small amount of water until onion sweats. Add flour and blend well. Add broth and bring to a boil, stirring until thickened. Add mustard and honey and blend well. Serve immediately.

*Makes 1¼ cups, or 4 5-tablespoon servings.*

**Nutrition Information per Serving:** *21 calories; 0.5 grams (18%) fat; 16% protein; 66% carbohydrates.*

# Chili Pepper Water

*This sauce will add zip to your favorite dishes, such as Hawaiian Savory Stew (page 230) or Chickenless Long Rice (page 150). It is very hot, so use it with caution!*

1 2-inch piece fresh ginger, peeled and chopped
½ cup fresh red chili peppers, stems removed
1 tablespoon sugar
2 tablespoons sea salt
7 cloves garlic

Blend all ingredients together in a food processor or blender with enough water to achieve the desired consistency.

*Makes 1 cup, or 16 1-tablespoon servings.*

# TWENTY-ONE

# Desserts

## Fruit Compote

2 whole pears, nectarines, peaches, or apples
Approximately 1 cup apple juice
½ cup raisins
½ teaspoon cinnamon
2 pinches sea salt
2 tablespoons water
1 teaspoon arrowroot dissolved in 2 teaspoons water
3 tablespoons toasted slivered almonds
Fresh mint leaves for garnish

Cut fruit into chunks. In a saucepan, combine fruit and enough apple juice to come ½ inch up the sides of the pan. Add raisins, cinnamon, and salt. Bring to a boil, reduce heat, and simmer for 1–2 minutes, or until fruit is slightly tender but still firm. Thicken the juice by adding arrowroot, then simmer 2 minutes longer. Serve in a dish or sherbet glass. Sprinkle with almonds and garnish with a sprig of mint.

*Makes 2 servings.*

**Nutrition Information per Serving:** *173 calories; 3.1 grams (15%) fat; 4% protein; 81% carbohydrates.*

# Strawberry-Banana Pudding

10½ ounces extra-firm silken tofu

1½ cups sliced fresh strawberries

1 banana

1 teaspoon vanilla extract

1 tablespoon freshly squeezed lemon juice

¼ teaspoon salt

2 tablespoons honey

In a food processor or blender, combine all ingredients and blend until smooth and creamy. Pour into individual serving dishes and chill overnight.

*Makes 4 servings.*
**Nutrition Information per Serving:** *109 calories; 1.2 grams (15%) fat; 23% protein; 62% carbohydrates.*

# Pineapple Sorbet

2 cups fresh pineapple chunks

1½ cups ice cubes

6 sprigs fresh mint for garnish

6 maraschino cherries for garnish

In a food processor fitted with an S blade, mince pineapple. Feed in ice cubes and process until frosty. Transfer to 6 chilled glass serving dishes and return to freezer for a few minutes. Just before serving, garnish each dish with a sprig of mint and a maraschino cherry.

*Makes 6 servings.*
**Nutrition Information per Serving:** *26 calories; 0.2 grams (7%) fat; 3% protein; 90% carbohydrates.*

# A's Baked Apples

*The A in the title stands for Alouette's Custom Catering, who contributed this recipe.*

8 medium cooking apples
1 cup apple juice
1 tablespoon cinnamon, plus more for garnish
½ teaspoon nutmeg, plus more for garnish
16 dried apricots
4 teaspoons honey (optional)
½ cup raisins (optional)

Preheat oven to 350°F. Cut a thin slice from top of apples. Cut out the core and seeds, leaving the apple whole. Place apples in a baking dish. Combine apple juice, cinnamon, nutmeg, and apricots and pour mixture into baking dish. Spoon some of this liquid into the center of each apple. Cover with aluminum foil and bake for 10 minutes. Remove from oven, uncover, and pour more liquid from the dish into the center of each apple. Cover again and cook 20 minutes more. Remove dish from oven, uncover, and add liquid to the center of apples again. Cook, uncovered, for 5 minutes. Apples should be soft but not mushy. Transfer apples to a platter or individual serving dishes. Remove apricots from sauce. Chop apricots and stuff them into the center of the apples. Place baking dish on top of the stove and heat over medium heat. Cook sauce until liquid is reduced to ½ cup. Pour reduced sauce over apples. Garnish apples with additional cinnamon and nutmeg and drizzle with honey and raisins, if desired. Serve warm or cold.

*Makes 8 servings.*

**Nutrition Information per Serving:** *125 calories; 0.7 grams (4%) fat; 2% protein; 95% carbohydrates.*

# A's Poached Pears

4 medium pears, firm but ripe
1 cup water
3 cinnamon sticks
1 teaspoon vanilla extract
2 tablespoons honey
1 banana, mashed
1 teaspoon cinnamon

Cut pears in half lengthwise. Scoop out seeds. Place pears, skin side down, in a saute pan. Add water, cinnamon sticks, and vanilla. Make sure liquid comes halfway up the sides of the pears. If it does not, add more water or transfer to a smaller pan. Poach pears over low heat for approximately 5 minutes. Do not allow liquid to evaporate. If needed, add more water. Turn pears over gently and cook for 1 more minute. Pears should be soft but not mushy. Transfer pears to a serving plate and arrange them skin side up. Heat 1 cup of the poaching liquid and add honey and banana. Stir until this liquid is reduced to ½ cup, then pour over pears. Arrange cinnamon sticks over pears and sprinkle with ground cinnamon.

*Makes 8 servings.*
**Nutrition Information per Serving:** *83 calories; 0.4 grams (4%) fat; 2% protein; 94% carbohydrates.*

# Fruit Strudel

2 large firm, ripe mangoes, peaches, or apples
Juice and zest of ½ lemon
1 tablespoon rum
3 tablespoons honey
¼ teaspoon cinnamon
¼ teaspoon vanilla extract
1 tablespoon cornstarch
¼ cup raisins (optional)
6 large sheets phyllo dough, about 14 × 18 inches each
½ cup bread crumbs

Peel, core, and cut fruit into ¼-inch slices. In a medium bowl, combine lemon juice, lemon zest, rum, honey, cinnamon, vanilla, and cornstarch. Add raisins, if desired, and fruit. Marinate for 10–15 minutes. Preheat oven to 375°F. Place the fruit in a strainer over a small saucepan. When liquids have been drained, put fruit back into the bowl and set aside. Cook marinade over medium heat, stirring constantly, until it thickens. Cool 2 minutes, then gently stir into fruit. Set aside. Place a sheet of phyllo dough on a work surface. Cover remaining sheets with plastic wrap and a damp towel until you are ready to work with them. Spray entire phyllo sheet lightly with cooking spray, then lightly sprinkle with bread crumbs. Repeat process with remaining phyllo sheets, layering them on top of the first. Place fruit mixture in a line on one short side of the phyllo sheets, leaving 1 inch of room on each side. Roll dough from the filled short side to form a tube. Spray top and sides of roll with cooking spray. Score top into 12 equal sections. (This will allow you to slice through it cleanly after baking.) Transfer to a baking sheet with seam side down. Bake for 25–30 minutes, or until golden brown. Cool slightly. Slice and serve warm or at room temperature.

*Makes 6 servings.*

**Nutrition Information per Serving:** *170 calories; 1.5 grams (8%) fat; 6% protein; 86% carbohydrates.*

# Carob-Dipped Strawberries

3 cups fresh strawberries, chilled
¼ cup honey
Pinch of cinnamon
Pinch of cardamom
¼ cup carob powder
1 tablespoon creme de cacao (optional)

Remove tops of strawberries. In a small saucepan, heat honey and spices, then stir in carob powder and creme de cacao, if desired. Remove from heat and let mixture thicken for a few minutes. If sauce is too thin, place it in the refrigerator for a few minutes. Arrange strawberries in a design of your choice on a chilled glass serving dish with a bowl of the carob sauce in the center.

*Makes 6 servings.*
**Nutrition Information per Serving:** *74 calories; 0.3 grams (3%) fat; 3% protein; 94% carbohydrates.*

# Kona Coffee Ice Dream

1 teaspoon raisins
¼ cup brewed decaffeinated Hawaiian Kona coffee, chilled
1 teaspoon rum extract
1 frozen banana
1 tablespoon carob powder (optional)

Soak raisins in water until soft, about ½ hour. Use the slicing blade of your food processor to slice frozen bananas, then put them into a separate mixing bowl and remove the slicing attachment from processor. Put in the S blade. Quickly return newly sliced and still frozen bananas to processor bowl (they'll thaw quickly now). Blend until the bananas have the texture of a very rich ice cream (this takes just a few minutes). Add coffee and rum extract, then blend until well mixed (another minute or two). Stir in the carob powder, if desired. Transfer to the mixing bowl and put in coldest part of freezer for about 5 minutes, or until slightly set. Serve topped with raisins.

*Makes 8 servings.*

**Nutrition Information per Serving:** *107 calories; 0.6 grams (4%) fat; 4% protein; 92% carbohydrates.*

# Honey Almond Fruit Cocktail

6 tablespoons powdered agar (seaweed)

2 cups water

1 cup soy milk

3 tablespoons honey

Almond extract to taste

1 cup watermelon cubes

1 cup honeydew melon cubes

1 cup apple cubes

½ cup cantaloupe cubes or fresh pineapple chunks

1 peach or pear, cut into cubes

In a saucepan, stir agar into water and heat on low. When agar is completely dissolved, add soy milk, honey, and almond extract. Chill until firm. Cut the resulting gelatin into ½-inch cubes. Combine gelatin and fruit; toss gently for an unusual and colorful fruit cocktail.

*Makes 8 servings.*

**Nutrition Information per Serving:** *85 calories; 0.6 grams (6%) fat; 8% protein; 87% carbohydrates.*

# Crispy Apricot Turnovers

¼ cup no-sugar-added apricot preserves
6 sheets phyllo dough, about 14 × 18 inches each

Preheat oven to 400°F. Lay a sheet of phyllo dough on a work surface with the narrow end toward you. Cover remaining sheets with plastic wrap and a damp towel until you are ready to work with them. Spray phyllo sheet with butter-flavored cooking spray. Fold in thirds lengthwise. Spray again. Spoon 2 tablespoons of apricot preserves onto the sheet about 1½ inches from the bottom edge. Fold the bottom 1½-inch flap over the filling. Fold the lower left-hand corner of phyllo diagonally to the right side of dough, covering the filling. Continue folding flag-style until the end of the sheet. Spray both sides of the turnover with cooking spray and place on a baking sheet. Repeat with remaining phyllo and apricot preserves. Bake for 15 minutes, or until golden brown.

*Makes 6 servings.*

**Nutrition Information per Serving:** *151 calories; 1.1 grams (7%) fat; 3% protein; 90% carbohydrates.*

# Apple Bran Cake

*This can also be made in a muffin tin. Other fruit, such as bananas, may be substituted for the apples.*

2 cups whole-wheat flour

2 cups bran

1 teaspoon allspice

1 teaspoon cinnamon

½ teaspoon ground cloves

½ teaspoon ground ginger

2 teaspoons baking powder

2 teaspoons egg substitute (optional)

1 cup honey

1 cup peeled and diced apples

½ cup applesauce

½ cup raisins (optional)

½ teaspoon vanilla extract

Preheat oven to 350°F. Combine dry ingredients and mix well. In a separate bowl, combine all remaining ingredients and blend well. Add flour mixture to moist ingredients; stir gently until well mixed. Pour into a 9-inch square nonstick baking pan. Bake for 40–50 minutes, or until cake pulls away from sides of pan.

*Makes 12 servings.*

**Nutrition Information per Serving:** *213 calories; 0.9 grams (4%) fat; 8% protein; 88% carbohydrates.*

# Spice Cake

3 cups whole-wheat pastry flour

2 tablespoons baking powder

2 teaspoons baking soda

½ teaspoon ground ginger

½ teaspoon mace

¾ teaspoon nutmeg

¼ teaspoon allspice

16 ounces extra-firm tofu

½ cup frozen apple juice concentrate

½ cup freshly squeezed orange juice

1 cup maple syrup

2 teaspoons vanilla extract

*Topping*

1 cup raisins

1 tablespoon orange zest

½ teaspoon cinnamon

1 8-ounce jar no-sugar-added orange marmalade

6 toasted pecan halves

Preheat oven to 350°F. In a large bowl, combine all dry ingredients and mix well. Blend tofu with apple juice, orange juice, maple syrup, and vanilla. Fold this mixture into the dry mixture until completely blended. Pour into a 9-inch cake pan coated with cooking spray and bake for 30 minutes, or until a toothpick inserted in the center comes out clean. Combine raisins, orange zest, cinnamon, and marmalade. Spread on warm cake and top with pecan halves.

*Makes 16 servings.*

**Nutrition Information per Serving:** *195 calories; 3 grams (13%) fat; 12% protein; 75% carbohydrates.*

# Carrot Cake

2 cups whole-wheat flour

1½ teaspoons baking soda

2 teaspoons baking powder

2 teaspoons cinnamon

½ teaspoon nutmeg

½ teaspoon ground cloves

½ teaspoon allspice

¾ cup honey

1¼ cups applesauce

4 teaspoons egg substitute well blended with 8 tablespoons water

3 cups grated carrots

1 8-ounce can crushed pineapple, partially drained

½ cup raisins

1 cup chopped walnuts (optional)

Preheat oven to 350°F. Combine flour, baking soda, baking powder, and seasonings; mix lightly. Add honey, applesauce, and egg substitute; mix well. Add carrots, pineapple, raisins, and nuts; mix well. Turn into a 13 × 9-inch nonstick baking pan. Bake for 1 hour.

*Makes 12 servings.*

**Nutrition Information per Serving:** *218 calories; 3.5 grams (14%) fat; 8% protein; 78% carbohydrates.*

# Mango Lychee Spoon Cake

1½ cups mango nectar
¼ cup freshly squeezed lemon juice
1 pound sliced mango
1 cup shelled and pitted lychee
2 teaspoons grated lemon zest
1 cup whole-wheat pastry flour
1½ teaspoons baking soda
¼ teaspoon salt
¼ cup vanilla-flavored rice milk

Preheat oven to 350°F. Combine juices, fruits, and lemon zest; set aside. Combine dry ingredients in a bowl. Add rice milk and stir only until moistened. Spray a 2-quart round baking dish with cooking spray. Spread the flour mixture into the dish and spoon the juice-and-fruit mixture over the batter. Bake for 40–50 minutes, or until golden brown. Remove from oven, cool on a rack, and serve warm.

*Makes 8 servings.*
**Nutrition Information per Serving:** *149 calories; 0.9 grams (4%) fat; 7% protein; 89% carbohydrates.*

# Conclusion: HawaiiDiet™ for the Health of the World

*A* diet and lifestyle based on traditional ways and spiritual values is the key to both physical and spiritual health.

I believe that diet is the most important element of physical health. Faith, prayer, and an understanding and practice of the concepts of *lokahi* and *aloha* are the most important elements of spiritual health.

When an individual becomes truly whole, that is, healthy in all aspects of his or her life, that individual also has a great potential to influence all of humanity. It is our hope that this book will inspire more individuals to seek this wholeness. In this way, they may enhance their contribution to the health of the community, the nation, and the world.

The ultimate state of global health, ideally, includes world peace. While this may seem an unachievable goal, humanity has proven time and again that what we can believe, we can indeed achieve. Matthew 17:20 tells us:

> If you have faith as a grain of mustard seed, you will say to this mountain, "Move from here to there," and it will move; and nothing will be impossible to you.

If we have faith—if we believe in world health and world peace—these beliefs can become a reality.

But—and I cannot stress this enough—world health and world peace must begin with the healing of the individuals who make up the world. It can occur only when people begin to heal themselves, and this healing will take place one step, one day, one person at a time. Diet and lifestyle changes are essential, at the individual level, if this is ever to occur.

In the end, we realize that the future of the world depends on the understanding of *lokahi*, the practice of *aloha*, and faith in God. We must come to a realization that the source of healing is the Almighty, who heals through the laws of nature. Only then will we fully understand that it is sheer vanity and arrogance to think that our high-tech procedures and designer drugs provide anything that resembles true health. In an age when bacteria and viruses increasingly resist antibiotics; where AIDS, heart disease, cancer, and other devastating diseases are beyond the healing abilities of modern medicine, we must look for new ways. We must take the responsibility upon ourselves to do what is necessary to heal ourselves and our world.

We are finding new hope in the old ways, in an integration of ancient concepts with modern science and in a renewed faith and a return to the source. The HawaiiDiet™ provides a tool with which we can begin the process of healing ourselves. Now it is up to us.

# List of Recipes

**Salads and Dressings**

# Dr. Shintani's Mass Index of Food (SMI)

| Food | SMI Value | Food | SMI Value |
|------|-----------|------|-----------|
| Almonds | 0.9 | Beans, kidney | 4.6 |
| Apples | 9.4 | Beans, lima | 4.9 |
| Apricots | 11.4 | Beans, navy | 4.6 |
| Artichokes | 26.0 | Beef, chuck | 1.4 |
| Asparagus | 21.0 | Beef, corned | 1.5 |
| Avocado | 3.3 | Beef, ground | 1.9 |
| Bacon | 0.8 | Beef, sirloin | 1.2 |
| Bagels, plain* | 3.8 | Beets | 12.7 |
| Bagels, whole-wheat* | 4.1 | Blackberries | 9.4 |
| Bamboo | 20.2 | Blueberries | 8.8 |
| Bananas | 6.4 | Bread, white* | 4.1 |
| Barley (cooked)* | 4.4 | Bread, whole-wheat* | 4.6 |
| Bass | 2.1 | Breadfruit | 5.3 |
| Bean sprouts, mung | 15.6 | Broccoli | 17.1 |
| Beans, dried white | 4.6 | Brussels sprouts | 12.1 |
| Beans, garbanzo (chickpeas) | 5.6 | Buckwheat (cooked) | 5.9 |
| | | Butter | 0.8 |
| Beans, green | 21.9 | Cabbage | 22.8 |

*SMI values adjusted upward to account for the increase in bulk of this food due to water absorption after ingestion.

| Food | SMI Value | Food | SMI Value |
|------|-----------|------|-----------|
| Cabbage, Chinese | 39.0 | French fries | 1.7 |
| Candy, chocolate | 1.0 | Garlic | 4.1 |
| Candy, hard | 1.4 | Ginger | 11.9 |
| Cantaloupe | 18.2 | Grapefruit | 27.3 |
| Carrots | 13.0 | Grapes | 11.9 |
| Cashews | 1.0 | Ham | 2.1 |
| Cauliflower | 20.2 | Ham sandwich | 1.6 |
| Celery | 32.8 | Hamburger, ¼ lb. | 2.2 |
| Cheese, blue | 1.5 | Hamburger, ¼ lb. w/cheese | 2.1 |
| Cheese, cheddar | 1.4 | Honey | 1.8 |
| Cheese, cream | 1.5 | Kale | 10.3 |
| Cherries | 8.7 | Kumquats | 22.8 |
| Chestnuts | 2.8 | Lamb, leg of | 2.9 |
| Chicken, dark meat | 3.1 | Lamb, loin chops | 2.2 |
| Chicken, white meat | 3.3 | Lemons | 30.4 |
| Coconut | 1.6 | Lentils | 5.2 |
| Collard greens | 12.1 | Lettuce | 39.0 |
| Corn | 6.5 | Lobster | 5.8 |
| Corn chips | 2.0 | Loganberries | 8.8 |
| Crab | 5.9 | Loquats | 14.8 |
| Crab salad | 3.8 | Lychee | 14.0 |
| Crackers, cheese* | 2.0 | Mackerel | 2.3 |
| Crackers, saltine* | 2.4 | Mangoes | 8.3 |
| Cranberries | 12.4 | Margarine | 0.8 |
| Cucumbers | 32.8 | Mayonnaise | 0.8 |
| Danish pastry | 1.5 | Melons | 18.2 |
| Doughnuts | 1.3 | Millet (cooked) | 4.6 |
| Eggs | 3.4 | Mushrooms | 19.5 |
| Eggplant | 28.8 | Mustard greens | 17.6 |
| Endive | 27.3 | Nectarines | 9.3 |
| Figs | 6.8 | Oatmeal | 9.9 |

*SMI values adjusted upward to account for the increase in bulk of this food due to water absorption after ingestion.

| Food | SMI Value | Food | SMI value |
|------|-----------|------|-----------|
| Oil/lard | 0.6 | Rice, brown* | 5.1 |
| Okra | 15.2 | Rice, white | 5.0 |
| Olives | 4.7 | Roll, dinner* | 3.2 |
| Onions | 14.8 | Roll, dinner, whole wheat* | 4.0 |
| Onions, green | 15.2 | Scallions | 15.2 |
| Oranges | 15.6 | Scallops | 4.9 |
| Papaya | 31.2 | Seaweed (konbu) | 12.7 |
| Pasta, buckwheat | 5.5 | Seaweed (wakame) | 12.1 |
| Pasta, semolina | 4.1 | Sesame seeds | 0.9 |
| Pasta, whole-wheat | 4.4 | Shrimp | 4.8 |
| Peaches | 16.6 | Shrimp, fried | 2.3 |
| Peanut butter | 0.9 | Soybeans | 4.2 |
| Peanuts | 0.9 | Soybean sprouts | 11.9 |
| Pears | 9.0 | Spaghetti | 4.8 |
| Peas | 6.5 | Spinach | 21.0 |
| Peppers, chili | 27.3 | Squash | 28.8 |
| Persimmons | 5.3 | Strawberries | 14.8 |
| Pineapples | 10.5 | Sturgeon | 3.4 |
| Pistachio nuts | 0.9 | Sugar | 1.5 |
| Pita bread, white* | 3.5 | Sunflower seeds | 1.0 |
| Pita bread, whole-wheat | 4.3 | Sweet potatoes | 5.4 |
| Plums | 9.1 | Tangerines | 16.1 |
| Poi | 9.1 | Taro | 5.6 |
| Pork | 2.1 | Tofu | 7.6 |
| Potatoes | 9.6 | Tomatoes | 27.3 |
| Potato chips | 2.0 | Tomato paste | 6.5 |
| Pretzels* | 2.8 | Tortilla, chupati | 3.4 |
| Prunes | 6.8 | Tortilla, corn* | 4.9 |
| Pumpkin | 16.6 | Tortilla, lowfat* | 4.3 |
| Radishes | 32.1 | Tuna (in oil) | 1.9 |
| Raspberries | 7.5 | Tuna (in water) | 4.3 |

*SMI values adjusted upward to account for the increase in bulk of this food due to water absorption after ingestion.

| Food | SMI value | Food | SMI value |
|---|---|---|---|
| Turkey | 2.1 | Watermelons | 21.0 |
| Turnips | 19.5 | Whole wheat* | 3.7 |
| Veal | 3.4 | Yams | 6.3 |
| Walnuts | 0.9 | Zucchini | 32.1 |
| Watercress | 27.3 | | |

*SMI values adjusted upward to account for the increase in bulk of this food due to water absorption after ingestion.

# Charts and Graphs

### 3A. Ten Leading Causes of Death in the U.S.

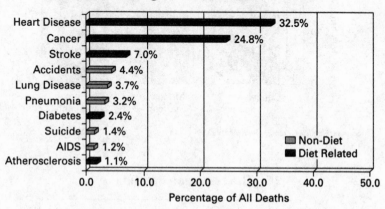

Source: National Center for Health Statistics, 1996

### 3B. Mortality Among Native Hawaiians
## As Compared to the Average Mortality Rates for All Races in the U.S.

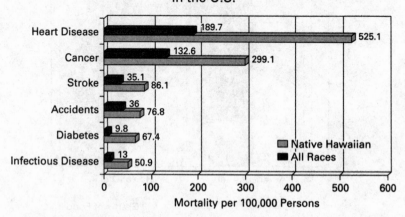

Source: Office of Technology Assessment, U.S. Congress, 1987.

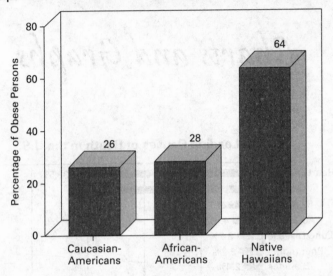

### 3C. Prevalence of Obesity Among Native Hawaiians
Compared to African-Americans and Caucasian-Americans

Source: *Annals of Internal Medicine,* 1993

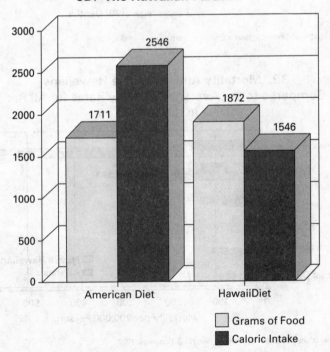

### 3D. The Hawaiian Paradox

## 3E. Dietary Fat and Coronary Mortality

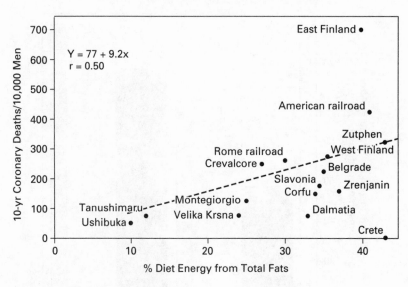

Adapted from Keys A. *Seven Countries Study*.
Cambridge: Harvard University Press, 1980.

## 3F. HawaiiDiet™ Spectrum of Healthy Traditional Diets

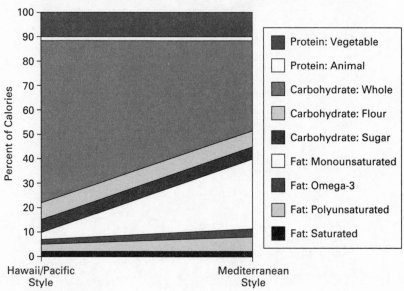

### 3G. Differential Insulin Response

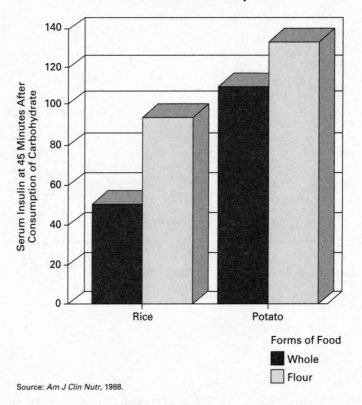

Source: *Am J Clin Nutr,* 1988.

### 3H.  Differential Glycemic Response

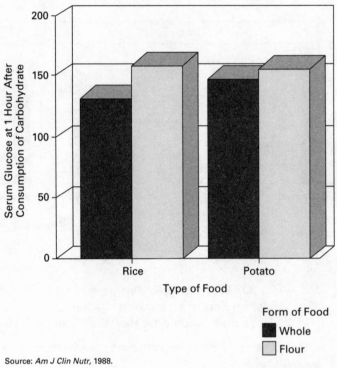

Source: *Am J Clin Nutr,* 1988.

## 3I. Average Results After 21 Days
### on a Traditional Hawaiian Diet

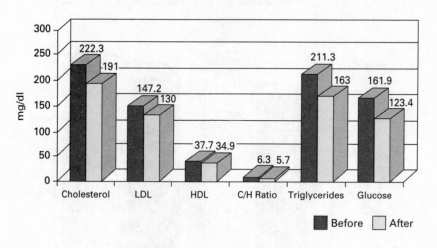

## 3J. Wai'anae Diet Program
### Fasting Serum Triglycerides After
### 21 Days on a Traditional Hawaiian Diet

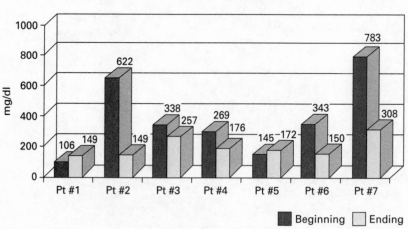

Shintani TT, Hughes CK, Beckham S, Kanawaliwali O'Connor H.
Copyright WCCHC 1991.

*280*

# Body Mass Index

## Body Mass Index* (BMI) Height and Weight Chart

"Overweight" = BMI of 25 or more "Obese" = BMI of 30 or more

### HEIGHT IN FEET/INCHES

| | 5'0" | 5'1" | 5'2" | 5'3" | 5'4" | 5'5" | 5'6" | 5'7" | 5'8" | 5'9" | 5'10" | 5'11" | 6'0" | 6'1" | 6'2" | 6'3" | 6'4" | 6'5" | 6'6" |
|---|---|---|---|---|---|---|---|---|---|---|---|---|---|---|---|---|---|---|---|
| **100** | 19.6 | 18.9 | 18.3 | 17.8 | 17.2 | 16.7 | 16.2 | 15.7 | 15.2 | 14.8 | 14.4 | 14.0 | 13.6 | 13.2 | 12.9 | 12.5 | 12.2 | 11.9 | 11.6 |
| **105** | 20.5 | 19.9 | 19.2 | 18.6 | 18.1 | 17.5 | 17.0 | 16.5 | 16.0 | 15.5 | 15.1 | 14.7 | 14.3 | 13.9 | 13.5 | 13.2 | 12.8 | 12.5 | 12.2 |
| **110** | 21.5 | 20.8 | 20.2 | 19.5 | 18.9 | 18.3 | 17.8 | 17.3 | 16.8 | 16.3 | 15.8 | 15.4 | 14.9 | 14.5 | 14.2 | 13.8 | 13.4 | 13.1 | 12.7 |
| **115** | 22.5 | 21.8 | 21.1 | 20.4 | 19.8 | 19.2 | 18.6 | 18.0 | 17.5 | 17.0 | 16.5 | 16.1 | 15.6 | 15.2 | 14.8 | 14.4 | 14.0 | 13.7 | 13.3 |
| **120** | 23.5 | 22.7 | 22.0 | 21.3 | 20.6 | 20.0 | 19.4 | 18.8 | 18.3 | 17.8 | 17.3 | 16.8 | 16.3 | 15.9 | 15.4 | 15.0 | 14.6 | 14.3 | 13.9 |
| **125** | 24.5 | 23.7 | 22.9 | 22.2 | 21.5 | 20.8 | 20.2 | 19.6 | 19.0 | 18.5 | 18.0 | 17.5 | 17.0 | 16.5 | 16.1 | 15.7 | 15.2 | 14.9 | 14.5 |
| **130** | 25.4 | 24.6 | 23.8 | 23.1 | 22.4 | 21.7 | 21.0 | 20.4 | 19.8 | 19.2 | 18.7 | 18.2 | 17.7 | 17.2 | 16.7 | 16.3 | 15.9 | 15.4 | 15.1 |
| **135** | 26.4 | 25.6 | 24.7 | 24.0 | 23.2 | 22.5 | 21.8 | 21.2 | 20.6 | 20.0 | 19.4 | 18.9 | 18.3 | 17.8 | 17.4 | 16.9 | 16.5 | 16.0 | 15.6 |
| **140** | 27.4 | 26.5 | 25.7 | 24.9 | 24.1 | 23.3 | 22.6 | 22.0 | 21.3 | 20.7 | 20.1 | 19.6 | 19.0 | 18.5 | 18.0 | 17.5 | 17.1 | 16.6 | 16.2 |
| **145** | 28.4 | 27.5 | 26.6 | 25.7 | 24.9 | 24.2 | 23.5 | 22.8 | 22.1 | 21.5 | 20.8 | 20.3 | 19.7 | 19.2 | 18.7 | 18.2 | 17.7 | 17.2 | 16.8 |
| **150** | 29.4 | 28.4 | 27.5 | 26.6 | 25.8 | 25.0 | 24.3 | 23.5 | 22.9 | 22.2 | 21.6 | 21.0 | 20.4 | 19.8 | 19.3 | 18.8 | 18.3 | 17.8 | 17.4 |
| **155** | 30.3 | 29.3 | 28.4 | 27.5 | 26.7 | 25.8 | 25.1 | 24.3 | 23.6 | 22.9 | 22.3 | 21.7 | 21.1 | 20.5 | 19.9 | 19.4 | 18.9 | 18.4 | 17.9 |
| **160** | 31.3 | 30.3 | 29.3 | 28.4 | 27.5 | 26.7 | 25.9 | 25.1 | 24.4 | 23.7 | 23.0 | 22.4 | 21.7 | 21.2 | 20.6 | 20.0 | 19.5 | 19.0 | 18.5 |
| **165** | 32.3 | 31.2 | 30.2 | 29.3 | 28.4 | 27.5 | 26.7 | 25.9 | 25.1 | 24.4 | 23.7 | 23.1 | 22.4 | 21.8 | 21.2 | 20.7 | 20.1 | 19.6 | 19.1 |
| **170** | 33.3 | 32.2 | 31.2 | 30.2 | 29.2 | 28.3 | 27.5 | 26.7 | 25.9 | 25.2 | 24.4 | 23.8 | 23.1 | 22.5 | 21.9 | 21.3 | 20.7 | 20.2 | 19.7 |
| **175** | 34.2 | 33.1 | 32.1 | 31.1 | 30.1 | 29.2 | 28.3 | 27.5 | 26.7 | 25.9 | 25.2 | 24.5 | 23.8 | 23.1 | 22.5 | 21.9 | 21.3 | 20.8 | 20.3 |
| **180** | 35.2 | 34.1 | 33.0 | 32.0 | 31.0 | 30.0 | 29.1 | 28.3 | 27.4 | 26.6 | 25.9 | 25.2 | 24.5 | 23.8 | 23.2 | 22.5 | 22.0 | 21.4 | 20.8 |
| **185** | 36.2 | 35.0 | 33.9 | 32.8 | 31.8 | 30.8 | 29.9 | 29.0 | 28.2 | 27.4 | 26.6 | 25.9 | 25.1 | 24.5 | 23.8 | 23.2 | 22.6 | 22.0 | 21.4 |
| **190** | 37.2 | 36.0 | 34.8 | 33.7 | 32.7 | 31.7 | 30.7 | 29.8 | 28.9 | 28.1 | 27.3 | 26.6 | 25.8 | 25.1 | 24.4 | 23.8 | 23.2 | 22.6 | 22.0 |
| **195** | 38.2 | 36.9 | 35.7 | 34.6 | 33.5 | 32.5 | 31.5 | 30.6 | 29.7 | 28.9 | 28.0 | 27.3 | 26.5 | 25.8 | 25.1 | 24.4 | 23.8 | 23.2 | 22.6 |
| **200** | 39.1 | 37.9 | 36.7 | 35.5 | 34.4 | 33.4 | 32.3 | 31.4 | 30.5 | 29.6 | 28.8 | 28.0 | 27.2 | 26.4 | 25.7 | 25.1 | 24.4 | 23.8 | 23.2 |
| **210** | 41.1 | 39.8 | 38.5 | 37.3 | 36.1 | 35.0 | 34.0 | 33.0 | 32.0 | 31.1 | 30.2 | 29.4 | 28.5 | 27.8 | 27.0 | 26.3 | 25.6 | 25.0 | 24.3 |
| **220** | 43.1 | 41.7 | 40.3 | 39.1 | 37.8 | 36.7 | 35.6 | 34.5 | 33.5 | 32.6 | 31.6 | 30.7 | 29.9 | 29.1 | 28.3 | 27.6 | 26.8 | 26.1 | 25.5 |
| **230** | 45.0 | 43.5 | 42.2 | 40.8 | 39.6 | 38.4 | 37.2 | 36.1 | 35.0 | 34.0 | 33.1 | 32.1 | 31.3 | 30.4 | 29.6 | 28.8 | 28.1 | 27.3 | 26.6 |
| **240** | 47.0 | 45.4 | 44.0 | 42.6 | 41.3 | 40.0 | 38.8 | 37.7 | 36.6 | 35.5 | 34.5 | 33.5 | 32.6 | 31.7 | 30.9 | 30.1 | 29.3 | 28.5 | 27.8 |
| **250** | 48.9 | 47.3 | 45.8 | 44.4 | 43.0 | 41.7 | 40.4 | 39.2 | 38.1 | 37.0 | 35.9 | 34.9 | 34.0 | 33.1 | 32.2 | 31.3 | 30.5 | 29.7 | 29.0 |
| **260** | 50.9 | 49.2 | 47.7 | 46.2 | 44.7 | 43.4 | 42.1 | 40.8 | 39.6 | 38.5 | 37.4 | 36.3 | 35.3 | 34.4 | 33.5 | 32.6 | 31.7 | 30.9 | 30.1 |
| **270** | 52.8 | 51.1 | 49.5 | 47.9 | 46.4 | 45.0 | 43.7 | 42.4 | 41.1 | 40.0 | 38.8 | 37.7 | 36.7 | 35.7 | 34.7 | 33.8 | 32.9 | 32.1 | 31.3 |
| **280** | 54.8 | 53.0 | 51.3 | 49.7 | 48.2 | 46.7 | 45.3 | 43.9 | 42.7 | 41.4 | 40.3 | 39.1 | 38.1 | 37.0 | 36.0 | 35.1 | 34.2 | 33.3 | 32.4 |
| **290** | 56.8 | 54.9 | 53.2 | 51.5 | 49.9 | 48.4 | 46.9 | 45.5 | 44.2 | 42.9 | 41.7 | 40.5 | 39.4 | 38.3 | 37.3 | 36.3 | 35.4 | 34.5 | 33.6 |
| **300** | 58.7 | 56.8 | 55.0 | 53.3 | 51.6 | 50.0 | 48.5 | 47.1 | 45.7 | 44.4 | 43.1 | 41.9 | 40.8 | 39.7 | 38.6 | 37.6 | 36.6 | 35.6 | 34.7 |

**WEIGHT IN POUNDS**

\* BMI is calculated as a quotient of weight in kilograms divided by height in meters squared. (kg/m2)

# Glossary of Medical and Scientific Terms

amino acid
An organic acid in which one of the hydrogen atoms on a carbon atom has been replaced by $NH_2$.

antioxidant
An agent that inhibits oxidation and thus prevents rancidity of oils or fats or the deterioration of other materials through oxidative processes (e.g., ascorbic acid, vitamin E).

carbohydrates
Class name for the aldehydic or ketonic derivatives of polyhydric alcohols, the name being derived from the fact that the most common examples of such compounds have formulas that may be written $C_n(H_2O)_n$ [e.g., glucose, $C_6(H_2O)_6$; sucrose, $C_{12}(H_2O)_{11}$], although they are not true hydrates and the name is in that sense a misnomer. The group includes compounds with relatively small molecules, such as the simple sugars (monosaccharides, disaccharides, etc.), as well as macromolecular (polymeric) substances such as starch, glycogen, and cellulose polysaccharides. The carbohydrates most typical of the class contain carbon, hydrogen, and oxygen only, but carbohydrate metabolic intermediates in tissue contain phosphorus.

cholesterol
5-cholesten-3β-ol; the most abundant steroid in animal tissues, especially in bile and gallstones, and present in food, especially food rich in animal fats; circulates in the plasma complexed to proteins of various densities and plays an important role in the pathogenesis of atheroma formation in arteries.

complex carbohydrate
A carbohydrate containing a large number of saccharide groups, long chains of carbon atoms; e.g., starch.

dietary fiber
The plant polysaccharides and lignin that are resistant to hydrolysis by the digestive enzymes in humans.

eicosanoids
A family of modified fatty acids, derived from a 20-carbon, polyunsaturated fatty acid, arachidonic acid, that regulate a number of cell functions, i.e., blood clotting, smooth-muscle contraction, neurotransmitter release and action, hormone secretion, and immune response.

fatty acid
Any acid derived from fats by hydrolysis (e.g., oleic, palmitic, or stearic acids); any long-chain monobasic organic acid; they accumulate in disorders associated with the peroxisomes.

glucagon
A hormone consisting of a straight-chain polypeptide of 29 amino acid residues (bovine glucagon), extracted from pancreatic alpha cells. Parenteral administration of 0.5 to 1 mg results in prompt mobilization of hepatic glycogen, thus elevating blood glucose concentration. It activates hepatic phosphorylase, thereby increasing glycogenolysis, decreases gastric motility and gastric and pancreatic secretions, and increases urinary excretion of nitrogen and potassium; it has no effect on muscle phosphorylase. As the hydrochloride, it is used in the treat-

ment of glycogen storage disease (von Gierke's) and hypoglycemia, particularly hypoglycemic coma due to exogenously administered insulin.

glycemic index
A ranking of foods based on their glycemic effect. The index has been used to classify carbohydrates for various applications, including diabetes, sports, and appetite research. The purpose of these tables is to bring together all of the published data on the indexes of individual foods for the convenience of users. In total, there are almost 600 separate entries, including values for most common Western foods, many indigenous foods, and pure sugar solutions. The tables show the glycemic index according to both the glucose and white bread (the original reference food) standard, the type and number of subjects tested, and the source of the data. For many foods there are two or more published values, so the mean +/- SEM was calculated and is shown together with the original data. These tables reduce unnecessary repetition in the testing of individual foods and facilitate wider application of the glycemic index approach.

HDL
Abbreviation for high density lipoprotein. See lipoprotein.

hemorrhagic stroke
The term "stroke" denotes the sudden development of focal neurological deficits usually related to impaired cerebral blood; more appropriate terms indicate the nature of the disturbance; e.g., thrombosis, hemorrhage, or embolism. Hemorrhagic stroke is characterized by hemorrhage; i.e., the escape of blood through ruptured or unruptured vessel walls.

homocysteine
A homolog of cysteine, produced by the demethylation of methionine, and an intermediate in the biosynthesis of L-cysteine from L-methionine via L-cystathionine.

indolamine

General term for an indole or indole derivative containing a primary, secondary, or tertiary amine group (e.g., serotonin).

insulin

A polypeptide hormone, secreted by beta cells in the islets of Langerhans, that promotes glucose utilization, protein synthesis, and the formation and storage of neutral lipids; obtained from various animals and available in a variety of preparations, insulin is used parenterally in the treatment of diabetes mellitus.

ketone body

One of a group of ketones that includes acetoacetic acid, its reduction product, $\alpha$-hydroxybutyric acid, and its decarboxylation product, acetone; high levels are found in tissues and body fluids in ketosis.

LDL

Abbreviation for low density lipoprotein. See lipoprotein.

lipoprotein

Complexes or compounds containing lipid and protein. Almost all the lipids in plasma are present as lipoproteins and are therefore transported as such. Plasma lipoproteins migrate electrophoretically with the $\beta$- and $\alpha$-globulins, but are presently characterized by their flotation constants (densities, in g/ml), as follows: chylomicra, <0.93; very low density (VLDL), 0.93–1.006; intermediate density (IDL), 1.006–1.019; low density (LDL), 1.019–1.063; high density (HDL), 1.063–1.21 (divided into two classes, HDL2 (1.063–1.125) and HDL3 (1.125–1.21); and very high density (VHDL), >1.21. They range in molecular weight from 175,000 to $1 \times 10^9$ and from 4 to 98% lipid (the higher the density, the lower the lipid content). The very low and low-density classes appear in the $\alpha_1$-globulin fraction and are particularly rich in triacylglycerols and cholesterol esters, respectively; the high-density and very high-density classes appear in the $\beta_1$-globulin fraction. Levels of lipoproteins are important in assessing the risk of cardiovascular disease.

macronutrients
Nutrients required in the greatest amount; e.g., carbohydrates, protein, fats.

micronutrients
Essential food factors required in only small quantities by the body; e.g., vitamins, trace minerals.

monounsaturated fatty acid
A fatty acid, the carbon chain of which possesses one double or triple bond (e.g., oleic acid, with one double bond in the molecule); called unsaturated because it is capable of absorbing additional hydrogen.

omega-3 fatty acid
A class of fatty acids that have a double bond, three carbons from the methyl moiety; reportedly, they play a role in lowering cholesterol and LDL levels.

osteoporosis
A condition of reduced bone mass, with decreased cortical thickness and a decrease in the number and size of the trabeculae of cancellous bone (but with normal chemical composition), resulting in increased fracture incidence. Osteoporosis is classified as primary (Type 1, postmenopausal osteoporosis; Type 2, age-associated osteoporosis; and idiopathic, which can affect juveniles, premenopausal women, and middle-aged men) and secondary (which results from an identifiable cause of bone mass loss).

phytochemistry
The biochemical study of plants; concerned with the identification, biosynthesis, and metabolism of chemical constituents of plants; especially in regard to natural products.

polyunsaturated fatty acid
A fatty acid, the carbon chain of which possesses two or more double or triple bonds (e.g., linoleic acid, with two double bonds in the mole-

cule); called unsaturated because it is capable of absorbing additional hydrogen.

retinoid
In plural form, a term used to describe the natural forms and synthetic analogs of retinol.

In experiments with rats, hamsters, and other animals, these vitamin A analogs have been shown to block carcinogenesis in a variety of epithelial tissues. Clinical trials have announced success of retinoid drugs in preventing actinic keratosis, bronchial metaplasia, cervical dysplasia, oral leukoplakia, tumors in the aerodigestive tract, and some skin cancers. Although the mechanism by which retinoids act is not fully understood, they may modulate gene expression and thereby slow or suppress the multistep process that leads to the creation, proliferation, and spread of cancerous cells.

saturated fatty acid
A fatty acid, the carbon chain of which contains no ethylenic or other unsaturated linkages between carbon atoms (e.g., stearic acid and palmitic acid); called saturated because it is incapable of absorbing any more hydrogen.

simple carbohydrate
A carbohydrate that cannot form any simpler sugar by simple hydrolysis; e.g., pentoses, hexoses.

triacylglycerol
Glycerol esterified at each of its three hydroxyl groups by a fatty (aliphatic) acid; e.g., tristearoylglycerol.

triglyceride
See triacylglycerol.

uric acid
2,6,8-Trioxypurine; white crystals, poorly soluble, contained in solution in the urine of mammals and in solid form in the urine of birds and

reptiles; sometimes solidified in small masses as stones or crystals or in larger concretions as calculi; with sodium and other bases it forms urates; elevated levels associated with gout.

vegan
A strict vegetarian; i.e., one who consumes no animal or dairy products of any type.

# Glossary of Foodstuffs and Hawaiian Words

aburage: A thin skin of deep-fried tofu that is often used as a sushi wrap. Aburage is available in the Asian section of most supermarkets.

adzuki beans: Tiny, hard red dried beans from Japan with a faintly sweet flavor.

agar: Also called agar-agar, this is a mineral-rich seaweed processed into a form that can easily substitute for gelatin.

*'ahi:* Hawaiian tuna, especially the yellowfin tuna. It is red when raw and turns white after cooking.

*aloha:* Love, mercy compassion, pity; a greeting; to love.

*'ano 'ano:* Seed, kernel.

barley malt syrup: Sometimes called malted barley syrup, this dark, thick sweetener (maltose being its principal sugar) is better tolerated by diabetics than refined white sugar. It is prepared from sprouted dried barley and can replace honey or molasses in baked goods.

basmati rice: This is a rich and aromatic grain from India. It is known as the king of rice and is eaten by India's elite. It is most healthful when eaten in the brown variety.

black bean paste: Salty fermented black beans used in Chinese cooking.

brown rice syrup: A sweetener made of rice that is found in health-food stores.

buckwheat: The seeds from the buckwheat plant, which is related to rhubarb, are used to make buckwheat flour. The plant's iron and mineral content is especially high, and this food has been a staple in Russia, Eastern Europe, and China for centuries. Buckwheat may be prepared in a variety of ways—as breakfast cereal (though is it not technically a cereal grain), pilaf, and other tasty treats. Hulled, crushed buckwheat kernels are also known as kasha, a food that is increasingly popular in health-food stores.

cellophane noodles: Also called long rice or bean threads, these are dried, transparent noodles made out of mung-bean starch that cook quickly.

chapati: An Indian unleavened flat bread that is much like a flour tortilla and that makes an excellent sandwich.

chickpeas: Also known as garbanzo beans, These legumes are highly popular in the Middle East. They are high in protein, and can be mashed into a paste with a bit of lemon, oil, and fresh garlic and used as a dip for pita bread or as a sandwich filler. They are also sometimes ground into flour.

chili paste: Chili peppers ground into a paste.

Chinese bean sauce: A sauce made from mashing Chinese fermented black beans and blending them with other ingredients. It can be found in the Asian section of most supermarkets.

Chinese mustard cabbage: A dark green cabbage with a mustardy flavor that is sold in Asian groceries and used in soups and vegetable dishes.

cilantro: Also called Chinese parsley. The dried fruit of this parsley-like plant is also known as coriander.

Congee: Chinese rice porridge or gruel, also known as jook.

daikon: A radish-flavored Japanese root in the turnip family. Daikon can be found raw in the produce section or pickled in the Asian section of your supermarket. Turnips are a good substitute for daikon in recipes.

fermented black beans: Whole fermented black beans that can be found in the Asian section of most supermarkets.

fiddlehead fern: A Native Hawaiian fern with tightly coiled fronds. Young fronds are eaten raw. The Japanese call this fern warabi.

fish sauce: A sauce made from fish extract, water, and salt.

five-spice powder: A Chinese seasoning blend of cloves, fennel, cinnamon, star anise, and szechuan pepper.

gandule: A tropical legume used by Puerto Ricans; also known as pigeon peas.

golden needles: The dried buds of the tiger lily, sold in Asian or Chinese markets.

goya powder: A Puerto Rican seasoning blend of monosodium glutamate, salt, dehydrated garlic, amato, coriander, and cumin.

gyoza: Japanese dumplings, usually fried in oil, that are eaten as appetizers.

*haupia:* Hawaiian coconut pudding.

Hawaii: The breath and the water of life from God (*ha:* to breathe; *wai:* water, to flow like water; *i:* God).

hoi sin sauce: A delicious Chinese sweet and tangy sauce made from fermented and seasoned yellow beans and red rice.

*huna:* Hidden secret. Minute particle; small, little.

jook: Chinese rice porridge; also known as congee.

kaffir lime: A Vietnamese or Thai lime tree, the leaves of which are used for flavoring in cooking.

*kahea:* To call, cry out; to name; recital of the first lines of a stanza by a dancer as a cue to a chanter; to greet.

*kahuna:* Keeper of the secret. A priest, minister, sorcerer, expert in any profession; to act as a priest or expert.

kalo: Taro, the staff of life, a main staple of the Native Hawaiian people past and present. Good taro is a prized food in Hawaii.

*kaona:* Hidden meaning in Hawaiian poetry.

*kumu:* The source. Bottom, base, foundation, basis; beginning, origin.

*Kumulipo:* The Dark Source. The origin or source of life; name of the Hawaiian chant of creation.

ko choo jung: A Korean sauce made of cooked mochi (rice), miso, and chili peppers.

konbu: A broad, thick Japanese seaweed also known as kelp or laminaria that is used both as a high-calcium food and as the basis of soup stock.

konyaku: A chewy Japanese product made from yam flour.

*laulau:* A bundle of food, usually fish, which has been wrapped in taro leaves, wrapped again in ti leaves, tied, and steamed in the imu, a Hawaiian underground oven.

*lehua:* A type of Hawaiian taro used to make poi or for cooking.

lemon grass: This herb with long green leaves and a sour flavor is used for tea and cooking. The root, which gives off a ginger-like flavor, is also used in cooking.

*lokahi:* Wholeness, unity, agreement, accord; in unity.

*lomi:* To rub, press, crush, massage, rub out; to work in and out.

lotus root: The root of the lotus plant, or Chinese water lily. This long, brown root reveals holes in the flesh when it is sliced. It is available fresh or canned in Chinese markets.

*lu'au:* Cooked taro leaves, usually boiled in water, with other ingredients added. This dish is a favorite at any Hawaiian party (*lu'au*).

lychee: A delicious fruit with sweet, soft, juicy meat surrounded by an inedible reddish woody shell. The fruit has a pit inside that is not eaten.

malt extract: See barley malt extract.

*mana:* Supernatural or divine power, miraculous power.

*manauwea:* A small, red *limu*, or seaweed, used for mixing with fish or in salads. It is called ogo by the Japanese.

Maui onion: A mild, sweet onion grown on the island of Maui.

mirin: A sweet Japanese rice wine used in cooking.

miso: A thick, fermented soybean paste that has a savory flavor suitable for soups and sauces.

*moi:* A type of Hawaiian taro used for cooking.

mu shu: Vegetables or meats seasoned with hoi sin sauce.

mun doo: Korean dumplings used in soups and for appetizers. Mun doo wrappers can be purchased in Asian grocery stores.

mung beans: These green or yellow beans are highly popular in Asia, where they are used in vegetable dishes. The sprouts are also widely used in Asian cuisine.

mustard cabbage: See Chinese mustard cabbage.

namasu: A Japanese raw vegetable salad with a sweet vinegar dressing that literally means "raw with vinegar."

namul: A Korean dish of slightly cooked vegetables in a sauce of vinegar, soy sauce, and sesame seeds.

*Nana i ke kumu:* Look to the source (*nana:* to look at, observe, see; *kumu:* bottom, base, foundation, basis, beginning, source, origin).

nori: A Japanese black seaweed, usually sold in thin sheets, found in Asian markets and used to wrap sushi.

*ogo:* See *manauwea.*

*'ono:* Delicious, tasty, savory; to relish, crave; deliciousness, flavor, savor. Also see wahoo.

oriental eggplant: A long eggplant that is about the shape and size of a small zucchini.

*Papa:* Earth Mother, wife of *Wakea* (Sky Father); also a flat surface, stratum, layer, level, foundation, reef, board.

papaya: A very popular pear-shaped fruit with yellow skin and yellow or sunrise-pink flesh inside.

phyllo: A Greek dough in very thin sheets that becomes flaky when baked.

pigeon peas: See gandule.

*poi:* A pudding-like substance made from cooked taro root; a staple starch of the Hawaiians.

*pono:* Goodness, morality, moral qualities, righteousness.

quinoa: Pronounced "keen-wah," this tiny fluffy grain was a staple of the Incan civilizations and was actually worshipped by them at one time. It has a rich nutty flavor, and is excellent in pilafs, casseroles, as a cereal, and in a variety of other dishes.

rice cheese: A new product made from rice milk that is lower in fat than dairy cheese.

rice-flour noodles: Also called rice sticks, these dried noodles are found in Asian markets. They can be presoaked and used in soups and stir-frys.

rice milk: Milk made by blending rice and water.

rice paper: Thin paper made from rice flour and water that is sold in dry form in Asian grocery stores. The paper must be hydrated by soaking it in water for five seconds. Rice paper is used to make Thai spring and summer rolls.

sea salt: Coarse salt, or rock salt. The Native Hawaiians used to have salt farms in which saltwater pools were dried and the remaining salt collected. The salty crust from tide pools is also collected and kept in bags to use in cooking.

seitan: A chewy, high-protein food made from boiled or baked wheat gluten mixed with water and seasonings. Seitan has the chewy texture of meat and is used as a meat substitute. Available in health-food stores.

shiitake mushroom: A delicious Japanese mushroom sold in either fresh or dried form. The dried variety is easily reconstituted by soaking it in water for ten minutes. The soaking water can also be used in the recipe.

soba: Long, thin buckwheat noodles used in a variety of Asian salads and soups.

somen: Small, fast-cooking Asian noodles made from various grains.

soy milk: A whitish, creamy drink made from soybeans.

tamari: Genuine tamari is soy sauce produced naturally, without wheat, as a byproduct of making miso. However, the term is commonly used to describe any naturally brewed soy sauce.

taro: A starchy tuber that is a staple of the Hawaiian diet; it is also known as *kalo*. Do not eat raw taro.

tempeh: A whole soybean food that is a good meat substitute. It is fermented, which minimizes its "beany" flavor and gassiness.

textured vegetable protein (TVP): A soy product made from extruded soy flour. It has the texture of ground beef, but without the cholesterol and the high fat content. TVP is used in making sauces, and its texture improves as it soaks in the sauce. It is available at health-food stores in minced, granulated, and chunky form.

Thai basil: Purple-leaf basil with a distinctive flavor.

ti leaves: Also known as ki in Hawaiian, this woody plant from the lily family has good-sized leaves that are smooth, dark green, and shaped like a long oval. Most Hawaiian families have ti plants growing in their yards because they have many uses, such as *lu'au* decoration, food wrapping, and lei making.

tofu: White fermented soybean curd with a mild flavor. Blocks of tofu are packed in water and come in extra-firm, firm, and soft textures. Tofu is available in most supermarkets. Be sure to drain and rinse tofu before using.

*'uala:* The Hawaiian word for sweet potatoes.

*'ulu:* Breadfruit. The word describes both the fruit and the tree, which was introduced into Hawaii by the Polynesian peoples who immigrated there. Its fruit is eaten either baked, boiled, or steamed, and can be made into poi.

wahoo: A fish similar to mackerel or tuna with white, delicate, flaky meat.

wakame: A tender, leafy Japanese seaweed, high in calcium.

*Wakea:* Sky Father, the husband of *Papa* (Earth Mother).

wasabi: A Japanese seasoning paste similar in taste to horseradish. It is available in Asian markets.

wheat berries: Whole kernels of wheat.

won bok: A cabbage used in Asian soups and other vegetable dishes. It is also known as Napa cabbage or Chinese cabbage.

wood ears: Dried black Chinese mushrooms sold in the Asian section of most supermarkets.

# Bibliography

## Introduction

Shintani, T. T., C. K. Hughes, S. Beckham, et al. "Obesity and Cardio-vascular Risk Intervention through the *ad libitum* Feeding of Traditional Hawaiian Diet." *Am J Clin Nutr* 53 (1991): 1647S–1651S.

## Chapter 2

Aluli, N. E. "Prevalence of Obesity in a Native Hawaiian Population." *Am J Clin Nutr* 53 (1991): 1556S–1560S.

Bray, G., and J. Bethune. *Treatment and Management of Obesity*. Maryland: Harper & Row, 1974.

Kumanyika, S. K. "Special Issues Regarding Obesity in Minority Populations." *Ann Intern Med* 119, no. 7, pt. 2 (1993): 650–654.

Shintani, T. T., C. K. Hughes, S. Beckham, et al. "Obesity and Cardio-vascular Risk Intervention through the *ad libitum* Feeding of Traditional Hawaiian Diet." *Am J Clin Nutr* 53 (1991): 1647S–1651S.

Snow, C. E. *Early Hawaiians*. Kentucky: University of Kentucky Press, 1974.

Stanndard, D. E. *Before the Horror*. Hawaii: Social Science Research Institute, 1989.

Stanndard, D. E., et al. "Experimental Obesity in Man." *Transactions of the Association of American Physicians* 81 (1968): 153–170; Sims, interview (September 14, 1979).

## Chapter 4

Abbott, R. D., D. S. Sharp, C. M. Burchfiel, et al. "Cross-Sectional and Longitudinal Changes in Total and High-Density Lipoprotein Cholesterol Levels over a 20-Year Period in Elderly Men: The Honolulu Heart Program." *Ann Epidemiol* 7, no. 6 (1997): 417–424.

Allan, T. M., and A. A. Dawson. "ABO Blood Groups and Ischaemic Heart Disease in Men." *Brit Heart J* 30 (1968): 377–382.

Bang, H. O., and J. Dyerberg. "Plasma Lipids and Lipoproteins in Greenlandic West Coast Eskimos." *Acta Med Scand* 192 (1972): 85–94.

Barnard, R. J., L. Lattimore, R. G. Holly, et al. "Response of Non-Insulin-Dependent Diabetic Patients to an Intensitve Program of Diet and Exercise." *Diabetes Care* 5, no. 4 (1982): 370–374.

Barnard, R. J., M. R. Massey, and S. Cherny. "Long-Term Use of a High-Complex-Carbohydrate, High-Fiber, Low-Fat Diet and Exercise in the Treatment of NIDDM Patients." *Diabetes Care* 6, no. 3 (1983): 268–273.

Bassett, D. R., M. A. Abel, R. C. Moellering, et al. "Dietary Intake, Smoking History, Energy Balance, and 'Stress' in Relation to Age, and to Coronary Heart Disease Risk in Hawaiian and Japanese Men in Hawaii." *Am J Clin Nutr* 22 (1969): 1504–1520.

Berrino, F., and P. Muti. "Mediterranean Diet and Cancer." *Euro J Clin Nutr* 43, supp. 2 (1989): 49–55.

Bruno, G., G. Bargero, A. Vuolo, et al. "A Population-Based Prevalence Survey of Known Diabetes Mellitus in Northern Italy Based upon Multiple Independent Sources of Ascertainment." *Diabetologia* 35 (1992): 851–856.

Burchfiel, C. M., A. Laws, R. Benfante, et al. "Combined Effects of HDL Cholesterol, Triglyceride, and Total Cholesterol Concentrations on 18-Year Risk of Atherosclerotic Disease." *Circulation* 92, no. 6 (1995): 1430–1436.

Campbell, T. C. "The Study on Diet, Nutrition, and Disease in the People's Republic of China." *Contemp Nutr* 14 (1989): 6.

Carroll, K. "Experimental Evidence of Dietary Factors and Hormone-Dependent Cancers." *Cancer Res* 35 (1975): 3374.

Cerqueira, M. T., M. M. Fry, and W. E. Connor. "The Food and Nutrient Intakes of the Tarahumara Indians of Mexico." *Am J Clin Nutr* 32 (1979): 905–915.

Chen, J., T. C. Campbell, J. Li, and R. Peto. "Diet, Life-Style, and Mortality in China: A Study of the Characteristics of 65 Chinese Counties." Oxford: Oxford University Press, 1990: 750.

Chen, J., C. Geissler, B. Parpia, J. Li, and T. C. Campbell. "Antioxidant Status and Cancer Mortality in China." *Int J Epidemiology* 21 (1992): 625–635.

Connor, W. E., M. T. Cerqueira, R. W. Connor, et al. "The Plasma Lipids, Lipoproteins, and Diet of the Tarahumara Indians of Mexico." *Am J Clin Nutr* 31 (1978): 1131–1142.

Council on Scientific Affairs. "Dietary Fiber and Health." *JAMA* 262 (1989): 542–546.

Creasey, W. A. *Diet and Cancer.* Pennsylvania: Lea & Febiger, 1985.

Crews, D. E., and P. C. MacKeen. "Mortality Related to Cardiovascular Disease and Diabetes Mellitus in a Modernizing Population." *Soc Sci Med* 16 (1982): 175–181.

"Current Health Status and Population Projections of Native Hawaiians Living in Hawaii." Office of Technology Assessment, U. S. Congress, April 1987.

D'Adamo, P. J. *Eat Right for Your Blood Type.* New York: G. P. Putnam's Sons, 1996.

Doll, R., and R. Peto. "The Causes of Cancer: Quantitative Estimates of Avoidable Risks of Cancer in the United States Today." *J Natl Cancer Inst* 66, no. 6 (1981): 1191–1308.

"Eskimo Diets and Diseases." *Lancet* 8334 (1983): 1139–1141.

Fan, W., R. Parker, B. Parpia, et al. "Erythrocyte Fatty Acids, Plasma Lipids, and Cardiovascular Disease in Rural China." *Am J Clin Nutr* 52 (1990): 1027–1036.

Ferro-Luzzi, A., and S. Sette. "The Mediterranean Diet: An Attempt to Define Its Present and Past Composition." *Euro J Clin Nutr* 43, supp. 2 (1989): 13–29.

Force, R. W. "Health-Related Effects Consequences and Results of Social Change in the Pacific." *Am J Tropical Med and Hygiene* 24, no. 5 (Sept. 1975): 721–728.

Forman, M. R., S. Yao, B. Graubard, Y. Qiao, et al. "The Effect of

Dietary Intake of Fruits and Vegetables on the Odds Ratio of Lung Cancer among Yunnan Tin Miners." *Int J Epidem* 21 (1992): 437–441.

Glomset, J. A. "Fish, Fatty Acids, and Human Health." *New Engl J Med* 312 (1983): 1253–1254.

Gore, I., T. Nakashima, T. Imai, and P. D. White. "Coronary Atherscle-rosis and Myocardial Infarction in Kyushu, Japan, and Boston, Massachusetts." *Am J Cardiology,* Sept. 1962: 400–406.

Grundy, S. M. "Monounsaturated Fatty Acids, Plasma Cholesterol, and Coronary Heart Disease." *Am J Clin Nutr* 45 (1987): 1168–1175.

Hankin, J., D. Reed, D. Labarthe, M. Nichaman, et al. "Dietary and Disease Patterns Among Micronesians." *Am J Clin Nutr* 23, no. 2 (March 1970): 346–357.

Hirayama, T. "Relationship of Soybean Paste Soup Intake to Gastric Cancer Risk." *Nutr and Cancer* 3 (1982): 223–233.

Holmes, M. D., B. Zysow, and T. L. Delbanco. "An Analytic Review of Current Therapies for Obesity." *J Fam Prac* 28 (1989): 610–616.

Iribarren, C., D. M. Reed, R. Chen, et al. "Low Serum Cholesterol and Mortality: Which Is the Cause and Which Is the Effect?" *Circulation* 92, no. 9 (1995): 2396–2403.

James, W. P. T., G. G. Duthie, and K. W. J. Wahle. "The Mediterranean Diet: Protective or Simply Non-Toxic?" *Euro J Clin Nutr* 43, no. 2 (1989): 31–41.

James, W. P. T., A. Ferro-Luzzi, B. Isaksson, and W. B. Szostak, eds. *Healthy Nutrition: Preventing Nutrition-Related Diseases in Europe.* WHO Regional Publications, European Series, No. 24. Copen-hagen: WHO.

Jenkins, D. J. A., T. M. S. Wolever, R. Venketeshwer, et al. "Effect on Blood Lipids of Very High Intakes of Fiber in Diets Low in Satu-rated Fat and Cholesterol." *New Engl J Med* 329, no. 1 (1993): 21–26.

Kagawa, Y. "Impact of Westernization on the Nutrition of Japanese: Changes in Physique, Cancer, Longevity, and Centenarians." *Preventive Medicine* 7 (1978): 205–217.

Kannel, W. "Cholesterol in the Prediction of Atherosclerotic Disease." *Ann Intern Med* 90 (1975): 85.

Katsouyanni, K., W. Willett, D. Trichopoulos, et al. "Risk of Breast Cancer among Greek Women in Relation to Nutrient Intake." *Cancer* 61 (1988): 181–185.

Keys, A. *The Seven Countries Study*. Massachusetts: Harvard University Press, 1980.

Koike, G., O. Yokono, S. Iino, M. Adachi, et al. "Medical and Nutritional Surveys in the Kingdom of Tonga: Comparison of Physiological and Nutritional Status of Adult Tongans in Urbanized and Rural Areas." *J Nutr Sci Vitaminol* 30 (1984): 341–356.

Kushi, L., E. B. Lenart, and W. C. Willett. "Health Implications of Mediterranean Diets in Light of Contemporary Knowledge. 2: Meat, Wine, Fats, and Oils." *Am J Clin Nutr* 61 (1995): 1416S–1427S.

Lindholm, L. H., A. D. Koutis, C. D. Lionis, et al. "Risk Factors for Ischaemic Heart Disease in a Greek Population: A Cross-Sectional Study of Men and Women Living in the Village of Spili in Crete." *European Heart J* 13 (1992): 291–298.

McDougall, J., K. Litzau, E. Haver, et al. "Rapid Reduction of Serum Cholesterol and Blood Pressure by a Twelve-Day, Very Low Fat, Strictly Vegetarian Diet." *J Am Coll Nutr* 14, no. 5 (1995): 491–496.

McGarvey, S. T., and P. T. Baker. "The Effects of Modernization and Migration on Samoan Blood Pressures." *Human Biology* 51, no. 4 (1979): 461–479.

McGarvey, S. T. "Obesity in Samoans and a Perspective on Its Etiology in Polynesians." *Am J Clin Nutr* 53 (1991): 1586S–1594S.

Mori, M., and M. Hirotsugu. "Dietary and Other Risk Factors of Ovarian Cancer among Elderly Women." *Jpn J Cancer Res* 79 (1988): 997–1004.

Muir, C., J. Waterhouse, T. Mack, et al. *Cancer Incidence in Five Continents. Vol. V. IARC, Lyon*. National Center for Health Statistics, 1995.

O'Dea, K. "Diabetes in Australian Aborigines: Impact of the Western Diet and Life Style." *J Internal Med* 232 (1992): 103–117.

Oiso, T. "Changing Food Patterns in Japan." *Nutrition in Health and Disease and International Development: Symposia from the XII International Congress of Nutrition*. Alan R. Liss, Inc., 1981: 527–538.

Ornish, D., S. E. Brown, L. W. Scherwitz, et al. "Can Lifestyle Changes Reverse Coronary Heart Disease?" *Lancet* 336 (1990): 129–133.

Pennington, J. A. *Bowes & Church's Food Values of Portions Commonly Used,* 16th ed. Pennsylvania: J. B. Lippincott Co., 1994.

Peto, R., J. Boreham, J. Chen, et al. "Plasma Cholesterol, Coronary Heart Disease, and Cancer." *BMJ* 298, no. 6682 (1989): 1249.

Popkin, B. M., G. Keyou, Z. Fengying, et al. "The Nutrition Transition in China: A Cross-Sectional Analysis." *Euro J Clin Nutr* 47 (1993): 333–346.

Prior, I. A. M., Davidson. "The Epidemiology of Diabetes in Polynesians and Europeans in New Zealand and the Pacific." *New Zeal Med J* 65 (1966): 375.

Reaven, G. M. "Do High Carbohydrate Diets Prevent the Development or Attenuate the Manifestations (or Both) of Syndrome X? A Viewpoint Strongly Against." *Curr Opin Lipidol* 8, no. 1 (1997): 23–27.

Reaven, G. M. "Pathophysiology of Insulin Resistance in Human Disease." *Physiol Rev* 75, no. 3 (1995): 473–486.

Reddy, B. S., A. Engle, B. Simi, et al. "Effect of Low-Fat, High-Carbohydrate, High-Fiber Diet on Fecal Bile Acids and Neutral Sterols." *Prev Med* 4, no. 17 (1988): 432–439.

Reed, D. M. "The Paradox of High Risk of Stroke in Populations with Low Risk of Coronary Heart Disease." *Am J Epid* 131 (1990): 579–588.

Rimm, E. B., E. L. Giovannucci, W. C. Willett, et al. "Prospective Study of Alcohol Consumption and Risk of Coronary Disease in Men." *Lancet* 331 (1991): 464–468.

Rosenthal, M. B., R. J. Barnard, D. P. Rose, et al. "Effects of a High-Complex-Carbohydrate, Low-Fat, Low-Cholesterol Diet on Levels of Serum Lipids and Estradiol." *Am J Med* 78, no. 1 (1985): 23–27.

Salmon, D. M. W., and J. P. Flatt. "Effect of Dietary Fat Content on the Incidence of Obesity among *ad libitum* Fed Mice." *Intl J Obesity* 9 (1985): 443–449.

Shapiro, L. "Do Genes Determine What Foods We Should Eat?" *Newsweek*, August 9, 1993, p. 4.

Shintani, T. T., C. K. Hughes, S. Beckham, et al. "Obesity and Cardiovascular Risk Intervention through the *ad libitum* Feeding of Traditional Hawaiian Diet." *Am J Clin Nutr* 53 (1991): 1647S–1651S.

Shintani, T. T., and C. K. Hughes. "Traditional Diets of the Pacific and Coronary Heart Disease." *J Cardio Risk* 1 (1994): 16–20.

Shintani, T. T. *Dr. Shintani's Eat More, Weigh Less® Diet.* Honolulu: Halpax Publishing, 1993.

Snowdon, D. A. "Animal Product Consumption and Mortality Because of All Causes Combined: Coronary Heart Disease, Stroke, Diabetes, and Cancer in Seventh-Day Adventists." *Am J Clin Nutr* 48 (1988): 739–748.

Taylor, R. J., and P. Z. Zimmet. "Obesity and Diabetes in Western Samoa." *Int J Obesity* 5 (1981): 367–376.

Teas, J., M. L. Harbison, and R. S. Gelman. "Dietary Seaweed (Laminaria) and Mammary Carcinogenesis Rates." *Cancer Res* 44 (1984): 2758–2761.

Trichopoulou, A., A. Tzonou, C. C. Hsieh, N. Toupadaki, et al. "High Protein, Saturated Fat and Cholesterol Diet, and Low Levels of Serum Lipids in Colorectal Cancer." *Int J Cancer* 51 (1992): 386–389.

Trowell, H., and D. Burkitt, eds. *Western Diseases: Their Emergence and Prevention.* Massachusetts: Harvard University Press, 1981.

Tsunehara, C. H., D. L. Leonetti, and W. Y. Fujimoto. "Diet of Second-Generation Japanese-American Men with and without Non-Insulin-Dependent Diabetes." *Am J Clin Nutr* 52, no. 4 (Oct. 1990): 731–738.

Ueda, H. "Cardiovascular Diseases in Japan." *Am J Cardiology,* Sept. 1962: 371–379.

Watts, G. F., B. Lewis, J. N. H. Brunt, et al. "Effects on Coronary Artery Disease of Lipid-Lowering Diet, or Diet Plus Cholestyramine, in the St. Thomas's Atherosclerosis Regression Study (STARS)." *Lancet* 339 (1992): 563–569.

West, K. M. "Diabetes in American Indians and Other Native Populations of the New World." *Diabetes* 23 (1974): 841–855.

Worth, R. M., H. Kato, G. G. Rhoads, et al. "Epidemiological Studies of Coronary Heart Disease and Stroke in Japanese Men Living in Japan, Hawaii, and California: Mortality." *Am J Epidemiology* 102 (1975): 481–490.

Wynder, E. L., E. Taioli, and Y. Fujita. "Ecologic Study of Lung Cancer Risk Factors in the U.S. and Japan, with Special Reference to Smoking and Diet." *Jpn J Cancer Research* 83 (1992): 418–423.

Yano, K., D. M. Reed, and C. J. MacLean. "Serum Cholesterol and Hemorrhagic Stroke in the Honolulu Heart Program." *Stroke* 20 (1989): 1460–1465.

Young, T. K., and G. Sevenhuysen. "Obesity in Northern Canadian Indians: Patterns, Determinants, and Consequences." *Am J Clin Nutr* 49 (1989): 786–793.

Zimmet, P., M. Arblaster, and K. Thoma. "The Effect of Westernization on Native Populations: Studies on a Micronesian Community with a High Diabetes Prevalence." *Aust NZ J Med* 8 (1978): 141–146.


***Chapter 5***

Abelow, B. J., T. R. Holford, and K. L. Insogna. "Cross-Cultural Association between Dietary Animal Protein and Hip Fracture: A Hypothesis." *Calcif Tissue Int* 50 (1992): 14–18.

Abraham, G. "Nutritional Factors in the Etiology of the Premenstrual Tension Syndromes." *J Reprod Med* 28 (1983): 446.

Acheson, K. J., Y. Schutz, T. Bessard, et al. "Glycogen Storage Capacity and de novo Lipogenesis during Massive Carbohydrate Overfeeding in Man." *Am J Clin Nutr* 48 (1988): 240–247.

Acheson, K. J., Y. Schutz, T. Bessard, et al. "Nutritional Influences on Lipogenesis and Thermogenesis after a Carbohydrate Meal." *Am J Physiol* 246 (*Endocrinol Metab* 9) (1984): E62–E70.

Aldercreutz, H. "Diet and Plasma Androgens in Post Menopausal Vegetarian and Omnivorous Women and Post Menopausal Women with Breast Cancer." *Am J Clin Nutr* 49 (1989): 433.

Aluli, N. E. "Prevalence of Obesity in a Native Hawaiian Population." *Am J Clin Nutr* 53 (1991): 1556S–1560S.

Anderson, J. W. "Hypolipidemic Effects of High-Carbo, High-Fiber Diets." *Metabolism* 29 (1980): 551–558.

Bahna, S. *Allergies to Milk*. New York: Grune & Stratton, 1980.

Bang, H. O., and J. Dyerberg. "Plasma Lipids and Lipoproteins in Greenlandic West Coast Eskimos." *Acta Med Scand* 192 (1972): 85–94.

Bonanome, A., A. Visona, L. Lusiani, et al. "Carbohydrate and Lipid Metabolism in Patients with Non-Insulin-Dependent Diabetes

Mellitus: Effects of a Low-Fat, High-Carbohydrate Diet vs. a Diet High in Monounsaturated Fatty Acids." *Am J Clin Nutr* 54 (1991): 586–590.

Booyens, J., and C. F. Van Der Merwe. "Margarines and Coronary Artery Disease." *Med Hypos* 37 (1992): 241–244.

Boushey, C. J., S. A. A. Beresford, and G. S. Omenn. "A Quantitative Assessment of Plasma Homocysteine as a Risk Factor for Vascular Disease: Probable Benefits of Increasing Folic Acid Intakes." *JAMA* 274 (1995): 1049–1057.

Brand, J. C., B. J. Snow, G. P. Nabhan, et al. "Plasma Glucose and Insulin Responses to Traditional Pima Indian Meals." *Am J Clin Nutr* 51 (1990): 416–420.

Buzzard, I. M., E. H. Asp, R. T. Chlebowski, et al. "Diet Intervention Methods to Reduce Fat Intake: Nutrient and Food Group Composition of Self-Selected Low-Fat Diets." *J Am Diet Assoc* 90, no. 1 (1990): 42–50.

Carroll, K. K. "Experimental Evidence of Dietary Factors and Hormone-Dependent Cancers." *Cancer Res* 35 (1975): 3374.

Carroll, K. K., and H. T. Khor. "Dietary Fat in Relation to Tumorigenesis." *Prog Biochem Pharmacol* 10 (1975): 308.

Chrominn, N., and A. Green. "Epidemiologic Studies in the Upernavik District, Greenland." *Acta Med Scand* 208 (1980): 401–406.

Coulston, A. M., G. C. Liu, and G. M. Reaven. "Plasma Glucose, Insulin, and Lipid Responses to High-Carbohydrate, Low-Fat Diets in Normal Humans." *Metabolism* 32, no. 1 (1983): 52–56.

Council on Foods and Nutrition. "A Critique of Low-Carbohydrate Ketogenic Weight Reduction Regimens." *JAMA* 224 (1973): 1415.

De Graf, C., T. Hushof, J. A. Weststrate, et al. "Short-Term Effects of Different Amounts of Protein, Fats, and Carbohydrates on Satiety." *Am J Clin Nutr* 55 (1992): 33–38.

Donato, K. "Efficiency in Utilization of Various Energy Sources for Growth." *Am J Clin Nutr* 5 (1978): 164–167.

Dreon, D. M., B. Frey-Hewitt, N. Ellsworth, et al. "Dietary Fat: Carbohydrate Ratio and Obesity in Middle-Aged Men." *Am J Clin Nutr* 47 (1988): 995–1000.

Dyerberg, J., and H. O. Bang. "Lipid Metabolism, Atherogenesis, and Haemostasis in Eskimos: The Role of the Prostaglandin-3 Family." *Haemostasis* 8 (1979): 227–233.

Dyerberg, J., H. O. Bang, E. Stoffersen, et al. "Eicosapentaenoic Acid and Prevention of Thrombosis and Atherosclerosis?" *Lancet* i (1978): 117–119.

Eaton, S. B., and M. Konner. "Paleolithic Nutrition." *New Engl J Med* 312 (1985): 83–89.

Ellis, J. M., and K. S. McCully. "Prevention of Myocardial Infarction by Vitamin B₆." *Res Comm Mol Path Pharmacol* 89 (1995): 208–220.

Farquhar, J. W., A. Frank, and R. C. Gross. "Glucose, Insulin, and Triglyceride Responses to High and Low Carbohydrate Diets in Man." *J Clin Investigation* 45 (1966): 1648–1656.

Garg, A., J. P. Bantle, R. R. Henry, et al. "Effects of Varying Carbohydrate Content of Diet in Patients with Non-Insulin-Dependent Diabetes Mellitus." *JAMA* 271 (1994): 1421–1428.

Garg, A., A. Bonanome, S. Grundy, et al. "Comparison of a High-Carbohydrate Diet with a High Monounsaturated Fat Diet in Patients with Non-Insulin-Dependent Diabetes Mellitus." *New Engl J Med* 319 (1988): 829–934.

Giovannucci, E., E. B. Rimm, G. A. Colditz, et al. "Prospective Study of Dietary Fat and Risk of Prostate Cancer." *J Nat Can Inst* 85 (1993): 1571–1579.

Grundy, S. M. "Monounsaturated Fatty Acids, Plasma Cholesterol, and Coronary Heart Disease." *Am J Clin Nutr* 45 (1987): 1168–1175.

Grundy, S. "Recent Nutrition Research: Implication for Foods of the Future." *Ann Med* 23 (1991): 187–193.

Hamalainen, E. "Diet and Serum Sex Hormones in Healthy Men." *J Steroid Biochem* 20 (1984): 459.

Hardinge, M. C., H. Crooks, and J. Stare. "Nutritional Studies of Vegetarians." *J Am Dietetic Assn* 48 (1966): 25–28.

Havala, S., and J. Dwyer. "Position of the American Dietetic Association: Vegetarian Diets." *J Am Diet Assoc* 93, no. 11 (1993): 1317–1319. [Published erratum appears in *J Am Diet Assoc* 94, no. 1 (Jan. 1994): 19.]

Hegsted, D. M. "Calcium and Osteoporosis." *J Nutr* 116 (1986): 2316–2319.

Hill, P., P. Chan, L. Cohen, et al. "Diet and Endocrine-Related Cancer." *Cancer* 39, 4 supp. (1977): 1820–1826.

Hill, P. "Environmental Factors and Breast and Prostate Cancer: A Population-Based Study in 223 Untreated Patients." *Lancet* 41 (1981): 3817.

Hirsch, J., L. C. Hudgins, R. L. Leibel, et al. "Diet Composition and Energy Balance in Humans." *Am J Clin Nutr* 67 (1998): 551S–555S.

Hollenbeck, C. B., and A. M. Coulston. "Effects of Dietary Carbohydrate and Fat Intake on Glucose and Lipoprotein Metabolism in Individuals with Diabetes Mellitus." *Diabetes Care* 14, no. 9 (1991): 774–778.

Holt, S. H. A., J. C. Brand Miller, et al. "A Satiety Index of Common Foods." *Euro J Clin Nutr* 49 (1995): 675–690.

Howie, B. "Dietary and Hormonal Interrelationships among Vegetarian Seventh-Day Adventists and Nonvegetarian Men." *Am J Clin Nutr* 42 (1985): 127.

Ingram, D. "Effect of Low-Fat Diet on Female Sex Hormone Levels." *J Natl Cancer Inst* 79 (1987): 1225.

Jenkins, D. J. A., T. M. S. Wolever, J. Kalmusky, et al. "Low-Glycemic Index Diet in Hyperlipidemia: Use of Traditional Starchy Foods." *Am J Clin Nutr* 46 (1987): 66–71.

Jenkins, D. J. A., T. M. S. Wolever, and R. H. Taylor. "Glycemic Index of Foods: A Physiological Basis for Carbohydrate Exchange." *Am J Clin Nutr* 34 (1981): 362–366.

Jenkins, D. J. A., T. M. S. Wolever, S. Vukson, et al. "Nibbling versus Gorging: Metabolic Advantages of Increased Meal Frequency." *New Engl J Med* 321 (1989): 929–934.

Kannel, W. B., W. P. Castelli, and T. Gordon. "Cholesterol in the Prediction of Atherosclerotic Disease." *Ann Int Med* 90 (1979): 85–91.

Katahn, M. *The T-Factor Diet*. New York: W. W. Norton, 1989.

Katsouyanni, K., Y. Skalkidis, E. Petridou, et al. "Diet and Peripheral Arterial Occlusive Disease: The Role of Poly-, Mono-, and Saturated Fatty Acids." *Am J Epidemiol* 133, no. 1 (1991): 24–31.

Koonsvitsky, B. P., D. A. Berry, M. B. Jones, et al. "Olestra Affects Serum Concentrations of Alpha-Tocopherol and Carotenoids but Not Vitamin D or Vitamin K Status in Free-Living Subjects." *J Nutr* 127 (1997): 1636S–1645S.

Kromhout, D., E. B. Bosschieter, and C. de Leezenne Couland. "The Inverse Relation between Fish Consumption and 20-Year Mortality from Coronary Heart Disease." *New Engl J Med* 312 (1985): 1205–1209.

Kushi, L., E. B. Lenart, and W. C. Willett. "Health Implications of Mediterranean Diets in Light of Contemporary Knowledge. 2: Meat, Wine, Fats, and Oils." *Am J Clin Nutr* 61 (1995): 1416S–1427S.

Lichtenstein, A. "Trans Fatty Acids, Blood Lipids, and Cardiovascular Risk: Where Do We Stand?" *Nutr Rev* 51, no. 11 (1993): 340–343.

Lissner, L. L., D. A. Strupp, H. J. Kawlwarf, et al. "Dietary Fat Intake and the Regulation of Energy Intake in Human Subjects." *Am J Clin Nutr* 46 (1987): 886–892.

Lowenberg, M. E. *Food and Man.* New York: John Wiley & Sons, 1974.

Matsuoka, A., T. Yamaguchi, Y. Masuyama, et al. "Characteristics of Dietary Treatment of Diabetes Mellitus in Japan: Comparison of Dietary Habits and Diabetic Pathology in Japanese and American Diabetics." In S. Baba, Y. Goto, and I. Fukui, eds., *Diabetes Mellitus in Asia.* Amsterdam: Excerpta Medica, 1976: 265–269.

McCully, K. S., and R. B. Wilson. "Homocysteine Theory of Arteriosclerosis." *Atherosclerosis* 22 (1975): 215–217.

McCully, K. S. "Vascular Pathology of Homocysteinemia: Implications for the Pathogenesis of Arteriosclerosis." *Am J Pathology* 56 (1969): 111–128.

Messina, V. K., and K. I. Burke. "Position of the American Dietetic Association: Vegetarian Diets." *Am Diet Assoc* 97, no. 11 (1997): 1317–1321.

Metz, S., W. Fujimoto, and R. O. Robertson. "Modulation of Insulin Secretion by Cyclic AMP and Prostaglandin E." *Metabolism* 31 (1982): 1014–1033.

O'Connor, H. K., R. K. Teixeira, M. Tan, S. Beckham, and T. T. Shintani. *Wai'anae Diet Cookbook 'Elua, Volume II.* Waianae, Hawaii: Waianae Coast Comprehensive Health Center, 1995.

Phillipson, B. E., D. W. Rothrock, W. E. Connor, et al. "Reduction of Plasma Lipids and Lipoproteins, Apoproteins by Dietary Fish Oils in Patients with Hypertryglyceridemia." *New Engl J Med* 312 (1985): 1210–1216.

Renuad, S., M. De Lorgeril, J. Delaye, et al. "Cretan Mediterranean Diet for Prevention of Coronary Heart Disease." *Am J Clin Nutr* 61 (1995): 1360S–1367S.

Rolls, B. J. "Carbohydrates, Fats, and Satiety." *Am J Clin Nutr* 61 (1995): 960S–967S.

Sanchez, A. "A Hypothesis on the Etiological Role of Diet on the Age of Menarche." *Med Hypotheses* 7 (1981): 1339.

Sanchez, S. "Dietary Influences on the Growth and Sexual Maturation in Premenarchial Rhesus Monkeys." *Horm Behav* 22 (1988): 231.

Sears, B. *The Zone Diet.* New York: HarperCollins, 1995.

Shintani, T. T. *Dr. Shintani's Eat More, Weigh Less® Cookbook.* Honolulu: Halpax Publishing, 1995.

Shintani, T. T., S. Beckham, and J. G. Tang. *Hawaii Diet Study.* Unpublished manuscript.

Shintani, T. T., C. K. Hughes, S. Beckham, et al. "Obesity and Cardiovascular Risk Intervention through the *ad libitum* Feeding of Traditional Hawaiian Diet. *Am J Clin Nutr* 53 (1991): 1647S–1651S.

Shintani, T. T., and C. K. Hughes. "Traditional Diets of the Pacific and Coronary Heart Disease." *J Cardio Risk* 1 (1994): 16–20.

Swain, J. F., I. L. Pouse, C. B. Curley, and F. M. Sacks. "Comparison of the Effects of Oat Bran and Low-Fiber Wheat on Serum Lipoprotein Levels and Blood Pressure." *N Engl J Med* 332, no. 3 (1990): 147–152.

Weinsier, R. L., M. H. Johnston, D. M. Doleys, and J. A. Bacon. "Dietary Management of Obesity: Evaluation of the Time-Energy Displacement Diet in Terms of Its Efficacy and Nutritional Adequacy for Long-Term Weight Control." *Br J Nutr* 47 (1982): 367–379.

Whyte, J. L., R. McArthur, D. Topping, and P. Nestel. "Oat Bran Lowers Plasma Cholesterol Levels in Mildly Hypercholesterolemic Men." *J Am Diet Assoc* 92, no. 4 (1992): 446–449.

Willett, W. C., D. J. Hunter, M. J. Stampfer, et al. "Dietary Fat and Fiber in Relation to Risk of Breast Cancer." *JAMA* 268, no. 15 (1992): 2037–2044.

Wolever, T. M. S. "Relationship between Dietary Fiber Content and Composition in Foods and the Glycemic Index." *Am J Clin Nutr* 51 (1990): 72–75.

Wolever, T. M. S., et al. "Beneficial Effects of Low-Glycemic Index Diet in Overweight NIDDM Subjects." *Diabetes Care* 15 (1992): 562–564.

Wolever, T. M. S., D. J. A. Jenkins, A. A. Jenkins, et al. "The Glycemic Index: Methodology and Clinical Implications." *Am J Clin Nutr* 54 (1991): 846–854.

Yano, K., D. M. Reed, and C. J. MacLean. "Serum Cholesterol and Hemorrhagic Stroke in the Honolulu Heart Program." *Stroke* 20 (1989): 1460–1465.

# *Acknowledgments*

$\mathcal{P}$roducing this book required a great deal of effort and thought from many people, spanning a period of several years.

It would be impossible to recognize here every person who influenced this book or participated in some way in its production. However, I would like to give special thanks to the following organizations and individuals: The Waianae Coast Comprehensive Health Center, their owners, the Waianae Coast community, and their staff, especially Helen Kanawaliwali O'Connor and Sheila Beckham, M.P.H., R.D., who helped to develop the original Waianae Diet Program; Claire Hughes, Dr.P.H., R.D., whom I consider one of the cofounders of the Waianae Diet Program, and the leading expert in the world on the traditional Hawaiian diet; Kekuni Blaisdell, M.D., one of my professors and mentors, and one of the cofounders of the John A. Burns School of Medicine at the University of Hawaii; my Hawaii Diet Study research team, including Sheila Beckham, M.S., R.D., Steve Bradley, M.D., and Phuong Sutherland, R.D., M.S., whose work comparing Mediterranean and Pacific diets provided some of the scientific foundation of the HawaiiDiet™; T. Colin Campbell, Ph.D., of Cornell University, Walter Willett, M.D., Dr.P.H., of Harvard University, Antonia Trichopolou, M.D., of the Univerity of Athens, and Lawrence Kushi, Dr.P.H., of the University of Minnesota, who freely gave their advice on the Hawaii Diet Study to make the project as high in quality as possible; Na Pu'uwai, a community-based organization; Noa Emmett Aluli, M.D., who was one of those who pioneered the use of the traditional Hawaiian diet to control lipids in the Molokai Diet Study; the Office of Hawaiian Affairs (OHA), who helped to fund the Waianae Diet Program over the years and who was a cosponsor of the HawaiiDiet™ program; Ke Ola Mamo, the Native Hawaiian health organization that has helped with the Hawaii Health programs; Robert Oshiro, Esq., and the Queen Emma Foundation, who have always supported my efforts to promote health in Hawaii and around the world; Ho` oipo DeCambra, Kenneth Brown, Kamaki Kanahele, and Ronald Sakamoto, Esq., current board members of the Hawaii Health Foundation, and past board members Christian Gulbrandsen, M.D., Connie Black, and James Kumagai, Ph.D., who shared the dream of Hawaii as a world center for health; Rodney Sato, Esq., the current vice president of the Hawaii Health Foundation, and former officers Keith Lee, Esq., and Mike Walsh, all of whom worked many hours to make the Hawaii Health Foundation a reality; Dr. Diane Nomura, the administrator of the Hawaii Health Foundation, who has always helped to keep me and the foundation moving in the right direction; David McDonald, the managing editor of the first version of this book, who was the best editor that ever worked for me; Barbara Burke, Janice Miller, and Lindsey Pollock, who helped edit the early version of this book; all the participants in the Hawaii-Diet™ study, who by their commitment helped to provide some of the scientific data for the HawaiiDiet™; the Honorable Benjamin J. Cayetano, governor of the state of Hawaii; lieutenant governor Mazie Hirono; members of the governor's cabinet, including Charles Toguchi, Susan Chandler, Herman Aizawa, and Joseph Blanco; state senator Calvin Kawamoto; all the participants in the Hawaii Health Program, who by their participation helped to demonstrate the application of the science behind the program and bring it to the public; all the contributors to the Hawaii Health Foundation—especially the Hawaii Medical Service Association, the McInerny Foundation, Maybelle Roth, Frear Eleemosynary Trust, AlohaCare, and Bank of America—who by their generosity help us promote health and peace in Hawaii and ultimately around the world; all the organizations and individuals that supported us or our programs in kind, such as Diagnostic Laboratory Services, the Mokichi Okada Association, the Hawai Department of Business, and the Department of Economic Development and Tourism; all the volunteers at the Hawaii Health Foundation, who by their personal commitment and work have made many of the accomplishments of the foundation possible; Jack Ha'o, my first publisher; Jan Foster, my desktop publisher, who has helped me produce educational materials over the years; Lindsey Pollock and Lauree Nakata, who helped to design the early version of this book; Tracy Sherrod and Emily Bestler, editors at Pocket Books, whose excellent editing kept this book high in quality, easy to read, and accessible to readers, and who moved the project along to keep it on schedule; Dan Green, my agent, who in his own right is an excellent editor whose advice and wise counsel I will always appreciate; and Rick Cesari, the "dean of infomercials," who introduced me to the infomercial business, who is a pioneer in this rapidly expanding field, and whose work I have admired for years.

I would also like to thank the following individuals and organizations who are at the top of their fields and were kind enough to take notice of our work: Bob Arnot, M.D., and the staff at NBC; Carolyn O'Neil and the staff at CNN; Laura Shapiro and the staff at *Newsweek;* Ben DiPietro, Meki Cox, and the Associated Press; Dick Allgire, Paula Akana, and TV station KITV; Leslie Wilcox, Mary Zanakis, John Yoshimura, and TV station KHON; Jade Moon and TV station KGMB; Emmie Tomimbang; Linda Tomchuck and the staff at the Encyclopedia Brittanica; Barbara Ann Curcio and *Eating Well* magazine; *Vegetarian Times* magazine; Steven Pratt and the *Chicago Tribune; Tufts Newsletter;* Diana Sugg and the *Sacramento Bee;* Dave Donnelly, Catherine Enomoto, Linda Hosek, Becky Ashizawa, and the *Honolulu Star Bulletin;* Joan Clarke, Beverly Creamer, Chris Oliver, and the *Honolulu Advertiser;* Debbie Ward and *Ka Wai Ola o OHA;* Janice Otaguro and *Honolulu* magazine; Ciel Sinnex and *MidWeek* magazine; Sally-Jo Bowman and *Aloha* magazine; Gwen Bataad and the *Hawaii Herald;* Betty Fullard-Leo and *Hawaii* magazine; Tracy Orillo-Donovan and the University of Hawaii, and many others whom I have forgotten to thank.

I would also like to thank my *hanai* (adoptive) family, especially my mother, Agnes Cope, and adoptive brother, Kamaki Kanahele, who have always given me wise counsel.

Thanks also to my brother, Arthur Shintani, and his company, Trends of Hawaii, who are always helping me with their support.

Thanks are also due to my wife, Stephanie; our daughters, Tracie and Nickie, and their grandparents Henry and Peggy Hong for their support and patience while I was writing this book.

In addition, I would like this book to honor the memory of the following deceased people who touched the lives of so many others, including mine, with the spirit of *aloha*. It is my hope that in some small way, the good they accomplished during their lifetimes will be carried on through this book, and that the benefits readers derive from this book will be a reflection of their legacies on earth and the spirit of God within them all. Their names are: "Auntie" Myrtle Mokiau, *kupuna* (wise elder) from Nanakuli, Hawaii, board member of the Waianae Coast Comprehensive Health Center, and one of my *hanai* (adoptive) mothers, who was a pillar of spiritual strength in Hawaii and for our program; Rell Sunn, the legendary surfer from Makaha, whom I had the privilege of meeting while working with her on a cancer research project in Waianae, Hawaii; Mililani Allen, *kumu* (teacher of) hula from Waianae, Hawaii, who graced our early programs with hula performances and wrote a song about our program in its early years; Herman Aihara, master teacher of macrobiotics from Oroville, California, and one of my own teachers, who in the 1960s helped to pioneer the concept of the healthfulness of traditional diets in America; Edward Aikala, community activist and friend, a big and powerful man with an even bigger, more powerful heart who shared the message of health for all Hawaiian people with his gentle, simple ways and whose work for and success with the Waianae diet inspired many people to take responsibility for their own health; Dr. Frances Sydow, educator and founder of the Kahumana Farm and Community, whose vision of health helped create a place where the Waianae Diet Program could grow and who provided much practical and spiritual support for my efforts to promote the health of the Hawaiian people; Dr. Fred Gilbert, physician, researcher, and one of the founders of the Pacific Health Research Institute, who helped inspire me to become a physician, helped in my transition from the field of law to medicine, and supported me in my continued research; Dr. Georgeda

Buchbinder, physician, anthropologist, nutritionist, and my mentor in preventive medicine, who was always supportive of my efforts to promote health in the community and who taught me much about striving for excellence through her personal example; Ray Brosseau, a multitalented man who was the chief editor of *Dr. Shintani's Eat More, Weigh Less Diet* and who always generously shared with me his wisdom and creative ideas on writing and on how to promote health; *Kupuna* Katherine K. Maunakea, poet, composer, and practitioner of Hawaiian herbal medicine, who was a living example of what the spirit of *aloha* truly means through her selfless sharing of her gifts with everyone who was fortunate enough to have known her; my grandmothers, Yukie Otoide and Miyo Shintani, and my grandfathers, Kansuke Shintani and Gunichi Otoide; and my parents, Emi and Robert Shintani, whose love and support I continue to feel even years after they have left this earth.

The recipes in this book were created through the efforts of a number of people and were developed in a number of programs that I have conducted through my private practice and through the Hawaii Health Foundation. I would like to thank the following people for their help in producing these recipes: Carol Devenot, an award-winning consumer science teacher, who was my chief recipe editor, tester, and advisor; Lynne Lee, another award-winning consumer science teacher, who was one of the chief cooking instructors of the Hawaii Health Program Seminars; Jenny Choy, a consumer science teacher, who has worked for many years at Kamehameha Schools with Native Hawaiian children and is one of the chief cooking instructors of the Hawaii Health Program Seminars; and Ann Tang, a home cooking expert, who contributed some of the recipes and dressings.

Janice Miller, who also served as editor and writer for this book, is also a home cooking expert and contributed a number of recipes, including some of the delicious desserts.

Dick Allgire, a local TV celebrity with KITV News 4, allowed me to use his "Lazy Enchilada" recipe from his book *Cook Healthy Fast*.

Barbara Gray, our food consultant, helped edit the recipes, helped make the recipes easy to understand, and helped ensure that they were pleasing to a wide variety of tastes.

Sheila Beckham, M.P.H., R.D., was the chief dietitian for the HawaiiDiet™ Study, the Hawaii Health Program, and a member of our recipe committee.

Stephen Bradley, M.D., a remarkable physician who is an orthopedist, family practitioner, and, believe it or not, a certified chef!

Helen Kanawaliwali O'Connor wrote many of the traditional Hawaiian recipes which came from *Wai'anae Diet Cookbook 'Elua*, Volume II.

Rozalyn Kalei`aukai Teixeira wrote many of the traditional Hawaiian recipes, *Wai'anae Diet Cookbook 'Elua*, Volume II. *Mahalo* and Alouette's Custom Catering deserves credit for some of the delicious salsas and dressings that appear in the book.

Special thanks are also due to the Hawaiian regional chefs who contributed some of the fancier recipes: Peter Merriman, chef and owner of Merriman's Restaurant in Kamuela, Hawaii, and the chef and co-owner of the Hula Grill in Ka'anapali, Maui, who helped us plan the Hawaii Health Program and contributed some exotic recipes to this book; Mark Ellman, chef and owner of Avalon in Lahaina, Maui, and partner in six Maui Tacos restaurants on Hawaii, Maui, and Oahu, who helped plan the Hawaii Health Program and contributed a number of recipes, including the Maui Tacos selections; and Roy Yamaguchi, chef and owner of Roy's Restaurants in Honolulu, Maui, Waikaloa, Poipu, Pebble Beach, Seattle, Japan, Hong Kong, and Guam, who generously contributed a signature dish of his own and other recipes, and who allowed us to adapt them slightly for simplicity's sake.

Last, but most important, I thank the Lord, from whom all blessings and healings come forth.

# Index

acorn squash, rice-stuffed, 178
aerobic exercise, 88–90
ahi, blackened, with soy-mustard
 sauce, Roy's, 200–01
Allgire, Dick, enchiladas, lazy,
 188–89
aloha, spirit of, 26–27, 82, 263, 264
Alouette's Custom Catering, 252, 253
American Dietetic Association, 71
American Heart Association, 43, 56
*American Journal of Clinical Nutri-
 tion,* xv
amino acids, 71, 72, 283
animal protein. *See* meat
'ano 'ano (seed of all things), 28–29
antioxidants, 78, 283
antipasto salad, 119
appetizers and snacks
 eggplant spread, 135
 hummus, simple, 140
 pizza, quick Mexican, 139
 portobello mushrooms, stuffed,
  137
 potato garlic dip, 140
 pot stickers, 130–31

summer rolls with clear and amber
 dips, 132–33
sushi, pan, 138
vegetables with garden dip, 136
apple(s)
 baked, A's, 252
 cake, bran, 259
 chutney salad, 121
 quinoa cereal, cinnamon, 164
apricot turnovers, crispy, 258
artichoke(s)
 antipasto salad, 119
 asparagus salad, 115
asparagus artichoke salad, 115
atherosclerotic disease, 9, 42, 72
avocado, guacamole, Maui Tacos',
 187

balsamic vinaigrette, 128
banana
 bread, 170
 crepes, 168–69
 fruit salad, tropical, 121
 ice dream, Kona coffee, 256
 pudding, strawberry-, 251

salad(s)
antipasto, 119
asparagus artichoke, 115
barley, southwestern, 122
bean, three-, 123
Caesar, 114–15
chicken, Moroccan, 120
chutney, 121
cole slaw, Far Eastern, 116
confetti slaw with vinaigrette, 117
fern, mountain, 149
fruit, tropical, 121
Greek, 118
pasta, rasta, 112
potato, miso, 108
potato, red, 107
seaweed (manauwea), 148–49
somen, cold, 110–11
sweet potato, 113
vegetable, mixed green, with potatoes, Peter Merriman's, 109
watercress and bean sprout namul,
111
salad dressing
Caesar, 114–15
Dijon, tangy, 126
thousand island, 125
See also vinaigrette
salmon fillet with fresh tomato salsa,
203
salsa
pineapple-tomatillo, Maui Tacos',
187
tomato, fresh, salmon fillet with,
203
saturated fats, 44, 63–64, 288
sauce(s)
black bean, Peter Merriman's, 183
chili pepper water, 249
curry, simple, 247
garlic and red bell pepper, roasted,
246

ginger miso, 245
gravy, savory, 244
honey-mustard, 248
mushroom, cremini, 242
mushroom, marinara, for pasta, 210
mushroom, teriyaki, 243
soy-mustard, ahi, blackened, with,
Roy's, 200–01
stir-fry, 196–97
sweet-and-sour tofu with snow
peas and mushrooms, 204–05
tomato-herb, chicken breast in
phyllo with, 194–95
See also dipping sauce
scrambled tofu, 206
seafood
shrimp with snow peas and mushrooms, 202
squid lu'au, 148
See also fish
seaweed, 34
salad, 148–49
vinaigrette, 236
seed of all things ('ano 'ano), 28–29
selenium, 78
serving size, 84–86
Seven Countries Study, 43
sex hormones, 76–78
Shintani Mass Index (SMI), 8, 18,
24, 36–39, 54, 62, 271–74
shiitake mushrooms, rice, baked,
with, 175
shrimp with snow peas and mushrooms, 202
slaws
cole slaw, Far Eastern, 116
confetti, with vinaigrette, 117
snacks. See appetizers and snacks
snow peas
shrimp with mushrooms and, 202
tofu, sweet-and-sour, with mushrooms and, 204–05